THE PROFESSIONS IN AMERICAN HISTORY

THE PROFESSIONS
IN AMERICAN HISTORY

Edited with an Introduction by
Nathan O. Hatch

UNIVERSITY OF NOTRE DAME PRESS
NOTRE DAME, INDIANA

Library of Congress Cataloging-in-Publication Data

The Professions in American history.

  Includes bibliographies.
  1. Professions—United States—History. I. Hatch,
Nathan O.
HD8038.U5P76 1988   331.7'12'0973   87-40351
ISBN 0-268-01568-6

Manufactured in the United States of America

To
VINCENT P. GREGG,
professional extraordinaire

ministrare non ministrari

CONTENTS

ACKNOWLEDGMENTS

I am grateful to the Department of History at the University of Notre Dame for sponsoring the lecture series which made possible these eleven presentations. Generous funding from the Schurz Communications Foundation and the Indiana Committee for the Humanities enabled the department to bring to campus exceptionally able scholars to discuss the history of a given profession with practicing professionals as well as students and faculty. Two other persons also deserve a word of hearty thanks for their assistance with this project: Catherine Box in organizing the lecture series and Carol Bryant in preparing the book manuscript.

CONTRIBUTORS

LAURENCE VEYSEY holds degrees from Yale University, the University of Chicago, and the University of California, Berkeley. He has been awarded research fellowships from the National Endowment for the Humanities, the Guggenheim Foundation, and the Charles Warren Center, Harvard University. His extensive publications on the history of American higher education include *The Emergence of the American University* (Chicago, 1965); "The Plural Organized Worlds of Humanities," in *The Organization of Learning in Modern America, 1860–1920* (Baltimore, 1979); and "Graduate Education in an Age of Stasis," in *The Philosophy and Future of Graduate Education* (Ann Arbor, 1980).

MAXWELL H. BLOOMFIELD holds a law degree from Harvard and a Ph.D. in American History from Tulane. He was awarded a Fellowship in Legal History in 1968–69 from the American Bar Foundation and was Visiting Professor of American Legal History in 1973 at the University of Virginia. His publications include *American Lawyers in a Changing Society, 1776–1876* (Cambridge, Mass., 1976) and *Law and American Literature: A Collection of Essays* (Chicago, 1980).

RONALD L. NUMBERS has served as chairman of the Department of the History of Medicine at the University of Wisconsin. He holds a Ph.D. from the University of California, Berkeley, and has been a Fellow of the Institute of the History of Medicine, The Johns Hopkins University. His writings include *Almost Persuaded: American Physicians and Compulsory Health Insurance, 1912–1920* (Baltimore, 1978); *The Education of American Physicians: Historical Essays* (Berkeley, Calif., 1980); and *Prophetess of Health: A Study of Ellen G. White* (New York, 1976).

MARTIN E. MARTY is the Fairfax M. Cone Distinguished Service Professor at the University of Chicago where he teaches the history of modern Christianity. He has served as president of the American Society of Church History and the American Catholic Historical Association. An associate editor of *The Christian Century* and coeditor of *Church History*, Mr. Marty has also written more than a score of books, including *Modern American Religion*, vol. 1: *The Irony of It All, 1893–1919* (Chicago, 1986).

JOHN SHY, Professor of History at the University of Michigan, holds a B.S. from the U.S. Military Academy and a Ph.D. in History from Princeton. His pathbreaking studies of the relationship between American society and its military include *Toward Lexington: The Role of the British Army in the Coming of the American Revolution* (Princeton, 1965), which won the John H. Dunning Prize of the American Historical Association; and *A People Numerous and Armed: Reflection on the Military Struggle for American Independence* (New York, 1976).

DANIEL J. KEVLES is Professor of History at California Institute of Technology. He holds a B.A. and Ph.D. from Princeton University and spent a year at Oxford as a National Science Foundation Fellow. His book *The Physicists: The History of a Scientific Community in Modern America* (New York, 1978) received the National Historical Book Prize in American History for 1979. He is also the author of *In the Name of Eugenics: Genetics and the Uses of Human Heredity* (New York, 1985).

BRUCE SINCLAIR is Professor of History at Case-Western Reserve University. In 1975 he won the Dexter Prize in the History of Technology for his book *Philadelphia's Philosopher Mechanics* (Baltimore, 1974). His extensive publications also include *A Centennial History of the American Society of Mechanical Engineers, 1880–1980* (Toronto, 1980).

MICHAEL SCHUDSON is Professor in the Department of Communication and the Department of Sociology at the University of California, San Diego. He is the author of *Discovering the News: A Social History of*

American Newspapers (New York, 1978) and *Advertising: The Uneasy Persuasion* (New York, 1984) and coeditor (with Robert Karl Manoff) of *Reading the News* (New York, 1986) and has written numerous articles on the mass media, the profession of journalism, and popular culture.

Don K. Price is Weatherhead Professor of Public Management *emeritus* at Harvard University, where from 1958 to 1977 he served as dean of the Kennedy School of Government. A graduate of Vanderbilt University and a Rhodes Scholar, he served in various capacities as a consultant on public administration to presidents Roosevelt, Eisenhower, Kennedy, and Johnson. His numerous publications include *Government and Science* (1954) and *The Scientific Estate* (1965), which was awarded the Faculty Prize of Harvard University Press.

John C. Burnham is Professor of History and Lecturer in Psychiatry at Ohio State University. He holds degrees from the University of Wisconsin and Stanford University. His numerous publications include *Lester Frank Ward in American Thought* (Washington, D.C., 1956), and *Psychoanalysis and American Medicine, 1854–1918: Medicine, Science, and Culture* (New York, 1967).

Harold C. Livesay is a member of the History Department at Virginia Polytechnic Institute and State University. A Ph.D. from The Johns Hopkins University and a prolific author, he has twice received the Newcomen Society Award in Business History. His books include *Merchants and Manufacturers: Studies in the Changing Patterns of Nineteenth-Century Distribution* (Baltimore, 1971); *Andrew Carnegie and the Rise of Big Business* (Boston, 1975), and *American Made: Men Who Built the American Economy* (Boston, 1979).

INTRODUCTION: THE PROFESSIONS IN A DEMOCRATIC CULTURE

Nathan O. Hatch

> In a country where there is no titled class, no landed class, no military class, the chief distinction which popular senti-ment can lay hold of as raising one set of persons above another is the character of their occupation, the degree of culture it implies, the extent to which it gives them an honourable prominence.   James Bryce, 1895

In the last decade, scholars in history and the social sciences have manifested a fascination with the development of the professions in America. We are now gaining a mature understanding of the variety of roles that the profes-sions have played in American history and, in turn, of the evolving charac-ter of America's respective professions, such as law, medicine, business man-agement, engineering, and journalism.

The problem is that most of these insights, unearthed by scholars, have not been readily available to professionals on the job, to graduate stu-dents in professional schools, or to undergraduates contemplating a given profession. Schools of business administration, for instance, concentrate on effectively consolidating, organizing, and teaching the contemporary theory and practice of management. What time rarely permits is the intriguing story of how the "science" of business management came to develop in the first place and how such professionalization has come to shape the corporate world. This volume hopes to bridge the gap between the humanities and the workaday world by stimulating people to think about the historical forces that have shaped their own profession and the role which theirs and other professions have played in American society.

Definitions of a profession multiply without end, but most focus on three primary criteria. First, a profession is generally considered to be an occupation based on a definable body of organized knowledge, an expertise

1

that derives from extensive academic training. Professional training and universities are tightly linked in an institutional setting that certifies quality and competence. Second, a profession at some level involves a moral commitment of service to the public that goes beyond the test of the market or the desire for personal profit. The ideal of most professions, at least, is that the accepted measure of success is not merely financial gain but some larger purpose, whether it be the well being of the public, the advancement of science, the care of the infirm, or the maintaining of justice. "Pursue the study of the law rather than the Gain of it," Jeremy Gridley, the leading lawyer in Boston, advised the fledgling attorney John Adams before his admission to the bar.[1] The professional person, it has been said, does not work in order to be paid but is paid in order to work.

A third criteria involves the relative independence or autonomy of professional life. In the modern world professional organizations are generally granted the right as a separate entity in society to regulate their own affairs and define their own standards. Recognized for a given expertise, the professional is free to choose clients, set hours and fees, define ethical norms, and establish certain "gatekeeping" functions—such as determining entrance criteria and standards for professional behavior. In other words, professionals are granted something of a monopoly over the exercise of their work. For most professions, legal recognition is granted through forms of licensure and certification.[2]

Such neat and tidy definitions are a good starting point for understanding the professions, yet are clumsy instruments when trying to interpret the full sweep of the professions in American history. In this democratic culture, numerous occupations have come to be accorded professional status which, in one way or another, fail to conform to these definitions. At the same time, the professions in their distinct American form have loomed large as objects both of intense attraction and criticism. Americans have sustained a veritable love-hate relationship with the role of the expert in a democratic culture. The professions have offered a wide door of upward mobility and at the same time built imposing walls to legitimate vested interests and social inequality. They have furnished the kind of expertise that has made American efficiency the wonder of the world and at the same time served to entrench elites unresponsive to popular control. In the most vivid example of contradictory extremes, Americans admire professionals for their dedication to public service and revile them for the extent to which such claims serve as masks for financial greed.

Why have Americans, who espouse such deep egalitarian convic-

tions, become such inveterate professionals? In the United States, professional aspiration has stretched far beyond the three venerable professions:
medicine, law, and the church. Middle-class Americans have long dreamed
of upgrading their occupations, working to endow them with the respect,
power, and financial security available to recognized experts. Only in America, for example, did undertakers in the nineteenth century sever their ties
with cabinetmakers and liverymen. They enhanced their prestige by calling
themselves "funeral directors" and "morticians," a title suggesting the word
physician.[3] Only in America have the ancient professions been rudely de-
mocratized and their doors opened to those without traditional social standing. In the nineteenth century, states refused to set formal education requirements for lawyers, physicians, and the clergy and refused to certify the
exclusive claims of established professionals. In the field of medicine, for
instance, regular physicians found themselves competing without legal advantage against a host of sectarian practitioners—homeopaths, hydropaths,
eclectics, chiropractors, and the like—each assuming the universal title of
"doctor." At the same time, the rapid expansion of institutions of higher
education offered the promise of professional status to those who could
never make that claim on the basis of social standing, family, or wealth.
By 1870, there were more institutions in America awarding bachelor's degrees, more medical schools, and more law schools than in all of Europe.
In a nation without an effective apprenticeship system and without a significant gentry, a diploma—quite readily obtained—came to serve as the sur-
est route to standing and respectability.[4]

   In fact, the concept of *the professions* for a whole range of occupations
has arisen historically only in the Anglo-American world. Robert Dingwall
has called professionalism "the Anglo-Saxon disease" and notes that it is no
accident that even the theoretical literature on the professions is almost wholly
Anglo-American. In Europe, where the state was much more active in organizing training and employment, occupations were less obliged to scramble
competitively for a secure and privileged place in the economy. In Germany
and France, status and security have derived less from a given occupation
and more from attendance at a state-controlled, elite institution of higher
education.[5]

   Even in England, where professionalism flourished among the middle
class in the nineteenth century, the professions remained embedded in firm
class distinctions and were themselves sharply graded. In medicine there were
three ranks: the physician, a gentleman with a liberal arts education who
alone could assume the title "doctor"; the surgeon, an artisan who treated

external injuries and was trained by apprenticeship; and the apothecary, a tradesman who bought and sold drugs. Until 1833, English physicians were required to hold a degree from Oxford or Cambridge; and between 1771 and 1833 the Royal College of Physicians admitted only 168 fellows.[6] Similar distinctions stratified the legal profession. Barristers were lawyers with a university education. With privileges granted by the exclusive Inns of Court, they alone could argue cases in court. Below them, attorneys and solicitors, who trained merely through apprenticeship, could make no claim to gentlemanly status and spent their time merely preparing cases. The most rigid gradations in the professions were the orders within the church: bishops, priests, and deacons. All were university trained, but a vast gulf separated the status of bishops, who sat as noblemen in the House of Lords, and the lowly deacons.[7] British universities manifested similar gradation of rank among faculties. Whereas in America all regular college faculty came to assume the title "professor," in Great Britain it was reserved for the select few who held university chairs; the lesser faculty were known as readers and lecturers.

The officer class of the British military was even more aristocratic than these older professions. Virtually down to World War I, an ambitious middle-class boy had little hope of seeking entrance into the upper echelons of the army and the navy, where one required a patron, the right education, and sufficient funds to purchase commissions which were controlled by the senior officers of a regiment.[8] An Andrew Jackson or a Ulysses S. Grant would never have had the opportunity for military exploits in this more controlled environment. Well into the twentieth century, the ethos of the British officer class illustrated a more general point: in Great Britain professional relationships have generally implied a class relationship. The authority of a professional was reinforced by these more basic distinctions in society.

Unencumbered by such rigid barriers, Americans have clamored to better themselves by achieving professional status, a trend that has only increased since World War II. In America even the field of business management, once thought antithetical to a professional ethos, has become thoroughly professionalized. The 70,000 Americans who face the job market each year armed with an M.B.A. have been trained in their own "science" of management, belong to their own professional associations, partake of their own conventions, books, and magazines, and assume a "professional" air by their style of language, clothing, income, and style of work. Virtually unknown in this country before World War II and without parallel in either

Japan or West Germany,[9] the profession of business management attests to how thoroughly the quest for credentials of merit has become a central organizing principle in our society. In this "credentialed society," it is little wonder that the "young urban professional" has come to be a cultural symbol.[10]

Yet the same democratic culture that makes professional status so alluring also remains deeply suspicious of the claims and pretensions of professionals. In a culture where the quest for professional standing has been so strong, one finds that excessive admiration is woven together with deep antipathy. Time and again Americans have opted for equality over privilege, the commoner over the expert. In colonial America, the Puritans maintained a deep hostility to lawyers as those who profited by the distress of others and who found occupational reasons for encouraging disputes.[11] Their grandchildren at the time of the American Revolution lobbied with equal fervor to keep America free from the control of a resident Anglican bishop. Jacksonian America witnessed a major assault upon established elites in politics, law, medicine, and the church. Claiming that these offices required no special professional qualification, ordinary people rushed to take these matters into their own hands.

In our own day, the ascendancy of the professions is accompanied by equally strident attack from at least four quarters: from consumer groups who complain of escalating professional fees and unequal distribution of professional service; from critics of professional schools who lament an exclusively utilitarian curriculum; from those who fault the strictly academic standards of access to the professions; and from those who find that professionalism serves to reinforce and extend the inequalities of American society.[12] These criticisms are part of a wider skepticism that has emerged toward all kinds of professional experts in the last twenty years. Public opinion research reveals, for instance, that from 1966 to 1983 the number of Americans saying that they have "a great deal of confidence" in professional institutions declined precipitously: from 61 percent to 36 percent in higher education, from 73 percent to 30 percent in medicine, from 41 percent to 23 percent in organized religion, and from 62 percent to 35 percent in the military.[13]

All of this is not meant to imply that American history is an unrelenting story of clear-cut antagonism between advocates of democracy and those of professionalism. For one thing, the very process of relying on expertise easily breeds new kinds of ambivalence and uneasiness about its role. For another, professionals in America have often claimed that democracy, whether in medicine, religion, or civil government, could degenerate into the worst kind of hierarchy and abuse of popular rights. In such cases, professionals have often defended themselves as the true saviors of democracy.

In fact, the great allure of the professions in the period between 1880 and 1920 was that they could restore American democracy from the corruptions and excesses to which it was allowed to sink during the Gilded Age. Progressive reformers viewed the rise of bureaucratic organizations staffed by trained experts and employing scientific objectivity as the only way to sustain and renew the best of American democracy. For leaders such as Woodrow Wilson, representative government easily came to mean government by the ideal of nonpartisan expertise. "Nonprofessionalism is nonefficiency," he exclaimed.[14] The point is that advocates of professionalism often see no tension between expertise and democracy; they are committed to an ideal of the former as a way to achieve the latter.

The eleven essays included in this volume explore in detail the recurring tensions within a society strongly attached to values that are both democratic and professional. The professions selected do not represent a canonical list of those occupations which most fully conform to some prescribed criteria; instead, they include the "ancient" professions—law, medicine, the clergy—as well as a representative group of newer occupations that have come to be accorded professional status. Other professional groups might well have been chosen: architecture, forestry, accounting, or dentistry, for instance. The list also reflects those professions which have been explored by historians in interesting and significant ways. In fact, the principal impetus for the book was the realization that so many gifted historians were working to chart the development of specific professions. The value of this volume is the sterling quality of their respective work and the insights available in observing the parallel evolution of different professions within a common culture.

The essay on higher education by Laurence Veysey is an excellent place to begin for at least two reasons. First, Veysey questions the whole idea of the professions as an occupational category in modern society, or at least he proposes to give up the effort abstractly to define the term *professional.* He argues that the professions remain little more than a series of rather random occupations that have come to be accorded professional status. The point is well taken given Veysey's description of the modern American university as anything but a single profession. He concludes that the university may well be the most internally diverse institution in contemporary society, comprised of several major subcultures and hundreds of specialties within them.

Veysey's discussion of higher education is also valuable because the rise of the modern university had such an integral relationship to the development of professional groups. Quite simply, young people heading for the professions did much to create the demand for universities a century ago, and professional societies have done much to shape university curricula ever since. Veysey posits that three rival traditions vie for influence in the modern university: training for professional careers, basic research, and liberal education. He concludes that the most highly threatened of these are the liberal arts. Their acute vulnerability is evident even in the way they are currently being defended. To argue that a "core curriculum" would remedy the deficiencies of today's students may well save the liberal arts, but only on a remedial or auxiliary level. Sounding a note of alarm about the liberal arts involves a certain irony in a book on the professions. For centuries a liberal arts education was the hallmark of the professional and the only absolute requirement for entering professional ranks.

The next four chapters treat those professions which cover the entire sweep of American history, from colonial times to the present: law, medicine, the clergy, and the military. In one way or another, each of these authors addresses the kinds of professional change which have been wrought on the anvil of democracy. In law and medicine, it is the extremes that are noteworthy: how did professionals so thoroughly lose control of their sphere of influence in Jacksonian America only to regain it so completely early in the twentieth century? The role of the clergy underwent equally profound changes in shedding their mantle as public officials and adapting to the intensely competitive environment of the early nineteenth century. Yet unlike lawyers and physicians, the clergy as a whole have never been able to reassert professional control over the sphere of religion. As Martin Marty suggests, their own influence has been reduced to that of nurturing specific clienteles, and their professional authority challenged with great effect by popular religious leaders—those who short-circuit normal entrance requirements for respectable clergy and gain authority by direct popular appeal. David Martin has noted that both England and American culture share an anti-intellectual populism, but in the United States the populists are actively inside the churches rather than outside of it.[15]

John Shy also notes contradictory extremes between an egalitarian culture and the authoritarian structure of a profession. In the case of the military, he suggests that this tension has been unavoidable, having been woven into the fabric of American history over two centuries. The authoritarian nature of the military gives it an inherently unstable relationship with a democratic society. The result is that lack of respect coexists with excessive admiration. For all their fear of the military as corrupt and dangerous and their long-term hostility to large standing armies, Americans have also been surprisingly open to the blandishments of former generals, from George Washington to Andrew Jackson to Dwight Eisenhower—what Shy calls the "political magic latent in military heroism."[16]

The three chapters which follow treat science, engineering, and journalism, all professions whose origins are intimately tied to the powerful democratic impulses that were at work in Jacksonian America. In the fields of science and engineering, professional organizations came into being as a way to defend the claims of experts against popular notions that scientific matters were accessible to all. The noted scientist Joseph Henry lamented in the 1840s: "Our newspapers are filled with puffs of quackery and every man who can . . . exhibit a few experiments to a class of young ladies is called a man of science."[17] Science and engineering as professions depended upon careful distinctions being drawn between experts and amateurs.

The field of journalism, on the other hand, came to assume professional status by riding the wave of democracy rather than trying to withstand it. Until the 1830s, newspapers were not self-supporting commercial ventures. Their circulation was small and dependent upon subscriptions from political and commercial elite rather than upon street sales. In addition, they had to be subsidized by political parties or factions, political opinion being the heart of the newspaper. During the 1830s, a new kind of publication emerged, the "penny press." Aimed at a wider public, this new form of journalism sought to break the hold of given political interests by focusing on news rather than on political commentary. In this environment, newspapers for the first time hired reporters to gather "news," the kind of nonpartisan information that could attract a wider public. The possibility of a professional "reporter" came about only as journalism broadened its audience, allowing the market rather than any single vested interest to shape its content.

The final three chapters of *The Professions in American History* deal with professions that have come to maturity in the twentieth century, most dramatically since World War II. Don K. Price points out that for reasons that are deep within American history a profession of public administration or public policy has been very slow to develop. How could anyone plan a career in public administration if the general assumption prevailed that performance of public duties was so simple a matter that it required no special qualifications and that rotation in office was an essential of democratic politics? Even the Civil Service reforms of the 1880s remained tangled in the dogmas of direct democracy. By requiring that every job be open to anyone from outside the service at any age, the system rendered impossible any system of career development. The system was incapable of treating government service as a coherent profession. These developments stand in marked contrast to the British Civil Service, which reserved top jobs for an elite set of university graduates and attempted to mold them into a distinct class of talented experts for long-term government service.

The demands of World War II, more than anything else, convinced those in government of the necessity of a distinct cadre of trained experts in public service. A decisive influence on the war's outcome was provided by mobilization of the sciences for the development of weapons and for operations research and systems analysis. What became clear was that policies grew incrementally out of specific decisions which required staff work based on the analytic sciences. While contemporary Washington may seem awash with experts in systems analysis and applied economics, Price notes the weakness of the country's career system of professional generalists. For all the allure of the Potomac, few gifted and well-educated Americans choose government service as a profession, dedicating themselves to a long-term career and avoiding the temptation to look for the next job in related firms from the private sector.

World War II also enhanced dramatically the role of professionals in psychology and counseling. The war gave sudden impetus to a demand for outpatient psychiatric and counseling services—to understand such baffling disorders as "battle fatigue." Because of the sheer need for more practitioners, it also allowed psychologists to win the right to move from testing and diagnosis into therapy, most noticeably into performing psychotherapy, which previously had been the exclusive domain of those trained by medical schools in psychiatry. Even the field of pastoral counseling came into its own during the 1940s. Before the war only one in ten seminaries had qualified psychological faculties; by midcentury three out of four did.

The modern profession of counseling, if it can be called that, represents the convergence of at least four streams: psychiatry, clinical psychology, pastoral counseling, and social work. The hesitancy of states to set precise boundaries for the field results in an extremely pluralistic and dynamic environment, one that draws counselors from a broad range of educational paths: schools of medicine, education, home economics, and social work as well as the liberal arts discipline of psychology. The real monitor of the field turns out to be less state regulation and more the decision of insurance companies about which kinds of professional training they will recognize for third-party payment.

It is appropriate to conclude with a discussion of business management, what Harold Livesay calls the most quintessentially American of the professions. Livesay's essay makes plain the deep unresolved tension of professionalism in democratic America. The very culture which many have identified with the business entrepreneur and the "self-made man" has now given rise to "scientific" management, a kind of expertise thought to exist independent of specific business situations and transferable from one firm to the next. Twenty years ago Americans were confident that they had successfully mastered the arts of engineering efficiency, cost control, and market forecasting, and were ready to share the blessings of this expertise with the world. The assumption was that businesses could successfully implant entrepreneurial energy into bureaucratic structures.

In recent years basic American industries such as steel, railroads, and automobiles have been shaken to the very foundations. Serene self-confidence has given way to handwringing and bitter complaint in the very industries from whose halls the clarion call for "scientific management" had gone forth. The utter collapse of the gospel of American management is evident in Livesay's wry remark that the survival of the American automobile industry seems dependent on learning to build cars that blend European design with Japanese engine technology. What happened?

Harold Livesay's answer to this question does not follow the lines of response most often heard from American business leaders: the problems of intractable labor at home, cheap workers abroad, and foreign governments that subsidize their own producers. He argues, rather, that the central difficulty remains with managers themselves and the patterns of professionalism that have come to characterize American industry. American managers, he suggests, have chosen to remain aloof from the workplace, have refused to tap the reservoir of experience and the imagination of "blue collar" workers, and have themselves slipped into patterns of conformity and caution rather than of daring and innovation.

If American management has failed, Livesay suggests, it is because it has lost touch with the very best of its own traditions. The sharpest irony is that the miracle of Japanese management is premised on low costs and high quality, virtues that are so little exclusively Japanese and which used to be the hallmark of American business. As we note contemporary statistics showing the clamor of American M.B.A.'s to become investment bankers, removing themselves yet another step from where work is actually done, it seems appropriate to ask whether business professionalism in this country does threaten to extinguish the very best of American entrepreneurial traditions.

In America it is clear that professional status largely has replaced land, family, or social status as the primary indicator of achievement. Yet professional boundaries in this society have rarely been static and inflexible, partly as the result of a democratic educational environment which prohibits any one small group of universities from monopolizing access to the professions, and partly due to the entrepreneurial tactics of newly emerging professions in staking out their own claims to expertise.

Yet a crucial and much-debated question remains: the extent to which professions in this society serve as agents of privilege, limiting access and monopolizing service, or of democracy, permitting vertical mobility and basing authority on knowledge and skill rather than on inherited status. The role of women in the professions is a good case in point, providing interesting but conflicting evidence. Some data, for instance, point to a range of significant professional advances that women have made in recent years: a tenfold increase in the percentage of women law students from 1960 to 1980 (from 1,883 or 3.8 percent to 42,045 or 33.8 percent);[18] a tripling of the percentage of women medical students since 1960,[19] an increase in the percentage of Ph.D.'s awarded to women from 13 percent in 1970 to 36 percent in 1985,[20] the doubling of the number of women executives and managers in the last decade, the percentage of M.B.A. candidates rising to about 20 percent; the increase in the number of business firms owned by women from 5 percent in 1972 to almost 20 percent now;[21] and the increase in women in the physical sciences from 5 percent in 1968 to over 15 percent today and in the life sciences from 15 percent to well over 30 percent.[22] On the other hand, the recent report of the National Research Council, *Women's Work, Men's Work: Sex Segregation on the Job (1986)*, concludes that the overall degree of sex segregation in the workplace has been a remarkably stable phenomenon since at least 1900 and that women for the most part continue to face discrimination and institutional barriers to achieving professional status.

Such contrasting pictures of the social role of the professions point up the need to reject simple and one-dimensional depictions of professional roles. As the same time they point to the difficulty of depicting accurately in so brief a space the dimensions of a subject which is so thoroughly a part of the American experience. In the final analysis, our perspective on the professions in American history is linked tightly to a larger interpretive issue: whether the story line of the American experience should be found in the achievements of those who found in this society ample opportunity for advancement or in the experience of the vast majority of citizens, those who have been dependent, for good or for ill, upon the claims of professionals to dispense their services justly.[23]

NOTES

1. Quoted in Edmund S. Morgan, *The Meaning of Independence* (Charlottesville, Va., 1976), p. 11.

2. The essays below by Don K. Price and Laurence Veysey deal extensively with the thorny problem of defining a profession. There is a vast sociological literature on the professions. See Talcott Parsons, "Professions," in *International Encyclopedia of the Social Sciences*, ed. David L. Sills (New York, 1968) 12:545. Helpful introductions to this literature are Michael Schudson's essay review of Magali Sarfatti Larson, *The Rise of Professionalism: A Sociological Analysis* (Berkeley, Calif., 1977) in *Theory and Society* 9 (1980): 215–28; and Robert Dingwall and Philip Lewis, *The Sociology of the Professions: Lawyers, Doctors and Others* (London, 1983). For excellent historical discussions on the issue of definition, see Samuel Haber, "The Professions and Higher Education in America: A Historical View," in *Higher Education and the Labor Market*, ed. Margaret S. Gordon (New York, 1974), pp. 237–80; and the introduction to Gerald L. Geison, ed., *Professions and Professional Ideologies in America* (Chapel Hill, N.C., 1983), pp. 3–11.

3. Burton J. Bledstein, *The Culture of Professionalism: The Middle Class and the Development of Higher Education in America* (New York, 1976), pp. 4–5.

4. Ibid., p. 33.

5. Robert Dingwall and Philip Lewis, *Sociology of the Professions*, pp. 24–26.

6. W. J. Reader, *Professional Men: The Rise of Professional Classes in Nineteenth-Century England* (New York, 1966), pp. 1–24.

7. For an excellent summary of the gradations in the British professions, see Haber, "The Professions and Higher Education in America," pp. 238–40.

8. W. J. Reader, *Professional Men*, pp. 73–84. For a provocative comparison of the British and American military, which notes the absence of an American officer class, see John Keegan's review of T. Harry Williams, *The History of American Wars from 1745 to 1918* (1980) in *New Republic*, 27 June 1981, pp. 32–34.

9. Robert B. Reich, "The Profession of Management," *New Republic*, 27 June 1981, pp. 27–32.

10. Randall Collins, *The Credential Society: An Historical Sociology of Education and Stratification* (New York, 1979).

11. John M. Murrin, "The Legal Transformation: The Bench and the Bar

of Eighteenth-Century Massachusetts," in *Colonial America: Essays in Politics and Social Development*, ed. Stanley N. Katz (Boston, 1971), p. 417.

12. For an illuminating discussion of this recent wave of criticism, see Nathan Glazer, "The Attack on the Professions," *Commentary* 66 (November 1978): 34–41. A stinging attack on the legal profession is Philip M. Stern, *Lawyers on Trial* (New York, 1980). On professional education, see Irwin C. Lieb, "Professional Education: Who's in Charge?" *Chronicle of Higher Education*, 7 July 1980, p. 48; and Andrew Hacker, "The Shame of Professional Schools," *Harper's* October 1981, pp. 22–28; and Commission on the Humanities, *The Humanities in American Life* (Berkeley, Calif., 1980), pp. 81–85. Three recent academic books sharply criticize professionalism as an attempt by middle-class groups to monopolize certain occupations: Bledstein, *Culture of Professionalism*; David F. Noble, *America by Design: Science, Technology, and the Rise of Corporate Capitalism* (New York, 1978); and Magali Sarfatti Larson, *The Rise of Professionalism: A Sociological Analysis* (Berkeley, Calif., 1978).

13. Based on polling by Louis Harris and Associates, these statistics are found in Howard R. Bowen and Jack H. Schuster, *American Professors: A National Resource Imperiled* (New York, 1986), p. 132.

14. For an excellent discussion of these issues, see Donald T. Critchlow, *The Brookings Institution, 1916–1952: Expertise and the Public Interest in a Democratic Society* (DeKalb, Ill., 1985), pp. 1–40, quotation from p. 10.

15. David Martin, *A General Theory of Secularization* (New York, 1978), p. 30.

16. See below, p. 99.

17. See below, p. 108.

18. Cynthia Fuchs Epstein, *Women in Law* (New York, 1981), p. 53.

19. Mary Roth Walsh, *"Doctors Wanted: No Women Need Apply": Sexual Barriers in the Medical Profession, 1835–1975* (New Haven, Conn., 1977), p. 269.

20. Bowen and Schuster, *American Professors*, p. 58.

21. Marilyn Loden, *Feminine Leadership* (New York, 1986).

22. Significant books on the role of women in science are Margaret W. Rossiter, *Women Scientists in America: Struggles and Strategies* (Baltimore, 1982); Evelyn Fox Keller, *Reflections on Gender and Science* (New Haven, Conn., 1985); and Keller and W. H. Freeman, *Feeling for the Organism* (New York, 1982), a widely acclaimed biography of Nobel prizewinner Barbara McClintock.

23. The subject of professional ethics is attracting increased attention. See Alan H. Goldman, *The Moral Foundations of Professional Ethics* (Totowa, N.J., 1980); Dewey J. Hoitenga, "Christianity and the Professions," *Christian Scholar's Review* 10, no. 4 (1981), pp. 296–309; Donald B. Kraybill and Phyllis Pellman Good, eds., *Perils of Professionalism: Essays on Christian Faith and Professionalism* (Scottdale, Pa., 1982); and Dennis M. Campbell, *Doctors, Lawyers, and Ministers: Christian Ethics in Professional Practice* (Nashville, 1982).

1. HIGHER EDUCATION AS A PROFESSION: CHANGES AND CONTINUITIES

Laurence Veysey

The somewhat loose and imprecise concept of higher education as a profession must first of all be placed in the context of the idea of the professions as a whole and the historical process that is called professionalization. Too often, I believe, these terms have been taken for granted, as if they had a meaning that is self-evidently clear to everyone. In fact, one is entitled to puzzle a good deal over this vocabulary, as it has been used both to distinguish an element in the American labor force and a tendency in twentieth-century American social history.

According to Census Bureau definitions, about 4 percent of the American labor force consisted of professionals in 1900, rising to about 13 percent in 1970. One may ask what truly sets this minority, relatively small in both years, apart from the rest of the working population. What characteristics do professionals share in common? What entitles so many diverse occupations, such as those represented in this volume, to be lumped together under a single label, *the professions?* The answer that probably leaps to one's mind is specialized training. But specialization, when one thinks about it, is a much broader phenomenon. It is not confined to professionals, or even to the middle class. No one is more specialized in function than an automobile assembly-line worker. So we are really talking not about specialization *per se*, but about specialization of a kind that seems intricate and somewhat intellectually interesting, often awesomely arcane to outsiders, and which it requires a long time to acquire. These qualifications right away introduce an element of subjectivity into the definition.

It is not always easy to pin down the kind of learning process that occurs in creating a "professional" man or woman. During the course of

15

the twentieth century, the university has emerged as the principal seat of professional training of various kinds in the United States. But even now it would be wrong simply to equate professional standing with an advanced academic degree. Actors, who are thought of as professionals both by the census and by general acclaim, still often train in very informal ways, without set time limits. Professional athletes do not always, even today, consider a college education a necessary part of their preparation for their speciality. Perhaps these are exceptions, but their existence serves as a reminder of the difficulty of defining the role of higher education as basic to all professions, rather than as simply a sector of a broader "professional" world.

Even the term *professional*, as related to the pursuit of an arcane, specialized calling, is still sometimes inconsistently applied. For instance, do we ever use the phrase *professional* to describe poets? Yet poets follow a highly intellectual pursuit, requiring great specialization and intense "training" of a certain kind. To take a rather different example, are funeral directors entitled to be called professionals? They think so, and the Census Bureau now agrees. Is their work intellectually interesting? As one conjures more and more examples, doubts about the definition of the term *professional* grow. It comes to seem more and more like an arbitrary historical usage, conferring high status on a privileged but somewhat random group of occupations that cannot satisfyingly be defined as an entire entity.

Does business belong with the professions? Historically, and again according to the Census Bureau, the answer is no. Yet business management is included in this volume. The reason that business has usually been contrasted with the professions, rather than considered to be among them, is that business operates for profit, while the professions, according to some sociologists who have labored hard to define the term, are characterized by their altruism, the dedicated performance of some needed social service by trained experts. I have little trouble in rejecting this motivational conception of the professions out-of-hand. Some of the most notoriously venal occupations, such as much of law, medicine, and dentistry, as well as the funeral industry, are counted among the professions. A great many people go into the professions to make money, as much as does any business executive. But if one recognizes this, the line gets further blurred between professionals and the rest of the middle class.

Further attempts have been made to define the term *profession* as an outcome of a specific historical process, called professionalization, during the course of which a band of experts comes together, creates a specialized organization such as the American Medical Association or the American

Historical Association, and then goes on to restrict membership (and therefore the practice of the profession) to those who can meet its standards, as self-determined. But this will not do either, for, to name just one prominent and highly relevant exception, academics have never been able to set their own terms of employment. They grant the Ph.D. degree to aspirants, but their professional expertise is only given a certain amount of weight in deciding whether they will actually be allowed to teach. Institutional bureaucracies, which may in their own way call themselves professional (by an allusion to a profession of management) but which stand outside the academic specialty, ultimately make those decisions. Various other professions that are included in this volume, among them scientists, journalists, and engineers, find themselves routinely in the same situation, that is, as employees of private or public corporations headed by outsiders. What is called professionalization happened in the full sense only to a few of what are known as "the professions."

Finally, we should not lose sight of the fact that in plain, everyday usage, we continue to employ the word *professional* very often in a still broader and vaguer way. When we use the phrase *professional soldier*, or *professional musician*, we mean nothing other than that the person performs the activity to earn a living, rather than merely doing it occasionally or on the side. In this sense, *professional* connotes only a paid employment status, in contrast to the more aristocratic notion of dipping one's hand in something while one is really standing outside and above it. This distinction, of course, lies behind the continuing tension between amateurism and professionalism in athletics. The term *professional*, in this context, becomes almost invidious rather than honorific.

If these thoughts produce confusion, it is somewhat deliberate on my part. I think we ought to be more confused about what a profession is than we sometimes are. The sociologist Eliot Freidson has pointed out still another interesting fact. The concept of the professions as a blanketing term for a broad range of occupations has arisen historically only in the Anglo-American world. This collective label has no equivalent on the continent of Europe. On top of everything else, it is thus culture-bound.

I propose, therefore, that it is best simply to give up the effort abstractly to define the term *professional*. That is, I propose to define the professions as nothing more than a series of rather random occupations that have historically been called that in our own culture (recognizing that the occupations thought appropriate to the label have also changed over time), and that have conferred at least fairly high social status on their practitioners and their families, while demanding some kind of extended training, usually—though not always—in universities. But even so, one should not forget that poets do not seem to require the label *professional*, even though they have developed a skill with words certainly equal to that of lawyers.

An awareness of the loose, shifting, and culturally provincial nature of the concept of *the professions* may help us to avoid undue rigidity in now considering our main subject, higher education as a profession. I would like to suggest, first of all, that, both historically and still today, the term *professional* does not carry equal resonance within all areas of what is known as higher education. The word is in fact only heard frequently, and given explicit deference, in three concrete locations within the university: among social scientists; among the nonacademic professional schools, such as those for law, medicine, engineering, forestry, and so forth; and, lastly, among high-level academic administrators in perceiving their own managerial role within the overall institution. So what has been left out? The humanities, on the one hand, and the natural sciences, on the other.

In the latter case, the term *professional* is not much used (for instance, we never bother to say, "he is a professional chemist") because, in a way, it is so taken for granted. One does not have to use the phrase *professional physicist*, because to be a physicist at all must mean that, and everyone knows it. Yet the standing of professional economists, even now, is not quite that secure. Economists who teach in universities and/or advise corporations and governments must still consciously gather the mantle of professionalism around themselves to distinguish themselves from people they regard as quacks and usurpers, just as the American Medical Association must still guard itself from advocates of laetrile.

On the other hand, humanists (for instance, literary critics) still often regard the term *professional* with a certain distance bordering on disdain, for they are thinking of it in another of its meanings, which I referred to earlier, as the performance of an activity as one's paid job. Humanists in America even now often look back to a more aristocratic or at least free-lance self-conception, in which one's calling as a poet, novelist, artist, or critic is grounded in the deepest part of the self, and a university paycheck is only an incidental necessity. Yet natural scientists and humanists have this in common: they tend to reject a utilitarian definition of the university. They are interested in the pursuit of truth, artistic or scientific, for its own sake. This is in contrast to both social scientists and academic administrators, who, for reasons of political and social commitment on the one hand and institutional posture and strategy on the other, tend to see the university as directly serving the society in a utilitarian fashion. So we arrive at another interesting conclusion: the term *professional*, rather than blanketing the entire university, as is often more crudely thought, adheres with special explicit force only to those elements within it which reflect a utilitarian worldview.

It would be helpful to stand back and think about how we, each of us, tend to envision the university. Each of us owns not just a sense of identification with the university as a whole, but a sharper, more particular identification with some discipline or specialty which we may also think of as a profession. Probably more than we realize, our view of the entire university is colored by the specific occupation within it that we pursue. Indeed, this is expected. A "good" department chair fights for the budget and the interest of his or her department as if it were the only cause within the university that mattered—whether it be philosophy, chemistry, or athletics. Only perhaps when threatened by outside forces, such as the Reagan administration, do we suddenly galvanize ourselves into a community for the purpose of trying to ward off a common threat. More routinely, we use the university for the pursuit of some particular interest within it, with which we passionately identify ourselves as our very lifeblood—always excepting the escape hatch of the pursuit of the particular interest known as administration. The university is in fact, then, like an umbrella, sheltering an incredible variety of these concrete interests or callings. Indeed it never happens that its artists, scientists, social scientists, athletic coaches, and administrators, much less its undergraduates, secretaries, and janitors, all sit down in the same room together, or go out at night to see the same play or film or hear the same lecture.

For instance, my own campus at Santa Cruz, California, is rather small-sized; we have only about sixty-eight hundred students. I like to think, having been there for over fifteen years—almost since it opened—that I know it intimately. I do know its roadways, its perspectives, and many of its rooms, which carry the memory of particular events and episodes. But every once in a while, on this same campus, I find myself on totally unfamiliar terrain. I stumble into offices which I never knew existed, staffed by people who are performing strange functions, and who, I suddenly realize, are no doubt just as acclimated to their specific corners of the campus as I am to mine, indeed no doubt just as inclined to visualize the campus as radiating outward from their own doorsteps. A medium-to-large campus in some ways is like a city. No matter how long one stays within it, following one's specialized routines, one never can get to know all of it, or all of it equally well.

The internally divided nature of the university may seem obvious, but at another level it is profound. The university may well be the most internally diverse institution there is. While a number of other institutions (a hospital, for instance) shelter a wide group of specialties, in none other that I can think of is their range so extremely diverse and numerous, indeed incongruous. These incongruities are widely perceived. What is scandalous to many, the buying of football players, is merely the expected pursuit of excellence to those within the university who are attached to that particular interest. But one need not fasten on such a notorious example. Entirely within the academic landscape, there are not just "two cultures," as in the simplification of the late C. P. Snow, but at least several major subcultures and hundreds of specialties within them.

Now, when called upon to regard higher education as if it were *one* of the professions, I find that this incredibly complex internal diversity stands in the way of generalizations, to a degree that I doubt any of the other authors in this volume will experience. What defines the university? Suppose, for example, that one were to say that teaching constitutes the common ground on which all the various special occupations within the university meet and function. One is tempted to claim that this is or should be the case. Yet the university as an institution dedicated across the board to teaching is threatened, as we all know, by the claims of research. Indeed, it is often tacitly maintained that the better the university it is, the worse the quality of its undergraduate teaching. We are all familiar with how difficult it is, in particular, to find scientists who enjoy teaching elementary courses. Somehow the university fosters these two distinct enterprises, along with athletics and advisers to government agencies and everything else. Clark Kerr coined the term *multiversity* to describe the entire mix that forms the conglomerate, but decades earlier the new University of Chicago, under William Rainey Harper, was already being facetiously labelled "Harper's Bazaar." Where in all this mixture can one pin down the notion of higher education as a single profession, even if we claim clearly to know what a profession is? The university shelters a multitude of what are called professions, and of people with varying degrees of attachment to the somewhat cloudy concept of professionalism.

If this extreme internal diversity is the outcome, what should we say of the history of the American university? The university in the United States is now approximately a century old. Just about all the elements that contribute to its diversity were present from the start—including, incidentally, big-time athletics, which got under way during the 1880s. Almost from the very outset, the university was characterized by a departmentalized, bureaucratic structure. And again from the beginning, it was inhabited by advocates of conflicting persuasions so far as the goals of the entire institution were concerned. While it has grown enormously in size, especially in the post-World War II period and most especially in the 1960s, a historian has to be astonished by the many continuities.

Let me identify the several major persuasions that have operated in the minds of academics, a hundred years ago and ever since, and which it has been the duty of administrators to attempt to reconcile and somehow present to the public as a single, attractive package. Even this summation will be oversimplified, as my side glances at still further concrete interests such as athletics must remind you. It confines itself to the academic side of the university and, perhaps in a partisan spirit, assumes its centrality. Each of these versions of what the university ought to be which I am about to sketch for you is relatively idealistic, even though the ideals conflict with each other. In common, they all assume that students are or ought to be interested in some kind of substance in their education, rather than primarily in obtaining a degree which will then give them financial rewards and social standing. Someone inclined toward a harsh realism might question the extent to which any of these academic ideals have succeeded in capturing the minds of wide numbers of undergraduates. They have tended to be the ideals prevalent among various sectors of the faculty. What follows, then, is in large part a faculty-oriented perspective on the history of the aims of higher education in America during the past hundred years.

Three differing academic persuasions have dominated debate over the function of higher education throughout the course of the last century. The first has been the utilitarian view that the university ought to train people in the technical expertise necessary to qualify them to pursue a wide variety of practical careers, in a society which has ever greater need of such specialized talent. Cornell University was founded on these premises in 1868 and is generally honored as the first major institution to embody this aim explicitly. The state universities, as they gradually arose, especially in the Midwest, identified themselves with the same readily understandable sense of purpose. University-trained experts would design bridges, help farmers to obtain greater crop yields, advise legislators on tax reforms, and so on, indispensably contributing in endless ways to the practical construction of the increasingly complex and technological society whose era seemed at hand. The president of the University of Illinois, Edmund J. James, caught the spirit of this kind of vision of the American academic world when he maintained, in the year 1905, that the university must "stand simply, plainly, unequivocally and uncompromisingly for training for vocation, not training . . . even for scholarship *per se*, except as scholarship is a necessary incident to all proper training of a higher sort for vocation, or may be a vocation itself, but training to perform an efficient service for society in and through some calling in which a man expresses himself and through which he works out some lasting good to society."[1] Here in a nutshell is the notion of the useful professional career, in whatever field, as the single desirable outcome of higher education in America.

This utilitarian idea of the university connects directly with what appears to be central tendencies in twentieth-century American life—the growth of nearly all the various professions, the flowering of technology, and the rise of bureaucratic organizations in both the private and public sectors, staffed by trained experts. It is interesting to ask whether and to what extent the university in America may in fact be credited with these enormous consequences, which would include the highly visible physical products that now dominate our lives, from skyscrapers to interstate highways to computerized equipment of all kinds. How much of this technology, and how much of the private and governmental bureaucracy, would have come into being without the existence of the university? Clearly it goes too far to say that the university is responsible for all of this. Technological inventiveness long preceded the initial appearance of the university in the nineteenth century. Bureaucratic organizational structure first appeared in the railroad industry, again before most business executives had college training. The idea of the university-trained expert really dates from the Progressive Era, by which time American society was already urbanized and industrially developed. Yet in recent decades, especially in such areas as architecture, engineering, social work, and, above all, medicine, the university really has been linked with the tangible material changes that everyone experiences in daily existence, whether or not they have been to college. And, just as clearly, the university is largely responsible for the substantial increase in the share of the American population which the Census Bureau labels professional.

Since the utilitarian vision of the American university has been allied with such powerful real forces in twentieth-century American life, it is understandable that both many of the academic participants and later historians have tended to see this linkage as the entire relevant account of the university in the United States. In this view, the meaning of the university lies in its role in furthering all the various professions. The university is seen to have created the professional expert as the central figure in the kind of society we actually have. The result may then be celebrated, as in the writings of Clark Kerr, or may be attacked, as in Burton J. Bledstein's book, *The Culture of Professionalism,* but the assumption that this is the whole important picture remains the same in both cases.

In fact, this conception of the university neither accounts for the entire academic side of the university nor explains the variety of responses in the society to its promises or to its tangible results. Both the university and the society are broader, and are more rent with internal strain and conflict, than this simple model of advancing professionalism allows for.

As regards American society, the elections of 1980 and 1984 have reminded us once again that forces unfriendly to academic expertise and to arcane professionalism have great staying power among the ordinary voters. Both from the left, as in the 1960s, and from the right, as in the 1980s, the model of a society governed by university-trained technocrats has come under attack. A plainer conception of American virtues, one that looks back longingly to the nineteenth century, proves to have surprising resilience. Property-oriented individualism, long pronounced dying or dead in an age of social "interdependence" by many liberal academics, reemerges as an American value with the widest resonance. One realizes that the entire conception of the technically oriented university as the font of American growth was joined only with a center zone of the political spectrum, ranging from New Dealers on the left to moderate Republicans on the right. The political center seemed to dominate America from 1933 through the 1970s. Thus it was understandable that historians, themselves usually friendly to the same outlook, should increasingly claim that it was the direction in which America was headed into the indefinite future, and that therefore the rise of the university, so defined, lay at the root of modern American society. But, both further to the left and further to the right, populism remained alive in the wings; and, in conflicting versions during the 1960s and 1970s, it reasserted itself. Now we can see a continuity between the rhetoric of the Populist politician "Pitchfork Ben" Tillman, promising to abolish the state university as part of his campaign for governor of South Carolina in 1890, and the Reagan administration's impulse to wipe out all appropriations for research in the behavioral sciences. Academically trained bureaucrats, technocrats, and professionals have grown accustomed all over again to being placed on the defensive, after an intervening period when everything seemed to be going their way.

Beyond this, one may inquire more closely into the characteristics of that intervening period, from the New Deal to the Great Society, from the point of view of the role of the academic expert within it. Though the physical transformation of America as a result of techical and professional expertise was enormous, and though the rise of bureaucracy was indeed real, some liberal historians have exaggerated the actual centrality of universities in realms of power, even during those decades. Franklin D. Roosevelt had his "Brains Trust," of course, but it is commonly agreed that he made his own decisions in a spirit of non-academic political realism. Again, the success of McCarthyism in the early 1950s showed the inability of what has often been called the East Coast or Ivy League establishment to maintain its power consistently. If its bastion was the State Department, the State Department has periodically suffered intrusions or has been bypassed in the making of foreign policy at the highest level. There was the sad self-deception involved in Arthur M. Schlesinger, Jr.'s role within the Kennedy administration. Only in the instance of Henry Kissinger is it undeniable that someone flaunting academic credentials achieved genuinely great power, and it was by expressing an outlook only marginally linked to the earlier academic liberalism. Much more often academics have been brought in, whether to government or to large private corporations, either to provide an agreeable window dressing for decisions already made by others, or to provide purely technical ways and means for accomplishing things, for instance in the military and profit-making realms.

Early in the twentieth century, much faith was often placed in the supposed neutrality and superior objectivity of the "expert." In the Progressive Era, a frequent demand was to replace partisan politicians with experts, so that decisions might be made fairly and impartially—"scientifically," as it was said—from then on into the future. But we have come to see that experts have their own partisanships, that they often hire themselves out to the highest bidder for their servics, and that if their views prove to be cantankerously independent they are characteristically shunted aside. Party politicians and corporate leaders seeking to maximize profit called the ultimate tune even during the decades when university-trained expertise appeared to have its maximum influence. The expertise, in many crucial areas, was indeed essential to the creation of the kind of society we have. But it did not exist in some kind of a vacuum. It was in harness to other, more familiar forces.

Expertise, I think it is fair to say, is not among the fundamental American values. We live among its fruits, but there is a widespread uneasiness and ambivalence about the phenomenon itself. The college professor, through much of the twentieth century, remained the target of a somewhat deroga-

tory popular stereotype, which pictured him or her as ineffectual, impractical, and marginal in terms of "real life," even though his or her self-image
(perhaps in direct response) was increasingly that of an expert. After the
Second World War this derogatory image softened, perhaps melted away.
But then, in the last fifteen years, a much wider skepticism has emerged
toward all kinds of professional experts, including professors. Only on the
East Coast, I believe, do academics routinely still enjoy a certain degree of
automatic deference, at least at leading private colleges and universities. In
my own neighborhood in northern California, a young man pumping gas,
learning I taught history at the university, thought it perfectly natural to
grin and cheerfully say, "History was the subject I hated the most in school."
It did not occur to him to defer to my feelings, nor was there any malice
in the remark. When, a couple of years ago, my campus seemed threatened
by closure, bumper stickers appeared in the town saying it would be a good
riddance; more significantly, the main argument used by townspeople in support of the university was the payroll it provided, rather than anything more
intrinsic. At best, higher education increasingly comes to symbolize butter
in an age of guns.

If professional expertise does not seem to have gained the kind of universal respect in American society predicted by its own representatives and
by some historians, an explicit emphasis on professional training for vocational service has never characterized the entire academic side of the American university itself. As I indicated earlier, the posture of a utilitarian professionalism has tended most often to assert itself among social scientists on
the arts and sciences faculty, among those teaching in professional schools
attached to the university, and among academic administrators seeking to
justify the university to the wider public. But this leaves other sectors of
the faculty not so well accounted for.

One may try to lump research-oriented scientists and scholars under
the label of professionalism, of course. Yet, both historically and right now,
I would argue that the ethos of science and of advanced scholarship in general is distinct from the service-oriented vocationalism that I have just been
talking about. The seeking of knowledge may captivate the mind as its own
end, and the intellectual systems that come into being as a result may have
little to do with any useful purpose. I do not think these are merely gran-
diloquent statements; rather I think they accurately reflect the intensity of
psychological commitment that some followers of a great many intellectual
specialties bring to their subject matter. There is such a thing as intellectual
curiosity. In fields like physics, astronomy, mathematics, or archaeology, its

lure would seem especially direct and undeniable, though one can find it in any academic discipline. It cannot be reduced to motives of careerism and self-promotion, though it is intertwined with them; nor, except on a very strained, artificial level, can intellectual curiosity be reduced to the idea of serving a society. The conflict between the two motives can be seen in the disappointment of astronomers that NASA funds were spent not on orbiting a huge telescope but on the showy, nationalistic goal of sending an American to the moon. Again, the fact that of late a number of the theoretical branches of science have made discoveries with portentous implications for human society—I need not name the examples—says nothing about the intellectual processes that led to them. The pursuit of basic science, or of scholarship as its own end, may be a profession, as that label is so often used, but there is an important sense in which it is "above" the more mundane, socially oriented aspects of professionalism conceived as public service. Like a game of chess, it is real, and when well done can strike people as awesome; but it is profoundly nonsocial, at times inhuman. No wonder then that it is often confusingly disguised by its own participants, to appear more humanly understandable and more socially useful than it is, especially in the context of pleas for funding.

The creation of the Johns Hopkins University in 1876 brought this kind of motivation to America for the first time in a deliberate institutional setting. And it is interesting that the circular announcing graduate work there in 1877 took pains to state that "the Johns Hopkins University provides advanced instruction, *not professional*, to properly qualified students, in various departments of literature and science."[2] This distinction has maintained itself in the common usage of the term *professional schools* for graduate schools other than in the arts and sciences, right down to the present. Clearly, in the minds of the most ardent devotees of science and scholarship, there has been something faintly demeaning about the term *professional*.

Perhaps the rhetoric about research as an academic ideal has been toned down just a bit since the enthusiastic days of the turn of the century, when G. Stanley Hall, the psychologist, called the researcher the "knight of the Holy Spirit of truth," and said that the university exists to keep alive "the holy fervor of investigation. . . . Research is its native breath, its vital air."[3] Hall and others freely compared the induction into an academic discipline by a young scholar with the process of religious conversion. "The young contributor becomes henceforth a member of the great body corporate of science, having his own function in the church militant yet invisible."[4] Today such language may seem overblown. Yet the stature later accorded an

Einstein stems from this same ethos. And the university, I think we would all admit, is supposed to represent the values of intellectual attainment, no matter what else it may also stand for. Even in the flattened climate of the 1980s one must still say this.

The problem with emphasizing the motive of intellectual curiosity and the goal of intellectual attainment in discussing the American university is that it sounds so elitist. It is far more elitist than the goal of vocational training for social service, yet even that other aim, involving the concept of professional expertise, has, as we have seen, come under recurrent populistic attack. In the face of all this, is there not a point where we must dig in and say that if the university does not stand for pure intellect, it stands for nothing? But I confess I ask this warily, and somewhat expecting a negative response. We live in an age not only of reduced means and budgets, but of increasing pessimism and loss of intellectual morale. The forces of the academic job market have become so discouraging as to produce much talk of a lack of will to go on. Faculties are being deprived of renewal through younger, more vital blood. The greatest age of the American university, in scholarly and scientific terms, may lie in the past. Perhaps to say this kind of thing is an overreaction; it is too early really to know. But I mention this second traditional ideal for the university, centered in intellectual discovery rather than in vocational training, aware not only of the great evils it has produced, such as nuclear weapons and scientific arrogance, but of what was precious and indispensable in it, and how it now seems genuinely threatened with decline.

There has always been yet another rival conception of the mission of higher education, however, and it forms the last of the three conflicting persuasions that have continually fought each other during the century-long history of the American university. This final view emphasizes the training of the mind (and therefore teaching) rather than the use of the mind to gain original knowledge (research). If the natural sciences are the most typical home of the research persuasion, then what we call the liberal arts, or sometimes of late more narrowly the humanities, usually form the bastion of this other, teaching-oriented outlook.

Until recently the position of the liberal arts within the American university has been surprisingly static. From the very beginning, a paradox presented itself: the liberal arts contained some of the most honored traditional disciplines, such as the classics, inherited from the earlier American college; yet they found themselves very much on the defensive, both from the advocates of utilitarian professional training and from the believers in a scientific style of research. In rebuttal to them both, those who spoke for liberal education claimed to represent timeless moral and intellectual values, often though not always allied to the cause of religion, and certainly always linked to what were believed to be the traditions of "Western civilization" (a phrase that came into currency at the time of the First World War, directed against Germany). Around the turn of the twentieth century, the defenders of the liberal arts invariably asserted that moral character was the desired end of teaching; needless to say, their hearts were in undergraduate teaching, rather than in the alien "scientific" world of the graduate or professional school. As Charles Eliot Norton, the famous art historian at Harvard, formulated these sentiments: "The highest end of the highest education is . . . the development of the breadth, serenity, and solidity of mind, and . . . the attainment of that complete self-possession which finds expression in character."[5] In social terms, the college existed to train gentlemen—a word that then had not yet passed out of existence. The future gentleman was to be taught those moral values, and those traits of character, that would enable him gracefully to become a civic leader. The model was the British upper classes. Clearly, in its own way, this ideal was even more elitist than that of scientific expertise or of professional standing. In an important sense, though they were allied with such older professional elites as the clergy and lawyers, the advocates of liberal education looked down upon the professions, particularly such upstart professions as engineering. They continued to defend an older conception of amateurism, or of the breadth that produced an ideal "Renaissance man," capable of effortlessly doing half a dozen different varied and honorable things at once. They did not want the curriculum to reflect vocational specialization; initially they attacked the elective system of studies. Dean Andrew F. West of Princeton sounded the typical note, in 1913, when he attacked "the break-up of the knowledge into pieces, the resulting dissevering of sympathy and dehumanizing of scholarship, the lowering of tone which comes from losing one's view of knowledge in its unified grandeur, and the literal 'provincialization' of learning."[6]

As time went on, during the course of the twentieth century, some of this older style of defending the liberal arts, essentially conceding nothing to science, professionalism, or the contemporary intellectual climate, remained present among humanists, at least until the 1960s. Maybe there are some echoes of this mood in the attempted revival of the humanities even now. But the believers in liberal education became increasingly fragmented, the victims of separation into their own specific disciplines, such as classics, art, literature, philosophy, and history, and of the varying currents of discourse within each of them. Religion became defended less and less. The idea of "Western civilization," stemming from the Greeks, became a substitute religion for some believers in the humanities; this was ardently pushed at Robert M. Hutchins's University of Chicago. But it too began to fade as a unified rallying point, amid the growing awareness of global ethnic diversity and cultural relativism which formed such a strong tide by the 1960s. Such other perspectives as Freudianism, Marxism, pragmatism, and logical positivism all captured bands of adherents within the humanistic fields. The liberal arts began to represent a multitude of conflicting voices. Today there is a demand to get "back to basics." But, when this cry is for something more than correct spelling, it becomes hard for a diverse faculty to agree as to what those basics really are.

There has even been talk lately of the death of the liberal arts. I think they are indeed in graver danger than ever before, as the economy threatens in a prolonged way to create a tone of anxiety that leads to the search for security through narrow pursuit of technically oriented careers, and as resources for the university dwindle at the same time. I think, however, that *death* is too extreme a term to use. Even in today's world, the liberal arts can remain strong at many institutions, such as those of the Ivy League, whose prestige is so high that they can still afford to set the conditions for a bachelor's degree. The problem is most acute at the large number of institutions of lesser renown, where, to survive as enrollments decline and competition becomes intense, the atmosphere may be in increasingly distinct danger of devolving into that of a trade school.

We have briefly looked at what I consider to be the three major rival traditions within the American academic world, those centered respectively in career training, basic research, and liberal education. We have seen that all have had a continuous existence in our universities ever since they were created roughly a hundred years ago. At various times in the past, each of them has enjoyed particular resonance, in a series of pendulum swings— utilitarian vocationalism in the decade from 1865 to 1875, again in the Progressive Era, and strongly once more in the last few years; basic research in the final quarter of the nineteenth century and again in the 1950s and early 1960s. The liberal arts have been more continuously on the defensive, but even they enjoyed notable revivals of esteem around 1910, in the mid-1940s, and, briefly, in the mid-1960s. But in the longer sweep it could always be said there was a steady balance among them, especially when taking into account the varying character of particular American colleges and universities. This balance prevailed during an age of growth, when slices of the expanding pie were available for everybody, helping to foster a frozen sense of the internal interests or constituencies within academia. Now that growth has ended, in an unfriendly political and economic climate, this long-time balance is indeed threatened, so far as the less elite institutions are concerned. All three aims for higher education have proved vulnerable to popu-listic attack. But this vulnerability differs in degree. Professional expertise can withstand the rather rhetorical assaults against it. Indeed, those assaults unfairly center on government bureaucrats, while the more venal profes-sions associated with the private sector of the economy are now once again being praised. Basic research is in a middle position, unable to command the kind of support it did in the 1960s, yet able to identify itself with utili-tarian goals such as national defense and thus able to maintain substantial capacity for resilience, at least in many areas. Most highly threatened are the liberal arts.

Our view of the situation will thus depend on our own position within the overall academic matrix. The academic world of the near future is apt to be marked by a curious mixture of satisfaction, mild concern, and out-right anguish, depending upon whether we represent such fields as business training, biology, or history. Those of us like myself who remain committed to the liberal arts will be placed increasingly in the position of pleading with administrations for survival on the basis of traditional conceptions of the need for balance. Our strongest argument, unfortunately, lies in the area of the demand for a return to "basics"—the perceived deficiencies of our students in such realms as effective writing and critical reasoning. In the movement to create survey courses under the label of *core curricula*, there is danger that the liberal arts may be saved, but only on a remedial or aux-iliary level.

I have postponed until the end the underlying question—does this variegated mixture of interests and outlooks that we lump together under the vague heading, *the academic profession*, deserve saving? It may seem to some of you a ridiculous question. But the populistic attack on academia has gained respectable adherents. Several years ago, in *The Culture of Profes-sionalism*—a book that attracted quite a bit of attention—Burton Bledstein blamed the university for the growth of professionalism in twentieth-century America, a professionalism he saw as elitist, self-seeking, and corrupt. "His-torically speaking," according to Bledstein, "the culture of professionalism in America has been enormously satisfying to the human ego, while it has taken an inestimable toll on the integrity of individuals." And he concluded,

"The culture of professionalism has allowed Americans to achieve educated expressions of freedom and self-realization, yet it has also allowed them to perfect educated techniques of fraudulence and deceit."[7] We are all aware of the seamier side of academic life, evident in career-seeking, intellectual politicking and one-upmanship, and in the occasional fabrication of scientific or scholarly evidence. Bledstein's book may be regarded as a symptom of the sometimes severe self-reproach that academics may engage in.

My defense of the academic world must necessarily be couched in very broad terms. I think that on the whole it is not a very bad world, especially when one compares it with other segments within the American social elite, which is the most directly relevant comparison. The incidence of outright corruption within academia is undoubtedly low in contrast to such fields as law or business. Moreover, to blame the university for the corruption present in these other professions is to exaggerate out of all proportion the university's role in our society, whether for good or for ill, and to neglect the role of the marketplace in setting standards, as against the much briefer impact of the training institution in any person's later life.

Indeed, to a remarkable extent, as I see it, the academic world has remained to one side of the rough-and-tumble of the more ordinary versions of American upper-middle-class life. This is not so true as it was before the Second World War, when very low salaries and less widespread respect for advanced training gave American academia an almost otherworldly tone. But this sense of loyalty to something higher than self-seeking remains very much alive. The academic world is probably second only to the world of American religion as a focal point for whatever idealism lingers in our society. It is the larger society which is failing us, not the academic world that is failing the society. It is the larger society which seems to have lost its compassion and its awareness of the need for equal human respect, and which appears to be moving dangerously close to tolerance for the idea of nuclear holocaust. Some academics may be found abetting these chilling tendencies. But the academic world remains one where the issues of peace and social concern, as well as of the value of intellect, are alive and at least debated. Many academics "burn out," lose their creativity and much of their idealism, at a discouragingly early age. And, amid the intense job pressures in many disciplines, this appears likely to be more frequent at present than it was in the securer if far leaner atmosphere of the turn of the century. The inability of universities to renew their vitality with younger scholars in the liberal arts is indeed ominous for the long-term future. Yet, for a time at least, and relative to the other worlds that are labelled as *the professions,* the academic world is, I would insist, not all that bad a place in which to find oneself, if one is so lucky.

NOTES

1. Edmund J. James, "The Function of the State University," *Science* 22 (1905): 615.

2. *Johns Hopkins University Register,* 1877–1878, p. 14; italics added.

3. G. Stanley Hall, "The University Idea," *Pedagogical Seminary* 15 (1908): 104.

4. G. Stanley Hall, "Confessions of a Psychologist," *Pedagogical Seminary* 8 (1901): 119–20.

5. Charles Eliot Norton, Arthur T. Hadley, William M. Sloane, and Brander Matthews, *Four American Universities* (New York, 1895), pp. 32–35.

6. Andrew F. West, *The Graduate College of Princeton* (Princeton, 1913), p. 4.

7. Burton Bledstein, *The Culture of Professionalism* (New York, 1976), pp. ix, 334.

HIGHER EDUCATION: SUGGESTIONS FOR FURTHER READING

Bledstein, Burton J. *The Culture of Professionalism.* New York, 1976.

Furner, Mary O. *Advocacy and Objectivity.* Lexington, Ky., 1975.

Gruber, Carol S. *Mars and Minerva.* Baton Rouge, La., 1975.

Haskell, Thomas L. *The Emergence of Professional Social Science in America.* Urbana, Ill., 1977.

Kerr, Clark. *The Uses of the University.* New York, 1963.

Oleson, Alexandra M., and Voss, John, eds. *The Organization of Knowledge in Modern America, 1860–1920.* Baltimore, 1979.

Veysey, Laurence. *The Emergence of the American University.* Chicago, 1965.

2. LAW: THE DEVELOPMENT OF A PROFESSION

Maxwell H. Bloomfield

George Bernard Shaw, in one of his less elfin moods, once remarked that all professions "are conspiracies against the laity."[1] Many people agreed with him at the time; still more would agree with him today. Professionals, by definition, hold themselves out to the public as the possessors of specialized knowledge and skills that the ordinary person lacks. The Industrial Revolution, accompanied by the emergence of a market-oriented society, established the preconditions for modern professional development in the United States, Great Britain, and western Europe during the nineteenth century. As professional training became standardized in colleges and universities, professional associations obtained licensing laws from compliant American legislatures that made them self-regulating guilds. Lesser occupational groups and trades similarly claimed professional status as a way of restraining competition, until the term *profession* has all but lost any intelligible meaning. Today, professionals include not merely doctors, lawyers, the clergy, and the other major groups discussed in this volume, but also manicurists, morticians, junk dealers (or "salvage consultants"), and even tree experts in some states. Consumer protection provides a common rationale for occupational licensing, and the rhetoric associated with one profession is often freely appropriated by another. Thus, the chair of the Illinois State Tree Expert Examining Board explained to a legislative commission in 1959 that the intent of the tree expert law was "primarily to protect the public against tree quacks, shysters, and inexperienced persons."[2]

Since licensed professions function as private governments—or "hidden hierarchies" of economic and political power, as one commentator has put it[3]—they threaten at times to evade public accountability and to subvert the legislative process. Critics have urged that some professions should be

33

deregulated and opened to unrestricted competition, while others should be more effectively controlled in the public interest through some external regulatory agency.[4] The tension between professionalism and democracy has been evident throughout our history, and lawyers in particular have been forced to reexamine their role on numerous occasions in the light of both external and internal criticism. I see this enduring tug-of-war between the lawyer and the public as a central theme in American legal history, and I should like to explore some of the ways in which the profession has adjusted, or failed to adjust, to the needs and aspirations of an evolving democratic society.

Lawyers as a group became prominent in the American colonies during the middle years of the eighteenth century. Prior to that time a decentralized agrarian society, loosely connected by poor roads and chance waterways, had little need for a class of trained practitioners. In places like New England, where Puritan values prevailed, early settlers commonly appealed to friendly mediators, rather than the courts, to resolve their disputes. In less godly areas, like Virginia, the lay judges of the county courts dispensed a discretionary justice that leaned heavily on local custom. Juries in every colony further represented the power of community opinion, and often ignored black-letter rules that conflicted with popular views of justice and fair play.[5]

By 1750 the expansion of long-distance trade and the maturing of colony-wide political institutions facilitated the rise of attorneys skilled in the drafting and interpretation of statutes and commercial documents. These "gentlemen of the bar," through birth or marriage, formed part of the colonial ruling elite and attempted to restrict legal practice to applicants from comparable social and educational backgrounds. For this purpose they established bar associations, some of which—like the Suffolk County organization in Massachusetts—developed into effective lobbying groups by the time of the Revolution.[6]

In the course of that successful struggle for independence, roughly one-fourth of all practitioners remained loyal to the Crown and either chose—or were forced into—permanent exile. Their departure weakened surviving bar associations and helped to check the prewar thrust toward corporate exclusiveness and a hierarchically structured profession on the English model. In the postrevolutionary decades young men, often hastily or superficially trained, swelled the ranks of the bar, despite conservative complaints against overcrowding and pettifoggery. Several states, including Massachusetts, New Jersey, and New York, did attempt for a time to restrict practice in the appellate courts to "barristers" or "counselors," while licensing "attorneys" to plead before inferior tribunals. But all such efforts to stratify the bar along class or functional lines failed, as did comparable efforts to regulate the medical profession.

In each case a genuine shortage of skilled technicians existed, there were multiple clienteles to be served, and the standards of professional orthodoxy had not been firmly established. Republican ideology, with its stress on aggressive individualism and laissez-faire government, further implied that the professions, like other employments, should be open to all male citizens on a competitive basis. By 1820, accordingly, eleven out of twenty-four states prescribed no specific term of study for prospective lawyers. This trend continued during the era of Jacksonian democracy in the 1830s and 1840s, and reached a climax of sorts in 1851, when the voters of Indiana approved a new constitution that provided: "Every person of good moral character, being a voter, shall be entitled to admission to practice law in all courts of justice."[7]

An open-door policy of professional recruitment did not, of course, guarantee success at the bar, nor did it lead to a significant decline in the quality of legal practice, as some outraged conservatives predicted that it would. Aspiring attorneys in the years before the Civil War prepared for a professional career by self-study and apprenticeship in the office of an established practitioner. The thoroughness of their training varied from office to office, and their qualifying bar examinations—which were administered in most states by committees of lawyers appointed on an ad hoc basis by the courts—were equally haphazard and unpredictable. Once admitted to practice, however, new attorneys were expected to establish their competence in the eyes of clients by winning cases against seasoned practitioners. Courtroom performance, rather than prior certification, was the key to professional success, and the competition for clients was keen, even in frontier areas. The town of San Augustine near the Texas-Louisiana border, for example, had a free population of 2,087 persons in 1850, including 15 lawyers, or a ratio of 1 lawyer for every 149 inhabitants. In such a competitive environment the visibility of lawyers made it relatively easy for potential clients to screen out the ignorant and the corrupt. Although the winnowing process was doubtless more difficult for those living in large Eastern cities, there, too, an open door to professionalism became a revolving door for would-be practitioners who lacked intelligence and energy.[8]

The absence of stringent admissions criteria did little to democratize the internal structure of the bar. Although lawyering, like other occupations in antebellum America, provided limited social mobility for the sons of small farmers and tradesmen, few attorneys climbed from rags to riches except in the pages of self-help manuals. A recent study of Massachusetts lawyers in the early nineteenth century uncovered a pattern of de facto stratification that undoubtedly prevailed in other states as well. At the top of a three-tiered legal profession stood a small group of wealthy practitioners, a cultured elite who associated familiarly with bankers and industrialists and served their interests in the courtroom and legislature. On the lowest level clustered a comparable body of marginal practitioners, including "pettifoggers" and part-time attorneys, who found it impossible to earn more than a bare subsistence from their professional labors and often abandoned the law entirely. Between these extremes lay a vast middle ground inhabited by most lawyers, who, without ever achieving real affluence, managed to support themselves and their families in varying degrees of comfort by handling a large number of routine cases. Elite practitioners further tended to marry into the families of other professionals, especially doctors and clergymen, thereby strengthening class divisions within the bar.[9]

To these early lawyers fell the task of adapting English legal doctrines and procedures to the developmental needs of a young republic. The creation of a distinctly American jurisprudence formed part of a movement toward decolonization in literature and the arts, as self-conscious Americans sought to assert their independence from England in cultural matters. At the outset legal nationalists faced a critical shortage of native legal publications. Although colonial assemblies had commonly provided for the occasional compilation and printing of statutes, few American law texts existed and published court decisions were simply unavailable. The first volume of American reports—Ephraim Kirby's *Connecticut Reports*—appeared in 1789, but the printing of state appellate court decisions did not begin in earnest until after the turn of the century. Federal court reporting followed a similar pattern: Alexander J. Dallas brought out the first volume of United States Supreme Court Reports in 1798, but regular and systematic federal reporting really began with William Cranch in 1804. By the 1820s, however, a substantial body of indigenous legal literature had been published, and practioners were already complaining that they could not keep up with the digests, statutes, and court reports that seemed to be pouring from the presses.

At this point several influential treatise writers appeared, who promised to synthesize these disparate materials into an overview of American law that would compare favorably with William Blackstone's celebrated exposition of English jurisprudence. Between 1826 and 1830 Chancellor James Kent of New York published his *Commentaries on American Law* in four volumes, an achievement that brought him immediate acclaim as the "American Blackstone." Shortly thereafter Joseph Story, a scholarly Associate Justice of the United States Supreme Court, produced the first of seven authoritative treatises on various fields of American law. The works of Kent and Story remained popular with law students and practitioners until the early twentieth century, and their success encouraged a horde of lesser authors to seek fame and fortune through the marketing of their own legal textbooks.[10]

Evolving American law, as described by these writers, combined republican political values with the economic theories of Adam Smith. An innovative judiciary, in particular, promoted the interests of bankers and entrepreneurs by overturning antidevelopmental English precedents in such areas of private law as contracts, property, and commercial law. Property law, for example, traditionally protected landowners in the exclusive enjoyment of their estates, but American judges refashioned the law of riparian rights to enable mill owners to appropriate water for business purposes without regard to the damage done to neighboring lands. A comparable shift from status to contract—from governmental restraint to the release of entrepreneurial energy—also occurred in public law, where the contracts clause of the federal Constitution was employed to prevent states from regulating the businesses they had chartered. By midcentury, courts and legislatures had done much to redistribute wealth from workers and consumers to a powerful business elite.[11]

The proliferation of antebellum treatises and practice manuals probably helped to delay the growth of law schools, since students could compensate for the deficiencies of their law office training by independent study. A more significant cause of low enrollments, however, lay in the professed goals and curricular requirements of early law schools. Prior to the 1830s most of these institutions—and especially those affiliated with colleges or universities—looked upon law as a humanistic discipline whose principles could not be mastered without a thorough knowledge of history, political theory, and philosophy. Like Blackstone in his classes at Oxford, American law teachers labored to produce not merely courtroom advocates but also enlightened statesmen and well-rounded citizens. Their curricula thus necessarily included many courses that were not directly related to the practice of law. To cite an extreme example: David Hoffman's *Course of Legal Study*, published in 1817 for use in the University of Maryland Law School, required at least four years for its completion.

Since most law students, then as later, preferred to dispense with all unnecessary learning and get on to the business of fee collecting, academic legal training foundered until Joseph Story began to moonlight as Dane Professor of Law at Harvard Law School in 1829. Story, too, believed that law should be taught as a "liberal science"; but financial deficits and low enrollments soon persuaded him to modify his traditional curriculum in some drastic ways. Yielding to the dictates of the marketplace, he restructured and compressed his program by eliminating all subjects that were not immediately useful to practitioners. His new curriculum encompassed little more than common law doctrines as developed by English and American judges and an exposition of the federal Constitution. Students were permitted to come and go as they pleased (provided they paid their fees), and examinations were abolished. Under these conditions the law school prospered and became a model for other institutions by the time of Story's death in 1845. The price of success was high, however; academic legal training was thereafter insulated from any fruitful contact with those humanistic and scientific subjects that Story's predecessors had considered essential to the formation of any lawyer above the level of a "mere technician."[12]

As the goals of legal education were redefined and narrowed by the middle of the nineteenth century, professional ethics underwent a comparable process of reevaluation. The first American code of legal ethics was David Hoffman's *Fifty Resolutions in Regard to Professional Department*, which the German-American lawyer and educator included as part of the revised edition of his *Course of Legal Study* in 1836. Intended to elevate the tone of professional life during an era of rampant democracy, Hoffman's *Resolutions* are most notable for their refusal to separate private from professional morality, or to admit that practitioners might ever be guided by norms that did not equally apply to all other citizens. "What is morally wrong, cannot be professionally right, however it may be sanctioned by time or custom," he asserted.[13] And neither loyalty to client nor compliance with the technicalities of the legal process could absolve an attorney from obeying the dictates of conscience and striving to do substantial justice to all parties. Hoffman carried the latter principle to the point of insisting that a practitioner was morally bound *not* to use all available legal defenses for the client when injustice would thereby result. "I will never plead the Statute of Limitations, when based on the *mere efflux of time*," he noted in a representative passage, "for if my client is conscious he owes the debt; and has no other defense than the *legal bar*, he shall never make me a partner in his knavery."[14]

Hoffman's fastidious and personalized approach to ethical questions seemed impractical to many of his contemporaries—a holdover from the more leisurely world of the eighteenth-century gentleman practitioner. Better attuned to the demands of an industrial age was George Sharswood's *Essay on Professional Ethics* (1854), which became the standard work on the subject for the next century. Sharswood, a Philadelphia judge, was familiar with Hoffman's *Fifty Resolutions* and agreed with many of their specific recommendations. But on such basic issues as the nature and extent of professional responsibility, the two men were poles apart. Where Hoffman referred all problems to practitioner's conscience—that mirror of universal morality—Sharswood opted for the external guidelines provided by the legal process itself. "The lawyer," Sharswood argued, "who refuses his professional assistance because in his judgment the case is unjust and indefensible, usurps the function of both judge and jury."[15] Because the justice or injustice of a cause could be determined only after all the technical rules of litigation had been fully satisfied, every client was entitled to the best possible legal representation. Sharswood thus severed the tie between public and private morality and replaced Hoffman's uniform moral standards with a set of professional norms that often clashed with the attitudes of the laity.[16]

By the time Sharswood's *Essay* appeared, the nation was entering a period of accelerated industrial growth that threatened to overwhelm established values and institutions, including the bar. With the completion of transcontinental rail and communications networks, giant corporations developed to serve and to exploit national markets, defying the competitive rules of classical economics. An unskilled immigrant work force, drawn increasingly from unfamiliar regions of southern and eastern Europe, provoked middle-class fears of alien domination and class war. Journalists warned that America was sinking into a "new feudalism," complete with robber barons and rebellious serfs; and the great labor upheavals of the late nineteenth century seemed to confirm such predictions. By 1900 the ideology of laissez-faire republicanism had largely collapsed, as social theorists hailed the advent of the welfare state, with its commitment to active governmental intervention in the economy on behalf of workers, consumers, and other disadvantaged groups.

For professionals the unsettling effects of massive industrialization provided opportunities for enhanced prestige. Lay people, aware of the limits of traditional knowledge in an era of rapid technological change, turned more readily to experts for guidance. The late nineteenth century was the seedtime of modern professional development in the United States, as one group after another created bureaucratic structures to impose order and control upon their respective disciplines. Contemporary observers saw in this trend a return to the corporativism of medieval society, in which power and status depended upon one's group affiliation. From the standpoint of middle-class professionals, however, the organizational impulse also represented an effort to stabilize social relationships by creating a body of professedly neutral technicians who might serve as mediators between capital and labor. Through the appointment of nonpolitical "experts" to serve on regulatory boards or investigative commissions, the actions of the administrative state might be legitimized and class hostility diluted.[17]

Lawyers contributed to the rise of the corporate society I have been describing in several important ways. As counsel to large corporations, they pioneered in the development of new business forms, such as the trust, and negotiated mergers and other types of corporate reorganization. They also borrowed the techniques of business management to rationalize the operations of their firms and to transform them from old-fashioned partnerships into disciplined "law factories." When Paul Cravath joined the Wall Street firm of Clarence Seward in 1899, for example, he promptly placed all associates on salary, installed telephones and typewriters, began a filing system, expanded the clerical staff, and centralized control of policy making in his own hands. Successful corporation lawyers like Cravath represented a new breed of elite bar leaders, whose ascendancy signaled a shift in the priorities of legal practice from litigation to office counseling and mediation.[18]

The growth of corporate power did not prove an unmixed blessing to the profession, of course. Certain businesses—notably title guaranty companies, collection agencies, insurance companies, and banks—began to offer routine, but profitable, services that had formerly been handled by the bar; and many general practitioners deplored the loss of independence and public esteem that seemed to accompany a specialized corporate practice. Prodded by both ethical and economic anxieties, elite bar leaders initiated a revitalized bar association movement that began with the formation of the Association of the Bar of the City of New York in 1870. Although earlier bar organizations had been denounced as monopolistic trade unions, the new groups flourished in the guildlike atmosphere of the late nineteenth century. The New York association lobbied successfully to replace several corrupt judges with honest ones, and provided a model for similar organizations of leading practitioners elsewhere. In less than a decade eight city and eight state bar associations arose in twelve different states, and their example in turn prompted the founding of the first national bar organization—the American Bar Association—in 1878.

Each of these groups, and those that followed, shared certain basic objectives and strategies. As select social clubs, they sought to enhance their public image by limiting membership to the most respectable and socially prominent practitioners; as trade unions, they lobbied to restrict access to the bar and to prevent lay competitors, such as title companies, from doing law jobs; and as public-spirited pressure groups, they advocated a variety of conservative reforms, including the adoption of uniform state laws and improvements in judicial procedure. Their efforts led to the introduction of standardized written examinations for all bar candidates by the early twentieth century, and to the centralized administration of those tests by state boards of bar examiners.[19]

Although the bar associations purported to speak for all reputable attorneys in their lobbying campaigns, they in fact reflected only the views of the narrow professional elite who controlled them. Those views, even when expressed in the language of disinterested reform, were often tinged with racism. Like other leadership groups in turn-of-the-century America, elite practitioners from old-stock backgrounds believed in Anglo-Saxon racial superiority and doubted the fitness of lesser breeds. Women, blacks, and some ethnic minorities were excluded from membership in many bar groups for years and formed their own associations for mutual support and advancement. Women lawyers founded the National Association of Women Lawyers in 1899; black attorneys established the National Bar Association in 1925; and many small ethnic organizations, such as the Bohemian Lawyers Association of Chicago (1911) and the Jewish Decalogue Society of Lawyers (1934), arose to protest the inhospitable temper of the major bar associations. Even the movement for an integrated (or compulsory) state bar, which began in 1913 under the aegis of the American Judicature Society, had some racist overtones. Although heralded as a mechanism for unifying and strengthening the bar, this "closed shop" for lawyers also promised to bring troublesome practitioners—especially black attorneys in the South and eastern European Jews in the urban Northeast—under more effective disciplinary control. By 1960 the bars in more than half of the states had adopted this model of professional organization.[20]

A comparable thrust toward consolidation and autonomy occurred in legal education, with the appointment of Christopher Columbus Langdell as dean of the Harvard Law School in 1870. Famous (or infamous) to generations of law students as the inventor of the case method of legal instruction, Langdell insisted that law was a theoretical science like geometry, and that its principles could only be mastered by rigorous academic training. "All the available materials of that science," he explained, "are contained in printed books. . . . The library is . . . to us all that the laboratories of the university are to the chemists and physicists, all that the museums of natural history is to the zoologists, all that the botanical garden is to the botanists."[21] Through the careful analysis of appellate court opinions a student might uncover a body of fundamental legal rules that were as timeless and unchanging as mathematical formulae. These rules, moreover, were few in number and could be deduced from a relative handful of leading cases. How was one to know which cases were worthy of serious study? Obligingly, Langdell unveiled yet another innovation: the first casebook. In his *Selection of Cases on the Law of Contracts* (1871) he included primarily English opinions, with a smattering of decisions from Massachusetts and New York. Although he arranged these cases in chronological sequences, he had no interest in their historical contexts. He sought rather to demonstrate the unfolding of transcendent legal truths, whose validity depended in no sense upon the needs of particular societies.

Langdell's jurisprudential theories and methods possessed an irresistible attractiveness for American lawyers in the late nineteenth century. At a time when treatise writers could no longer assimilate the increasing mass of reported cases, he proposed to simplify and systematize legal knowledge by developing a unitary set of rules to govern every field of private law. His controlled use of primary data—appellate court opinions—as a basis for generalization was in keeping with the scientific temper of the age, and brought the law school into line with other graduate schools that were becoming centers of specialized research. For judges the triumph of Langdellian principles encouraged a move away from the socially conscious jurisprudence of the antebellum years toward an arid formalism that relied upon precedents in a mechanical fashion. A new style of opinion writing developed, in which jurists avoided facts and policy arguments, justifying their adherence to the rules of a bygone agrarian age by merely citing a string of cases.[22]

Since the preparation and use of casebooks required a high level of scholarship, Langdell's system further produced a new class of full-time law professors. "What qualifies a person . . . to teach law," he maintained, "is not experience in the work of a lawyer's office, not experience in dealing with men, not experience in the trial or argument of cases, not experience, in short, in using law, but experience in learning law."[23] Instructors who taught by the case method could not rely on old lecture notes; their task was rather to train students in correct legal reasoning by engaging them in intensive discussion of case material—a process the early Langdellians modestly termed the "Socratic dialogue." The idea that law should only be taught by an intellectual elite was perhaps the most revolutionary plank in Langdell's program; but here, too, he gradually prevailed, despite bitter opposition. The appointment of James Barr Ames, a recent graduate, to the Harvard law faculty in 1873 signaled the beginning of the modern professoriat. By 1900 academic lawyers from thirty-two law schools founded the Association of American Law Schools to promote the continued Harvardization of legal training throughout the country.

Like the elite practitioners in the bar associations, the law professors of the AALS sought to upgrade and standardize educational requirements and to eliminate unworthy competitors, such as part-time and night law schools. These latter institutions, whose origins went back to the founding of the Iowa Law School as a night school in 1865, had increased enormously by the early twentieth century as a result of population growth and market demand. Catering to workingmen, women, blacks, and ethnic minorities, the marginal law schools were training almost as many students in 1916 as the regular day schools. Their success threatened to undermine the work of Langdell's disciples, who made vigorous efforts to drive them out of business.

Prodded by the AALS, the American Bar Association in 1913 persuaded the Carnegie Foundation to conduct an independent study of legal education in the United States. A similar inquiry into the conditions of medical training had already been made by Carnegie researchers, and the resulting Flexner Report on Medical Education (1910) had recommended the abolition of marginal medical schools. Anticipating an equally decisive vindication, elite law professors were dismayed by Alfred Z. Reed's report, *Training for the Public Profession of the Law*, which appeared in 1921. Although Reed recognized the deficiencies of the night law schools, he believed that they provided some essential services for low-income groups and should be preserved. American society was pluralistic, he noted, and a unitary model of legal education could not serve diverse markets effectively. Since stratification along functional and class lines already existed within the bar in practice, why not institutionalize this diversity by assigning different tasks to the several types of law schools? Thus, elite institutions might train students for corporate practice and for prestigious judicial and administrative posts, while the night schools would produce attorneys destined for probate work, criminal law, and trial practice. In the absence of a differentiated bar of this sort, Reed feared that students from poorer back-

grounds would be deterred from entering the profession, and that the practice of law would be monopolized by those from middle- and upper-income
groups. "The night school authorities," he concluded, ". . . see most clearly
that the interests not only of the individual but of the community demand
that participation in the making and administration of the law shall be kept
accessible to Lincoln's plain people."[24]

Predictably, the ABA and the AALS denounced Reed's proposals as
wrongheaded and undemocratic, although some elite practitioners openly
admitted their desire to restrict minority access to the bar by closing the
night schools. In 1921 the ABA invested its Council on Legal Education
with the power to accredit schools, and thereafter lobbied state bar associations and legislatures to adopt uniform educational standards, including a
period of prior college training as a prerequisite for entering any law school.
These efforts bore little fruit until the 1930s, when prolonged economic
depression forced the weakest schools to shut down and induced a majority
of state legislatures to approve some ABA proposals as a way of alleviating
an overcrowded job market.

Progress toward a unitary system of legal education proceeded in two
stages. During the 1930s states began to insist upon law school training as
the sole method of preparing for the bar. Apprenticeship in a law office,
with its clinical and idiosyncratic features, thus disappeared as a viable alternative mode of acquiring legal knowledge and experience. Then, in the
aftermath of World War II, state legislatures moved to standardize legal education still more, by requiring that students attend only those law schools
approved by the ABA or the AALS. The circle was now complete: Law
professors monopolized the field of legal education, and in most states applicants could not take the bar examination unless their competence had
already been certified by a diploma from an accredited law school.[25]

The triumph of academic legal training did not, however, insure the
perpetuation of Langdellian jurisprudence. By the 1920s Langdell's basic
assumptions and methods came under increasing attack from certain law
professors and judges, whom historians have labeled collectively as "legal
realists." Although these critics never formed a coherent group or movement, they shared common legal values that contrasted sharply with those
of the Langdellians. Skeptical and relativistic, the legal realists denied the
primacy of abstract principles and called instead for empirical studies to
measure the social impact of statutes and decisions. Law to them was not
a closed system of logical rules, but an ongoing and uncertain process that
had to be constantly reexamined in the light of data supplied by the social

sciences. Such an approach led to some interesting curricular innovations, from Columbia Law School's interdisciplinary courses in the 1920s to the widespread clinical programs of the 1960s and 1970s.

These problem-centered courses were offered as electives and did not supplant the traditional core subjects, which continued to be taught by the case method. The legal realists subverted Langdell's conceptualism, however, by creating a new type of casebook that incorporated much statutory and extralegal source material. Karl Llewellyn's *Cases and Materials on the Law of Sales* (1930), which sought to show how legal rules influenced societal behavior, was the prototype of the functionally oriented textbook which has since become dominant in the nation's law schools. Influenced by realist thinking, some law schools also hired adjunct professors from the social sciences to teach courses on contemporary social problems or established joint degree programs for their students.[26]

The Great Depression of the 1930s provided a ready-made testing ground for realist theories and methods. Encouraged by the pragmatic and experimental nature of the early New Deal, some leading realists, including William O. Douglas and Jerome Frank, traveled to Washington to work in one of the newly created federal agencies. Frank, Karl Llewellyn, and other realists also helped to found the National Lawyers Guild in 1937, as a liberal alternative to the ABA. Committed to the defense of New Deal values and programs, the guild actively recruited blacks, women, and members of ethnic minorites from the start. Although it soon became embroiled in bitter quarrels between liberal and communist factions, it did implement some significant realist proposals for the better delivery of legal services to middle- and low-income groups. Under guild auspices pioneer neighborhood law offices and legal clinics were set up in Chicago and Philadelphia to assist persons whose legal needs had been generally ignored by the profession in the past. These pilot projects succeeded in two ways: clients were educated in their legal rights and unemployed or under-employed lawyers were given rewarding work to do. The neighborhood law offices of the 1930s also served as models for the much more extensive legal services programs that were carried out through the Office of Economic Opportunity in the 1960s.[27]

Although legal realism no longer exists as a vigorous and self-conscious force in American jurisprudence, its vestiges linger in multiple forms, from law school curricula to the iconoclasm of a revitalized National Lawyers Guild. And its legacy, we can now see, has been profoundly ambiguous. On the one hand, the realists destroyed the myth of legal certainty and objectivity without constructing any alternative value system to replace it. They thus arguably intensified the fragmentation of American society and encouraged litigants to view the law as wholly political and manipulative. At the same time, their efforts to study the social effects of legal rules made them aware of the need to expand legal services to disadvantaged groups, and pointed toward the "new professionalism" of today's public interest lawyers, consumer advocates, and poverty lawyers. Through legal clinics and neighborhood law offices many low-income Americans became involved in the legal system for the first time and learned something of their legal rights.

Perhaps this educational byproduct of the legal realist movement more than compensates for its defects. Today there are hopeful signs that the profession at large acknowledges public responsibilities that far transcend the narrow loyalty-to-client ethic enunciated by George Sharswood. Bar associations have abandoned their earlier elitism and have supported the civil rights movement and other popular causes. A new *Code of Professional Responsibility,* adopted by the ABA in 1970, emphasizes the duties that lawyers owe to the community in which they live and work. These obligations include: educating laypeople to recognize their legal problems; providing professional assistance to everyone who needs it, whether rich or poor; and promoting constructive changes in the legal system, "without regard to the general interests or desires of clients or former clients."[28] Unfortunately, the *Code* provides no effective machinery for enforcing these precepts, and their practical impact remains uncertain. At the least, however, it may be said that lawyers in recent years have become increasingly concerned with the proliferating needs and novel demands of all classes in a postindustrial society. Issues of client representation and professional accountability have taken on new meaning in the crisis-ridden years of the 1960s and 1970s. As Learned Hand, a wise and humane jurist, warned his colleagues at the bar, "If we are to keep our democracy, there must be one commandment: thou shalt not ration justice."[29]

NOTES

1. Quoted in Ronald Gross and Paul Osterman, eds., *The New Profesionals* (New York, 1972), p. 9.

2. Quoted in Jethro K. Lieberman, *The Tyranny of the Experts* (New York, 1970), p. 17. On the evolution of modern professionalism, see Magali Sarfatti Larson, *The Rise of Professionalism: A Sociological Analysis* (Berkeley, 1977); Philip Elliott, *The Sociology of the Professions* (New York, 1972); and Burton J. Bledstein, *The Culture of Professionalism* (New York, 1976).

3. Corinne Lathrop Gilb, *Hidden Hierarchies: The Professions and Government* (New York, 1966).

4. See, for example, Lieberman, *Tyranny of the Experts*, pp. 245 ff.; Donald L. Martin, "Will the Sun Set on Occupational Licensing?" in Simon Rottenberg, ed., *Occupational Licensure and Regulation* (Washington, D.C., 1980), pp. 142–54.

5. Lawrence M. Friedman, *A History of American Law* (New York, 1973), pp. 81–88; A. G. Roeber, *Faithful Magistrates and Republican Lawyers: Creators of Virginia Legal Culture, 1680–1810* (Chapel Hill, N.C., 1981); William E. Nelson, *Americanization of the Common Law* (Cambridge, Mass., 1975), pp. 13–35.

6. Gerard W. Gawalt, *The Promise of Power: The Emergence of the Legal Profession in Massachusetts, 1760–1840* (Westport, Conn., 1979), pp. 7–35; Anton-Hermann Chroust, *The Rise of the Legal Profession in America*, 2 vols., (Norman, Okla., 1965), 1:141, 180–93, 204–6.

7. Quoted in James Willard Hurst, *The Growth of American Law: The Law Makers* (Boston, 1950), p. 250. For a general discussion of professional trends in the postrevolutionary decades, see Chroust, *Rise of the Legal Profession*, 2:3–51; and Joseph F. Kett, *The Formation of the American Medical Profession* (New Haven, Conn., 1968).

8. Friedman, *History of American Law*, pp. 275–78; Maxwell Bloomfield, "The Texas Bar in the Nineteenth Century," *Vanderbilt Law Review* 32 (1979): 261–76.

9. Gawalt, *Promise of Power*, pp. 109–15, 168–79.

10. Friedman, *History of American Law*, pp. 282–92; Grant Gilmore, *The Ages of American Law* (New Haven, Conn., 1977), pp. 19–29.

11. Morton J. Horwitz, *The Transformation of American Law, 1780–1860* (Cambridge, Mass., 1977).

12. William R. Johnson, *Schooled Lawyers: A Study in the Clash of Professional Cultures* (New York, 1978), pp. 3–13; Alfred Z. Reed, *Training for the Public Profession of the Law* (New York, 1921), pp. 142–59, 453–56.

13. David Hoffman, *A Course of Legal Study, Addressed to Students and the Profession Generally*, 2d ed., (Baltimore, 1836), p. 765.

14. Ibid., p. 754.

15. George Sharswood, *An Essay on Professional Ethics*, 6th ed., (Philadelphia, 1930), p. 84.

16. Maxwell Bloomfield, "David Hoffman and the Shaping of a Republican Legal Culture," *Maryland Law Review* 38 (1979): 673–88. For an incisive critique of both Hoffman and Sharswood and an alternative model of client representation, see Thomas L. Shaffer, *On Being a Christian and a Lawyer* (Provo, Utah, 1981).

17. Robert H. Wiebe, *The Search for Order, 1877–1920* (New York, 1967), pp. 111–63; Bledstein, *Culture of Professionalism*, pp. 318–31.

18. Hurst, *Growth of American Law*, pp. 295–305, 334–52.

19. Ibid., pp. 276–89, 319–22, 359–65; George Martin, *Causes and Conflicts: The Centennial History of the Association of the Bar of the City of New York, 1870–1970* (Boston, 1970).

20. Dayton David McKean, *The Integrated Bar* (Boston, 1963); Jerold S. Auerbach, *Unequal Justice: Lawyers and Social Change in Modern America* (New York, 1976), pp. 40–73.

21. Quoted in Gilmore, *Ages of American Law*, p. 42.

22. Ibid., pp. 41–48, 60–67.

23. Quoted in Joel Seligman, *The High Citadel* (Boston, 1978), p. 37.

24. Reed, *Training for the Public Profession of the Law*, p. 417; Auerbach, *Unequal Justice*, pp. 74–112.

25. Robert Stevens, "Two Cheers for 1870: The American Law School," *Perspectives in American History* 5 (1971): 405–548.

26. John W. Johnson, *American Legal Culture, 1908–1940* (Westport, Conn., 1981), pp. 93–150.

27. Auerbach, *Unequal Justice*, pp. 191–209.

28. *Code of Professional Responsibility* (1970), Canon 8, EC 8–1.

29. Quoted by Arthur J. Goldberg in a luncheon address of March 31, 1973, reprinted in *Legal Services Reporter*, 6 April 1973.

LAW: SUGGESTIONS FOR FURTHER READING

I. GENERAL WORKS

Friedman, Lawrence M. *A History of American Law*. New York, 1973.
Hurst, James Willard. *The Growth of American Law: The Law Makers*. Boston, 1950.
Nolan, Dennis R. *Reading in the History of the American Legal Profession*. Indianapolis, 1980.

II. COLONIAL ERA TO 1900

Bledstein, Burton J. *The Culture of Professionalism*. New York, 1976.
Bloomfield, Maxwell H. *American Lawyers in a Changing Society, 1760–1876*. Cambridge, Mass., 1976.
Calhoun, Daniel H. *Professional Lives in America: Structure and Aspiration, 1750–1850*. Cambridge, Mass., 1965.
Chroust, Anton-Hermann. *The Rise of the Legal Profession in America*. 2 vols. Norman, Okla., 1965.
Gawalt, Gerard W. *The Promise of Power: The Emergence of the Legal Profession in Massachusetts, 1760–1840*. Westport, Conn., 1979.
Horwitz, Morton J. *The Transformation of American Law, 1780–1860*. Cambridge, Mass., 1977.

Roeber, A. G. *Faithful Magistrates and Republican Lawyers: Creators of Virginia Legal Culture, 1680–1810*. Chapel Hill, N.C., 1981.

III. TWENTIETH CENTURY

Auerbach, Jerold S. *Unequal Justice: Lawyers and Social Change in Modern America*. New York, 1976.

Brill, Stephen. "The Law Firm of the Future." *American Lawyer*, November 1980, pp. 27–49.

Johnson, John W. *American Legal Culture, 1908–1940*. Westport, Conn., 1981.

Johnson, William R. *Schooled Lawyers: A Study in the Clash of Professional Cultures*. New York, 1978.

McKean, Dayton David. *The Integrated Bar*. Boston, 1963.

Martin, George. *Causes and Conflicts: The Centennial History of the Bar of the City of New York*. Boston, 1970.

Seligman, Joel. *The High Citadel: The Influence of Harvard Law School*. Boston, 1978.

3. THE FALL AND RISE OF THE AMERICAN MEDICAL PROFESSION

Ronald L. Numbers

Midway through the nineteenth century American medicine lay in a shambles. Addressing the first annual meeting of the American Medical Association, in 1848, president Nathaniel Chapman expressed the dejection felt by many physicians. "The profession to which we belong," he lamented, "once venerated on account of its antiquity—its varied and profound science —its elegant literature—its polite accomplishments—its virtues—has become corrupt and degenerate, to the forfeiture of its social position, and with it, of the homage it formerly received spontaneously and universally."[1] The golden age Chapman recalled may have been only an old man's fantasy, but American physicians had unquestionably fallen on hard times. For centuries, at least since the late Middle Ages, Western societies had commonly recognized medicine, along with divinity and law, as one of the prototypical professions, possessing an esoteric body of knowledge, requiring extensive training, and being entitled to exclusive rights protected by law.[2] Although many healers practiced outside the law and failed to acquire professional status, those who earned M.D. degrees or served a protracted apprenticeship formed an occupational elite. By the mid-nineteenth century, however, medicine had for many Americans degenerated into little more than a trade, open to all who wished to try their hand at healing. "Any one, male or female, learned or ignorant, an honest man or a knave, can assume the name of a physician, and 'practice' upon any one, to cure or to kill, as either may happen, without accountability," wrote one observer in 1850. "'It's a free country!'"[3]

Within a century American physicians and their allies effected a revolution. By 1950, and even earlier, medicine had emerged as the strongest and most influential profession in America. Aspiring physicians competed

intensely to enter the guild and studied for years to acquire the proper credentials and requisite knowledge. Powerful institutions guarded its interest
and regulated its behavior. Laws in every state protected its rights. Indeed,
as one lawyer noted enviously, no interest group in the country enjoyed
"more freedom from formal control than organized medicine."[4]

THE FALL

During the early nineteenth century American physicians viewed their
situation with optimism—and rightfully so. Although the country abounded
with self-appointed healers and poorly trained doctors, professionally ambitious physicians seemed to be improving their position. With the opening
of a medical school at the College of Philadelphia in 1765, Americans could,
without going abroad, supplement their apprenticeships with formal lectures and acquire medical degrees. By 1830 the United States boasted twenty-
two such institutions. By this time, also, thirteen states had awarded physicians special privileges, usually in the form of laws giving medical societies
exclusive rights to license practitioners. Few of these statutes granted licensed
practitioners more than the right to sue for unpaid bills; yet they did provide the medical elite with a modicum of social recognition.[5]

In the decades after 1830 several factors converged to undermine the
progress physicians seemed to be making: an epidemic of "medical school
mania" broke out, the profession fractured into rival sects, and physicians
lost the legal standing they had just acquired. Of course, physicians were
not the only professionals to suffer a loss of status at this time. As one historian has pointed out, the period from 1830 to 1880 witnessed the general
"disestablishment and humbling of the professions" in America.[6] Nevertheless, the particulars of the medical story are unique.

Encouraged by revised state laws that accepted a medical school diploma as the equivalent of a license from an approved medical society, physicians who fancied themselves as professors began flooding the country with
low-grade institutions. Already by 1830 the nation's twenty-two medical
schools exceeded by several times the number in European countries of
comparable size, and during the next three decades the quantity more than
doubled. To make matters worse, most of these institutions, even those
nominally affiliated with a college or university, were run for prestige and
profit by ill-equipped local practitioners, many of whom could not have
matriculated as students in the best European schools. Because of this com-

mercial orientation, requirements for admission—where they existed at all —remained low and graduation often depended more on a student's ability to pay than on his or her competence. Some medical students could barely read and write, and most had never sat in a college classroom. The best arts students aspired to careers in divinity or law and looked upon medicine as a last resort. "It is very well understood among college boys," wrote one dispirited physician, "that after a man has failed in scholarship, failed in writing, failed in speaking, failed in every purpose for which he entered college; after he has dropped down from class to class; after he has been kicked out of college, there is *one* unfailing city of refuge—the profession of medicine."[7]

Until the last quarter of the century students typically obtained their M.D. degrees by successfully completing eight months of formal training, the last half of which merely duplicated the first. During this brief period they were expected to learn not only the basic sciences like anatomy, physiology, and chemistry, but to acquire clinical skills as well. This became especially true as more and more schools dropped a previous apprenticeship as an entrance requirement. It was no wonder, commented the medical reformer Nathan Smith Davis in 1845, that 99 out of every 100 American physicians were poorly educated:

> With no *practical* knowledge of chemistry and botany; with but a smattering of anatomy and physiology, hastily caught during a sixteen weeks' attendance on the anatomical theater of a medical college; with still less of real pathology; they enter the profession having mastered just enough of the details of practice to give them the requisite *self-assurance* for commanding the confidence of the public; but without either an adequate fund of knowledge or that degree of mental discipline and habits of patient study which will enable them ever to supply their defects.[8]

Such practitioners, charged another contemporary, tended to pursue "medicine as a trade instead of a profession, [and to] study the science of patient-getting to the neglect of the science of patient-curing."[9]

A second development that undermined the status of medicine was its fragmentation into competing sects, each offering an alternative to the so-called heroic therapy of regular physicians. During the early nineteenth century practitioners gained considerable notoriety for copious bleeding and the almost routine prescribing of calomel, a mercury-based cathartic that often produced harmful and discomforting side effects. Such practices gave rise to a host of critics, among the most vocal and visible of whom were the homeopaths and the various botanics, such as the Thomsonians and eclectics.[10]

The pioneer among American sectarians was a New Hampshire farmer, Samuel Thomson, who learned much of his botanic lore from a local female herbalist. Early in his healing career he became convinced that the cause of all disease was cold and that restoring the body's natural heat was the only cure. This he accomplished by steaming, peppering, and puking his patients, relying heavily on lobelia, a botanical emetic long used by American Indians. Not one to ignore the commercial possibilities of his discovery, Thomson in 1806 began selling "Family Rights" to his practice, for which he obtained a patent in 1813. During the 1820s and 1830s his agents fanned out from New England through the southern and western states urging self-reliant Americans to become their own physicians. By 1840 approximately 100,000 Family Rights had been sold, and Thomson estimated that about three million individuals had adopted his system. In states as diverse as Ohio and Mississippi as many as one-half of the citizens reportedly cured themselves the Thomsonian way.

Unlike many sectarians, who simply wanted the public to exchange one kind of physician for another, Thomson saw no need for professional healers of any kind. It was high time, he declared, for the common man to throw off the oppressive yoke of priests, lawyers, and physicians and assume his rightful place in a truly democratic society. Contrary to his wishes, his disciples in the 1830s began opening medical schools and competing head-to-head with regular physicians. By the 1840s, however, the Thomsonians were rapidly losing ground to a rival botanical sect—the eclectics—who achieved great popularity in the Midwest, where, in Cincinnati, they operated one of the nation's largest medical schools. Eclectic physicians and surgeons denounced blood-letting and calomel-dosing, but, except for preferring vegetable to mineral remedies, their practice differed little from that of the regulars.

Homeopathy originated in the mind of a regularly educated German physician, Samuel Hahnemann, who during the last decade of the eighteenth century constructed a novel system of healing based in large part on the healing power of nature and two fundamental principles: the law of similars and the law of infinitesimals. According to the first law, diseases are cured by medicines having the property of producing in healthy persons symptoms similar to those of the disease. An individual suffering from fever, for example, would be treated with a drug known to increase the pulse rate of a person in health. Hahnemann's second law held that medicines are more efficacious the smaller the dose, even down to one-millionth of a gram. Though regular practitioners—or allopaths, as Hahnemann dubbed them—ridiculed this theory, many patients flourished under the mild homeopathic therapy and they seldom suffered harmful side effects.

Following its appearance in the United States in 1825, homeopathy quickly grew into the nation's largest medical sect, replete with its own medical schools, societies, and journals. Its practitioners, many of whom defected from the regular ranks, were often well educated and well received by the middle and upper classes. By 1860 there were an estimated 2,400 homeopaths nationally—compared with about 60,000 regular physicians, only a third of whom possessed M.D. degrees.[11]

The acrimonious debates between sectarians and regulars—to say nothing of bitter quarrels among the regulars themselves over the efficacy of drug therapy and bleeding—created an atmosphere in which it became fashionable, wrote one editor, "to speak of the Medical Profession as a body of jealous, quarrelsome men, whose chief delight is in the annoyance and ridicule of each other."[12] Although many individual physicians continued to enjoy the respect of their communities, the reputation of the profession as a whole does seem to have declined. Certainly public confidence in medicine was not bolstered when physicians like Harvard's Oliver Wendell Holmes suggested that, with few exceptions, "if the whole materia medica, *as now used,* could be sunk to the bottom of the sea, it would be all the better for mankind—and all the worse for the fishes."[13]

Indicative of the public's low esteem for the medical profession during the 1830s and 1840s was its stripping doctors of their privileged legal status. Although it is difficult to see how early-nineteenth-century licensing laws deterred anyone from practicing medicine, Thomsonians especially felt persecuted and led the fight to repeal the so-called Black Laws. Apparently they were not without popular support, because at one point during the legislative debate in New York, Samuel Thomson's son John arrived in the chamber dramatically pushing a wheelbarrow full of petitions. Swayed by such displays of anti-monopolistic sentiment, state legislatures one by one repealed the offending statutes, until by 1850 only two states retained laws in any way restricting the practice of medicine. Society, observed one dejected physician, had thrown the medical profession overboard, "to sink or swim as it can, without even a rope by which to sustain itself."[14]

Unhampered by legal prejudice, healers of every stripe assumed the title *doctor* and hung out their shingles. According to one 1850 survey, of the 201 practitioners in eastern Tennessee, 35 held M.D.'s from regular medical schools, 42 had taken only one course of lectures, 27 identified themselves as botanics, while the rest—nearly half of the total—had picked up their knowledge of medicine from casual reading.[15] With so many marginally qualified practitioners crowding the field, even medical school graduates often found it impossible to live on their medical income alone. It was high time, concluded professional leaders, to launch a counteroffensive—to protect the public health as well as their own pocketbooks.

EARLY REFORMS

Abandoned to their own devices by the states, medical reformers first explored what they could accomplish through self-regulation. As the editor of the *New York Journal of Medicine* wrote in 1845:

> The profession in almost every state in the union is now left, so far as legal enactments are concerned, to take care of itself; to make its own rules, and adopt its own standard of excellence. For if we cannot make rules or laws which will banish ignorance, stupidity, and empiricism, we can, at least, fix our *own* standard of qualification, and thereby say who *we* will recognize as *our* associates.[16]

To accomplish this end, members of the State Medical Society of New York in 1846 convened a national convention to explore ways of reducing internal discord, isolating sectarians, and, above all, elevating the quality of medical education. Although some medical professors denounced the movement as an "aristocratic" attempt to cripple medical schools, nearly 100 delegates from sixteen states showed up.[17] The following year this group launched the American Medical Association, the first national society of regular physicians.

One of the top items on the AMA's agenda was to draw up a code of ethics, outlining not only the duties of the "professional" physician toward patients and peers, but also the obligations of patients to obey their physicians and avoid quacks. Although the code dealt more with etiquette than ethics, it did establish guidelines governing economic behavior, a source of much contention. In addition to banning advertising, the selling of secret nostrums, and other practices associated with quackery, it recommended the adoption of fee bills in each community to regulate the price of medical services. These schedules of minimum fees were to be binding in all cases except those involving the indigent, other physicians, and certain public duties. American doctors commonly acknowledged an obligation to put their patients' welfare above personal gain, but they also recognized, as one practitioner explained, that "a physician must train himself to be a professional man when treating patients, and a business man when collecting his bills."[18]

To segregate sectarians and to assist the public in identifying regular physicians, the code stipulated that no AMA member could consult with anyone "whose practice is based on an exclusive dogma." Like the entire code, this provision remained advisory until 1855, when it became mandatory.[19]

No subject attracted greater attention among AMA members than medical education, the improvement of which, they hoped, would simultaneously produce better physicians and reduce the number of potential competitors. At its first meeting delegates adopted standards requiring medical schools to offer anatomic dissections and clinical instruction, to extend their terms from four to six months, and to require entering students to possess "a good English education, a knowledge of Natural Philosophy, and the elementary Mathematical Sciences, including Geometry and Algebra and such an acquaintance, at least, with the Latin and Greek languages as will enable them to appreciate the technical language of medicine, and read and write prescriptions." These standards were so unrealistically high that, in the opinion of one scholar, rigid enforcement "would have closed down practically every medical school in the country, and would have depleted the ranks of formally educated physicians in a few years."[20] Fortunately for medical educators, the AMA represented only a small percentage of American physicians and remained too weak and ineffective throughout the nineteenth century to reform much of anything.

Medical education did, nevertheless, improve significantly during the latter half of the century. Although the proliferation of substandard schools continued unabated, the best institutions lengthened their curricula to three years, offered a new set of courses each year, required some evidence of preliminary education, and, led by the Harvard Medical College, abandoned proprietary status to become an integral part of a university. The dramatic growth of laboratory-based medical science in the latter half of the century encouraged such reforms, as did the German training of approximately 15,000 American physicians between 1870 and 1914.[21]

No event symbolized the reformation of American medical education more than the opening in 1893 of the Johns Hopkins School of Medicine under the leadership of the German-trained pathologist William H. Welch. At a time when, according to Welch, no American medical school required a preliminary education equal to "that necessary for entrance into the freshman class of a respectable college," the Hopkins faculty, at the insistence of its patron, demanded a bachelor's degree. Modestly following the Hopkins example, more than twenty schools by 1910 raised their entrance requirements to two years of college. This reform, Robert E. Kohler has argued, had far-reaching effects: it "stretched the financial resources of the proprietary school beyond the breaking point. . . . Higher entrance requirements disrupted the established market relation with high schools, diminished the pool of qualified applicants, and resulted in a drastic plunge in enrollments. Medical schools could not survive on fees."[22]

A further prod to educational reform came not from within the profession itself, but from the states, every one of which passed some kind of medical licensing act between the mid-1870s and 1900. Although physicians generally led the crusade to restrict the practice of medicine, they were not without external support. As society came to rely on physicians to certify births and deaths, to control infectious diseases, and to commit the insane, it became increasingly apparent that licensing served a public as well as a professional function. In 1888 the Supreme Court in a landmark decision, *Dent v. West Virginia*, upheld the authority of the state medical examining board to deprive a poorly trained eclectic physician of the right to practice. In the opinion of Justice Stephen J. Field, no one had "the right to practice medicine without having the necessary qualifications of learning and skill," and no group had greater competency to judge these qualifications than well-trained physicians.[23] Thus society granted the medical profession one of its most cherished goals: the authority to exclude practitioners deemed unworthy. The fact that other professions won protective legislation at the same time suggests that the physicians' achievement resulted more from a change in social policy than from a recognition of the improved state of medical science, impressive though it may have been.

The state licensing boards influenced medical education in two ways. First, most of them required candidates to hold a diploma from a reputable medical school, that is, one requiring evidence of preliminary education and, perhaps, offering a three-year course of study, a six-month term, and clinical and laboratory instruction. This forced any school hoping to compete for students to upgrade its curriculum, at least superficially. Second, many states, especially during the late 1880s and 1890s, revised their laws to require all candidates, even those holding medical degrees, to pass an examination.

Although some of the weaker schools quickly learned how to coach students to pass these tests, graduates from strong institutions had a much better chance of passing. A shallow medical education no longer paid.[24] The success of the licensing laws convinced professional leaders of the great advantage of legal sanctions over moral suasion in reforming medical education. "It is our opinion," declared the editor of the *Journal of the American Medical Association* in 1895, "that notwithstanding the far-reaching influence of the medical press, and the support of the various medical societies of the country, medical legislation alone caused the healthy reform. It is also apparent that the enforcement of efficient medical legislation in a few States will do more in destroying the dangerous work of the low grade college than all other factors combined."[25]

Medical practice acts not only set standards for licensing physicians but defined the very practice of medicine. The Nebraska act, for example, stipulated that anyone "who shall operate on, profess to heal, or prescribe for, or otherwise treat any physical or mental ailment of another" was practicing medicine and thus subject to the provisions of the law. For various political reasons, the states often granted exceptions. Many laws specifically exempted dentists, midwives, medical students, and persons who gave emergency aid; and a few states, especially in New England, provided immunity for Christian Scientists and others who engaged in mental healing.[26] However, physicians, whose strategy called for the elimination or subordination of competitors, preferred to define the practice of medicine as broadly as possible. As the sociologist Eliot Freidson has argued, "An essential feature of a useful concept of profession is the possession of something of a monopoly over the exercise of its work."[27] American physicians would have agreed.

Since the appearance of rival sects in the first half of the century, regulars had sought to isolate and discredit them. Nevertheless, well-trained sectarians, especially homeopaths and eclectics, had prospered. During the latter part of the century it became increasingly difficult to distinguish between orthodox and heterodox practice, or to argue that one system was more efficacious than another. In the 1880s, for example, one life insurance company concluded that homeopathy was just as effective as allopathy in saving lives, while a comparative study at Cook County Hospital in Chicago showed the latter to have only a slight edge in mortality rates. Given the training, therapeutic success, and numerical strength of the sectarians, regulars found it impossible to legislate them out of existence; in fact, in at least twenty states they sat on the same licensing boards with homeopaths or eclectics—at a time when the AMA still banned professional inter-course. In only three or four instances did they obtain what they most de-sired: a single licensing board composed exclusively of regulars.[28]

Although orthodox physicians liked to describe their efforts to sup-press sectarians in humanitarian terms, evidence suggests that opposition stemmed as much from fear of competition as from a desire to safeguard the public. After all, as one homeopath perceptively noted, regulars made few attempts to police therapy among themselves:

> If you inform the people that you treat those who come to you ac-cording to Similia, so far as drugging goes, you are anathema with the "regular," but if you get inside his fold, you can use any old treat-ment you please—be it an "electro-therapeutist," a man of "suggestion," or of "serums," calomel, bleeding, anything, and be a "regular physi-cian." Curious, isn't it? Looks as though the real thing at issue was the "recognition of the union" rather than the "welfare of the public."[29]

In addition to battling sectarians, the regular medical profession zeal-ously fought to subordinate and control allied health personnel. As the num-ber of trained nurses increased after the Civil War, physicians expressed con-cern that these women would attempt to expand their role and presume to act as physicians. Thus doctors attempted to limit the amount of theo-retical training nurses received and insisted that nurses strictly obey their orders. As the *Boston Medical and Surgical Journal* explained, the physician's relationship to the nursing staff was to be "like that of the captain to his ship." To win acceptance and approval from the medical profession, nurses themselves went out of their way to reassure the doctors. For example, in her influential *Nursing Ethics* (1900) Isabel Hampton emphasized discipline as the key to success: "The head nurse and her staff should stand to receive the visiting physician, and from the moment of his entrance until his de-parture, the attending nurses should show themselves alert, attentive, cour-teous, like soldiers on duty."[30] Such an attitude posed no threat either to pocketbooks or egos.

Physicians experienced much greater difficulty trying to subdue male pharmacists, who not only sold medicines prescribed by doctors but fre-quently diagnosed minor ailments and suggested remedies. Pharmacists, warned one physician in the early 1880s, had "so industriously and ener-getically wedged themselves between the 'dear public' and the professional province of the physician" that they threatened to take over the practice of medicine. Incensed doctors denounced this intrusion as dangerous and illegal and sought to revise medical practice acts to ban practices such as over-the-counter prescribing. Their efforts, however, generally failed, and in at least one state (North Dakota) the pharmacists retaliated by securing passage of a law barring physicians from dispensing medicines. "If physicians wish to prevent encroachment on their domain," warned one pharmacist, "they should avoid invading others' property."[31]

Dentistry, which required mechanical skills more than medical knowledge, was one of the few healing activities that physicians attempted neither to crush nor to control. When dentists in the late 1830s tried to win a place for their specialty in the medical school curriculum, one physician quipped "that the author of such a plan, to be consistant, should not fill teeth but treat the constitutional causes of dental caries by bleeding, puring, and leeching his patients."[32] Thus rebuffed, a group of physician-dentists in 1840 established the Baltimore College of Dental Surgery, the first dental school in the country. Although some dentists fretted for decades about their identity ("If we are not medical specialists we are a set of carpenters," said one), the majority, believing that "dentistry was altogether too large to be made the tail end of the kite of medical practice," quietly created a set of institutions paralleling those of the medical profession: societies, schools offering D.D.S. degrees, and separate dental licensing boards. "A professional wall is now being built up," explained one dental leader, "and we hope it will be built so high and strong, that none can scale or break it down, but that all who enter will be compelled to do so through the legitimate and well-guarded gateways." Except for legal loopholes that often allowed physicians to practice dentistry, dentists succeeded by the end of the century in building their professional wall. They failed, however, to win equal standing among physicians, who regarded the filling and pulling of teeth as minor matters. "If dentists are ambitious to be considered medical specialists, they must undergo a general medical education," said one physician condescendingly. "An individual dentist who has taken the medical degree may assuredly be received as a brother practitioner, but a simple D.D.S. never."[33]

In spite of substantial improvements in medical education and the passage of licensing laws, the medical profession at the end of the century still contained, according to one knowledgeable physician, "a vast number of incompetents, large numbers of moral degenerates, and crowds of pure tradesmen." By 1900 there were 151 medical schools, and even the worst institutions sometimes managed to prepare their graduates to pass ineffectual licensing examinations. In one notorious case, the weakest of Chicago's fourteen schools—"a school with no entrance requirement, no laboratory teaching, no hospital connections"—outperformed its thirteen rivals on the state boards. The medical practice acts, complained one contemporary, allowed all but "the most flagrant quacks and charlatans from carrying on their business unmolested."[34] Thus after a half-century of reform much remained on the medical profession's agenda for elevating its status: the elimination of inferior medical schools, the enactment of stricter licensing laws, and the creation of a powerful national body to represent the interests of physicians.

THE REFORMATION COMPLETED

The professional leaders of American medicine faced the twentieth century determined to complete the reformation they had begun, that is, to reduce the quantity and increase the quality of medical practitioners. Although the ratio of physicians to patients had scarcely changed during the previous fifty years—in fact, it had actually decreased from 1:568 in 1850 to 1:576 in 1900—American doctors continued to view the overcrowding of their profession by poorly trained physicians as their greatest problem. Such individuals, argued the reformers, not only provided inadequate and sometimes dangerous care, but also depressed physician income. Well into the twentieth century, most American physicians earned less than $2,000 a year. In 1914, for example, less than 60 percent of Wisconsin's approximately 2,800 practitioners earned enough even to pay income taxes; and of those who paid, the average income was only $1,488—well below that of bankers, manufacturers, and lawyers, though more than twice what professors earned.[35]

The profession's first order of business was to create a united front. Since its founding in 1847, the AMA had remained virtually impotent; it had, noted its president sadly in 1901, "exerted relatively little influence on legislation, either state or national." Only about 7 percent of the country's physicians had joined the association, and independent state and county societies often operated at cross purposes to the will of the national body. In response to this situation, an AMA committee in 1901 recommended a complete reorganization: the welding of local, state, and national units into one representative society that would "foster scientific medicine and . . . make the medical profession a power in the social and political life of the republic." Henceforth, membership in a local (generally county) society would automatically carry membership in the state and national organizations. This plan, approved at the 1901 annual session, produced immediate results. Most state societies fell quickly into line, and membership in the AMA multiplied over sevenfold within five years. For the first time American physicians possessed an organization large enough and strong enough effectively to further its interests.[36]

Like its nineteenth-century parent, the reorganized AMA fought to control access to the profession by tightening the requirements for medical education and licensure. In 1904 it created a Council on Medical Education, which soon began inspecting and grading medical schools. A few years later the council cooperated with the Carnegie Foundation in producing Abraham Flexner's famous report on *Medical Education in the United States and Canada* (1910). This muckraking exposé described conditions—often abysmal—at each of the country's 155 medical schools. The adverse publicity generated by the AMA's inspections and the Flexner report, together with continuing pressure from licensing bodies and the growing expense of providing laboratory and clinical instruction, forced many institutions to shut down—and finally brought a halt to the overproduction of unqualified physicians. Between 1910 and 1920 the number of medical schools declined from 155 to 85, and it continued falling for the next two decades. In the same period the total number of physicians in the United States was dropping for perhaps the first time in history. The schools that survived this winnowing were, by 1930, generally requiring a bachelor's degree for admission and offering rigorous scientific and clinical training. Unlike the improvements of the nineteenth-century, which had little to do with the AMA, these changes often resulted from the AMA's cozy relationship with the state licensing boards, which delegated to the AMA (sometimes jointly with the American Association of Medical Colleges) the privilege of deciding which schools merited approval for the licensing of their graduates. By this means, and by accrediting hospitals for the training of interns, organized medicine gained considerable control over the education and supply of physicians.[37]

The medical profession enjoyed much less success in its efforts to monopolize the practice of medicine by outlawing rivals and controlling allies. As we have seen, during the last quarter of the nineteenth century regular physicians often united reluctantly with their old nemeses, the eclectics and homeopaths, to win passage of state licensing laws. In 1903 the AMA took additional steps toward unity by deleting its ethical ban against consulting with irregulars and by welcoming as members eclectics and homeopaths willing to forsake sectarian dogma for scientific truth. This latter act proved to be the kiss of death for eclectic and homeopathic organizations, which, though still numerically strong, were now struggling to survive. Weakened by internal discord, defecting members, and the lack of state-supported medical schools, they soon ceased to be a factor in American medicine.

The demise of eclectics and homeopaths did not, however, eliminate sectarian competition. During the late nineteenth century, Christian Science, osteopathy, and chiropractic made their appearance, and by the early twentieth century these new "cults," as the medical establishment insisted on calling them, began threatening the therapeutic consensus based on scientific medicine as well as the economic goals of physicians. Despite an intensive and protracted campaign by the medical profession to have these sects declared illegal, all three won the legal right to practice their form of healing. The nature of their victory varied from state to state, but their experience in Wisconsin illustrates the various means they used to thwart the medical profession's monopolistic designs.

Like their spiritual leader, Mary Baker Eddy, Christian Science practitioners denied the existence of disease and the need for physicians. Instead of prescribing drugs, they relied on prayer and verbal persuasion to cure individuals who imagined themselves to be ill. Christian Scientists began practicing in Wisconsin in the 1880s, but physicians could do little to stop them before the state passed a medical practice act in 1897. Following enactment of this bill, authorities in Milwaukee arrested two Christian Science practitioners for violating the new law. At their trial the defendants argued that they were not guilty of practicing medicine "because they never administered drugs, never performed surgery, never manipulated the body or even touched their patients." Nevertheless, the court convicted them—only to be overruled by a higher court, which agreed that Christian Science had little in common with medicine. Therefore, Christian Scientists in Wisconsin faced only the insults of physicians, not the threat of arrest. In some other states, as we have noted, legislators specifically exempted them in defining medical practice.

Osteopathy was founded by a Missouri physician, Andrew Taylor Still, who turned against regular medicine after drug therapy failed to save the lives of his children. Convinced that the human brain functioned as "God's drug store," he attributed all disease to obstructions inhibiting the flow of blood and nervous fluid, which he sought to cure using manual manipulation, particularly of the spine. The first osteopaths arrived in Wisconsin in the 1890s, and by 1900 nineteen had located in the state. Charged in that year with illegal practice under the 1897 statute, the osteopaths lost their first court case. Seeking relief, they petitioned the legislature to create a separate licensing board for osteopathy. Regular physicians lobbied instead for the addition of an osteopath to the existing licensing board, believing that the "requirements are so high it is safe to say that but few, if any, osteopaths will ever be able to meet them." The regulars got their wish, but discovered to their chagrin that the underrated osteopaths routinely qualified for licenses to practice. Elsewhere, in over half the states, regulars suffered even greater humiliation, as legislators ignored their pleas and set up separate boards composed only of D.O.'s.

Chiropractic, the brainchild of an Iowa grocer, Daniel David Palmer, explained disease in terms of dislocations of the spine, which allegedly impeded the circulation of nervous fluid. Like osteopaths, with whom they were frequently confused, chiropractors relied therapeutically on adjustments of the spinal column. When the first of them moved to Wisconsin in the early 1900s, they landed in jail for practicing *osteopathy* without a license. Undeterred, they continued to practice illegally until 1915, when the legislature granted them immunity to work as unlicensed practitioners. Ten years later it disregarded the will of the medical profession and, like legislatures in many other states, voted to create a separate chiropractic board of examiners.[38]

In the early 1930s one study of medical care in America reported that "the efforts of the medical profession to prevent legal recognition of the chiropractors have met with almost universal defeat." In fact, by this time nearly a quarter of American healers were Christian Scientists, osteopaths, chiropractors, or irregulars of some stripe. It was clear, concluded the same study, that "in the United States the legislative regulation of the healing art is not accomplishing its acknowledged purpose," that is, creating a monopoly for regular physicians.[39]

Medical doctors encountered equal difficulty keeping assorted other healthcare professionals from intruding on what they regarded as their rightful domain. Although they actually assisted podiatrists in achieving their independent status — on the grounds that corn-cutting like tooth-pulling was too trivial to control — they fought continually to limit the activities of such interlopers as optometrists, psychologists, and midwives, who competed directly with physicians specializing in ophthalmology, psychiatry, and obstetrics.[40] The medical profession hoped to restrict the practice of such individuals by defining medicine comprehensively; however, unsympathetic judges and legislators time and again sided with its opponents, as can be seen in the history of relations between physicians and optometrists.

Until the latter part of the nineteenth century physicians generally left the dispensing of spectacles to itinerant peddlers and other businessmen, who fitted eyeglasses on a trial-and-error basis. But after the 1860s, when a Dutch ophthalmologist showed how various visual disorders could be treated by prescribing glasses, physicians became increasingly active in the field — and resentful of opticians who continued to test for lenses. The issue came to a head in 1892, when a couple of New York ophthalmologists warned an optician named Charles F. Prentice that he was violating the state's medical practice act by performing such tests. If he wished to prescribe lenses rather than simply sell them, they argued, "he must first get a degree of M.D. and then a license to practice in this State." Prentice responded to this veiled threat by organizing a state optical society and appealing to the legislature to pass a special practice act for opticians.

During the ensuing debate it became clear that opticians (or optometrists, as they came to be called) sought a status equivalent to dentists, who functioned independently of the medical profession, whereas physicians wanted to relegate optometrists to a position analogous to pharmacists, who simply filled physicians' prescriptions. "The optician must be forbidden to prescribe spectacles," declared one medical journal, "and it should be as illegal for the optician to prescribe glasses as it is for the pharmacist to prescribe morphine or arsenic. Both the optical instrument and the drug are medical agents, and only a physician is fitted to judge of the propriety of their use." Retorted Prentice: "A lens is not a pill."[41]

Despite medical harassment, including occasional arrests for violating medical practice acts, optometrists eventually acquired full legal recognition. During the two decades between 1901 and 1921 they won judicial decisions declaring optometry to be outside the sphere of medical practice, and every state in the Union passed laws setting up examining boards for optometrists. These laws usually barred them from using drugs and, to their great irritation, allowed physicians to refract eyes and prescribe glasses; nevertheless, such statutes represented a clear victory for the optometrists and another humbling defeat for the medical profession, which continued into the 1950s to shun optometrists and to debate whether optometry was a cult or merely a medical sect.[42]

THE PROFESSION AND THE PUBLIC

A century after the founding of the AMA the American medical profession could look with pride on its various accomplishments. Although its efforts to monopolize the practice of medicine had fallen far short of its goals, it had, through its alliance with the law, eliminated overcrowding in the field, greatly reduced the number of incompetents practicing medicine, and acquired so much prestige and power that medicine became the envy of other professions. By the mid-twentieth century physicians had become the most admired professionals in the land, and, benefiting especially from the growth of health insurance, had passed bankers and lawyers to become the nation's highest paid workers.[43] Despite mounting criticism of the medical profession during the past couple of decades, physicians have, by and large, retained their elevated position in American society.[44] And despite the increasing intrusion of insurance companies, government agencies, and various allied health professionals into the medical domain, the gains physicians made during the first half of the twentieth century have, to a great extent, remained intact.

Medical apologists have long argued that professional advancement brought corresponding gains to the public. "There is nothing for the benefit of medicine unless it is for the benefit of the people," declared one medical society official. "The two interests are identical." In recent years, however, critics of the medical profession have increasingly questioned such assumptions, arguing instead that the reforms we have described "centralized, bureaucratized, modernized and expanded medicine and medical education in the interests of physicians' own professional needs and with little regard for the needs of the public."[45]

The truth, I believe, lies somewhere between these two extremes. On the one hand, there can be little doubt that physicians benefited handsomely from their efforts to regulate and monopolize the practice of medicine. It is equally apparent that the elevation of the profession, in conjunction with other factors, drove up the cost of medical care, created a shortage of American-trained doctors, and damaged the chances for the poor and minorities to pursue careers in medicine.[46] On the other hand, only the most prejudiced observer would argue that the public did not gain as well. Curative medicine may have contributed little to the dramatic reduction in mortality during the past century, but physicians using preventive and ameliorative measures did significantly improve the quality and length of life in America.[47] And although the profession continues to harbor its share of scoundrels, patients today enter doctors' offices with much less cause for fear—and much more hope of being helped—than did their grandparents and great-grandparents. The interests of the profession and the public may not be identical, but neither are they antithetical.

NOTES

1. N. S. Davis, *History of the American Medical Association* (Philadelphia, 1855), p. 56.

2. See, e.g., Vern L. Bullough, *The Development of Medicine as a Profession: The Contribution of the Medieval University to Modern Knowledge* (Basel, 1966).

3. [Lemuel Shattuck], *Report of the Sanitary Commission of Massachusetts* (Boston, 1850), p. 58.

4. "The American Medical Association: Power, Purpose, and Politics in Organized Medicine," *Yale Law Journal* 63 (1954): 1018.

5. See, e.g., Joseph F. Kett, *The Formation of the American Medical Profession: The Role of Institutions, 1780–1860* (New Haven, Conn., 1968); and William G. Rothstein, *American Physicians in the Nineteenth Century: From Sects to Science* (Baltimore, 1972).

6. Samuel Haber, "The Professions and Higher Education in America: A Historical View," in *Higher Education and the Labor Market*, ed. Margaret S. Gordon (New York, 1974), p. 251. The "mania" quotation comes from James H. Cassedy, "Why Self-Help? Americans Alone with Their Diseases, 1800–1850," in *Medicine without Doctors: Home Health Care in American History*, ed. Guenter B. Risse, Ronald L. Numbers, and Judith W. Leavitt (New York, 1977), p. 35.

7. "American vs. European Medical Science Again," *Medical Record* 4 (1869): 183. See also Martin Kaufman, "American Medical Education," in *The Education of American Physicians: Historical Essays*, ed. Ronald L. Numbers (Berkeley and Los Angeles, 1980), pp. 7–28.

8. Harris L. Coulter, *Divided Legacy: A History of the Schism in Medical Thought*, 3 vols. (Washington, 1973), 3:143.

9. Worthington Hooker, *Physician and Patient: or, A Practical View of the Mutual Duties, Relations and Interests on the Medical Profession and the Community* (New York, 1849), p. viii.

10. These paragraphs on sectarian medicine are extracted from Ronald L. Numbers, "Do-It-Yourself the Sectarian Way," in Risse, Numbers, and Leavitt, *Medicine without Doctors*, pp. 49–72.

11. Kett, *Formation of the American Medical Professions*, p. 186.

12. Richard Harrison Shryock, *Medicine in America: Historical Essays* (Baltimore, 1966), p. 151.

13. Rothstein, *American Physicians*, p. 178. For a positive view of medical prestige, see Barbara G. Rosenkrantz, "The Search for Professional Order in Nineteenth-Century American Medicine," 14th International Congress of the History of Science, *Proceedings*, 1974, pp. 113–24.

14. Kett, *Formation of the American Medical Profession*, pp. 13, 165.

15. Richard Harrison Shryock, *Medical Licensing in America, 1650–1965* (Baltimore, 1967), pp. 31–32.

16. Coulter, *Divided Legacy*, p. 182.

17. Davis, *History*, pp. 30–32.

18. J. J. Taylor, *The Physician as a Business Man; or, How to Obtain the Best Results in the Practice of Medicine* (Philadelphia, 1981), p. 94; "Code of Medical Ethics," American Medical Association 10 (1857): 607–20.

19. Ibid., p. 614.

20. Rothstein, *American Physicians*, p. 120.

21. Robert P. Hudson, "Abraham Flexner in Perspective: American Medical Education, 1865–1910," *Bulletin of the History of Medicine* 56 (1972): 545–61; Thomas Neville Bonner, *American Doctors and German Universities: A Chapter in International Intellectual Relations, 1870–1914* (Lincoln, Neb., 1963).

22. Simon Flexner and James Thomas Flexner, *William Henry Welch and the Heroic Age of American Medicine* (New York, 1941), pp. 219, 222–23; Robert E. Kohler, "Medical Reform and Biomedical Science: Biochemistry—A Case Study," in *The Therapeutic Revolution: Essays in the Social History of American Medicine*, ed. Morris J. Vogel and Charles Rosenberg (Philadelphia, 1979), p. 32.

23. Haber, "Professions and Higher Education in America," p. 260.

24. Kaufman, "American Medical Education," p. 19.

25. Donald E. Konold, *A History of American Medical Ethics, 1847–1912* (Madison, Wis., 1962), p. 30.

26. Alexander Wilder, *History of Medicine* (New Sharon, Maine, 1899), pp. 776–835.

27. Eliot Freidson, *Profession of Medicine: A Study of the Sociology of Applied Knowledge* (New York, 1970), p. 21.

28. John S. Haller, Jr., *American Medicine in Transition, 1840–1910.* (Urbana, Ill., 1981), pp. 126, 266; Rothstein, *American Physicians*, pp. 308–9.

29. Coulter, *Divided Legacy*, pp. 433–34. For confirmation of this opinion by a regular physician, see Hooker, *Physician and Patient*, p. 255.

30. Philip A. Kalisch and Beatrice J. Kalisch, *The Advance of American Nursing* (Boston, 1978), pp. 150–53; Mary Roth Walsh, *"Doctors Wanted: No Women Need Apply": Sexual Barriers in the Medical Profession, 1835–1975* (New Haven, Conn., 1977), p. 142; Janet Wilson James, "Isabel Hampton and the Professionalization of Nursing in the 1890s," in Vogel and Rosenberg, *Therapeutic Revolution*, p. 221.

31. Haller, *American Medicine in Transition*, pp. 268–72; James G. Burrow, *Organized Medicine in the Progressive Era: The Move toward Monopoly* (Baltimore, 1977), p. 114.

32. L. Laszlo Schwartz, "The Historical Relations of American Dentistry and Medicine," *Bulletin of the History of Medicine* 28 (1954): 545.

33. Robert W. McCluggage, *A History of the American Dental Association: A Century of Health Service* (Chicago, 1959), pp. 155, 169–71. See also William J. Gies, *Dental Education in the United States and Canada* (New York, 1926), pp. 39–40.

34. Shryock, *Medical Licensing*, p. 60; Abraham Flexner, *Medical Education*

in the United States and Canada (New York, 1910), p. 170; Rothstein, *American Physicians*, p. 310.

35. Ronald L. Numbers, *Almost Persuaded: American Physicians and Compulsory Health Insurance, 1912–1920* (Baltimore, 1978), pp. 4, 9; Committee on Social Insurance, *Statistics Regarding the Medical Profession*, Social Insurance Series Pamphlet No. 7 (Chicago, [1917]), p. 123.

36. Numbers, *Almost Persuaded*, pp. 27–28.

37. Ibid., pp. 4, 113; Kaufman, "American Medical Education," p. 20; Shryock, *Medical Licensing*, p. 63; "American Medical Association," pp. 969–70.

38. Elizabeth Barnaby Keeney, Susan Eyrich Lederer, and Edmond P. Minihan, "Sectarians and Scientists: Alternative to Orthodox Medicine," in *Wisconsin Medicine: Historical Perspectives*, ed. Ronald L. Numbers and Judith Walzer Leavitt (Madison, 1981), pp. 59–68; Louis S. Reed, *The Healing Cults: A Study of Sectarian Medical Practice – Its Extent, Causes, and Control* (Chicago, 1932). Regarding osteopathy, see Norman Gevitz, *The D.O.'s: Osteopathic Medicine in America* (Baltimore, 1982); and Erwin A. Blackstone, "The A.M.A. and the Osteopaths: A Study of the Power of Organized Medicine," *Antitrust Bulletin* 22 (1977): 405–40.

39. Reed, *Healing Cults*, pp. 1, 121.

40. See, e.g., Maurice J. Lewi, "Medicine and Podiatry in New York State," *New York State Journal of Medicine* 54 (1954): 536–40; John C. Burnham, "The Struggle between Physicians and Paramedical Personnel in American Psychiatry, 1917–41," *Journal of the History of Medicine and Allied Sciences*, 29 (1974): 93–106; Frances E. Kobrin, "The American Midwife Controversy: A Crisis of Professionalization," *Bulletin of the History of Medicine* 40 (1966): 350–63; and Judy Barrett Litoff, *American Midwives: 1860 to Present* (Westport, Conn., 1978).

41. Charles F. Prentice, *Legalized Optometry and the Memoirs of Its Founder* (Seattle, 1926), quotations on pp. 27, 55; James R. Gregg, *American Optometric Association: A History* (St. Louis, 1972), p. 47.

42. Ibid., pp. 56–58, 79–80; Louis S. Reed, *Midwives, Chiropodists, and Optometrists: Their Place in Medical Care* (Chicago, 1932), pp. 36–60; *1846–1958 Digest of Official Actions: American Medical Association* (Chicago, 1959), pp. 536–40.

43. Robert W. Hodge, Paul M. Siegel, and Peter H. Rossi, "Occupational Prestige in the United States, 1925–63," *American Journal of Sociology* 70 (1964): 290; Andrea Tyree and Billy G. Smith, "Occupational Hierarchy in the United States: 1789–1969," *Social Forces*, 56 (1978): 887; Ronald L. Numbers, "The Third Party: Health Insurance in America," in Vogel and Rosenberg, *Therapeutic Revolution*, pp. 192–93.

44. John C. Burnham, "American Medicine's Golden Age: What Happened to It?" *Science* 215 (1982): 1474–79.

45. Ronald L. Numbers, "Public Protection and Self-Interest: Medical Societies in Wisconsin," in Numbers and Leavitt, *Wisconsin Medicine*, p. 96; Gerald E.

Markowitz and David Karl Rosner, "Doctors in Crisis: A Study of the Use of Medical Education Reform to Establish Modern Professional Elitism in Medicine," *American Quarterly* 25 (1973): 107.

46. See, e.g., Herbert M. Morais, *The History of the Negro in Medicine* (New York, 1967); and Walsh, *Doctors Wanted,* pp. 192–94. Although the percentage of women in medical schools declined during the first half of the twentieth century, Walsh argues that they were not driven out of the profession by licensing laws and educational requirements (p. 237). Rather, she attributes the decline to overt discrimination against women.

47. On the relationship between medicine and mortality in America, see Judith Walzer Leavitt and Ronald L. Numbers, eds., *Sickness and Health in America: Readings in the History of Medicine and Public Health* (Madison, Wis., 1978), pp. 3–10.

Medicine: Suggestions for Further Reading

Bullough, Vern L. *The Development of Medicine as a Profession: The Contribution of the Medieval University to Modern Knowledge.* Basel, 1966.

Burrow, James G. *Organized Medicine in the Progressive Era: The Move toward Monopoly.* Baltimore, 1977.

Flexner, Simon, and Flexner, James Thomas. *William Henry Welch and the Heroic Age of American Medicine.* New York, 1941.

Freidson, Eliot. *Profession of Medicine: A Study of the Sociology of Applied Knowledge.* New York, 1970.

Gevitz, Norman. *The D.O.'s: Osteopathic Medicine in America.* Baltimore, 1982.

Haller, Jr., John S. *American Medicine in Transition, 1840–1910.* Urbana, Ill. 1981.

Kalisch, Philip A., and Kalisch, Beatrice J. *The Advance of American Nursing.* Boston, 1978.

Kett, Joseph F. *The Formation of the American Medical Profession: The Role of Institutions, 1780–1860.* New Haven, Conn., 1968.

Konold, Donald E. *A History of American Medical Ethics, 1847–1912.* Madison, Wis., 1962.

Leavitt, Judith Walzer, and Numbers, Ronald L., eds. *Sickness and Health in America: Readings in the History of Medicine and Public Health.* Madison, Wis., 1978.

McCluggage, Robert W. *A History of the American Dental Association: A Century of Health Service.* Chicago, 1959.

Morais, Herbert M. *The History of the Negro in Medicine.* New York, 1967.

Numbers, Ronald L. *Almost Persuaded: American Physicians and Compulsory Health Insurance, 1912–1920.* Baltimore, 1978.

Numbers, Ronald L., ed. *The Education of American Physicians: Historical Essays.* Berkeley and Los Angeles, 1980.

Rothstein, William G. *American Physicians in the Nineteeth Century: From Sects to Science*. Baltimore, 1972.

Shryock, Richard Harrison. *Medicine in America: Historical Essays*. Baltimore, 1966.

Shryock, Richard Harrison. *Medical Licensing in America, 1650–1965*. Baltimore, 1967.

Walsh, Mary Roth. *"Doctors Wanted: No Women Need Apply": Sexual Barriers in the Medical Profession, 1835–1975*. New Haven, Conn., 1977.

4. THE CLERGY

Martin E. Marty

A ministerial student at McCormick Theological Seminary had been working at the YMCA in a western metropolis. On her last day at work before
leaving for Chicago she bade farewell to the elevator operator. Where was
she going? To theological seminary. What was that? A school, she answered,
where one prepared to become a minister. The concept startled the operator, not because he was unfamiliar with women in ministry but because
he was remote from ministry. Well, not completely remote. He had an image of it. After learning that it would take her four years to complete studies
and enter ministry he said good-bye with a completely serious appeal: "Don't
forget me. As soon as you become a minister, let me know which television channel you're on!"

The elevator operator was sufficiently distanced from colonial concepts of the minister as a public figure and from later realizations of the
clergy as leaders of congregation to have no picture of what professionals
in those eras or fields might have been. His image of ministry came from
the image industries which determine much of culture and some of clerical
ministry in our time.

The McCormick student who told me that story could only find it
amusing because she had different expectations than the elevator operator. She knew something of biblical norms for ministry, and had some historical sense — otherwise she would not have found pathos and amusement
in his sincere comments. No doubt she also feels called to ministry by her
love for Jesus Christ and the church, pulled by the appeal and endowment of the Holy Spirit. She is eager to be sanctioned in the traditions of
her church and by the standards of scripture and the community she would
serve.

This minister-to-be and the incident on which she reported illustrate
the way the clerical profession lives within and between two sometimes com-

plementary and sometimes competing norms. On the one hand, the clerical ministry makes claims to be sanctioned by transcendent norms, by the
mandates and promises of God. Only in humanist wings of Unitarian-
Universalism would there be an exception to this basis for the profession.
In this sense it is unique. While Christians or people of other faiths may
have theological views of lay vocation, they do make distinctive claims for
the charter and regulation of ministry in the sacred sphere. Because of the
transcendent appeal, it is difficult to "check out" empirically some dimensions of ministry.

   While the ministerial profession is responsive to that divine call and
context, it is also very much a profession among the professions. In those
terms it is, willy nilly, subject to the instinctive or deliberate canons imposed by the public and the individuals who make up that public. Cultural
norms have an obvious impact on ministry. Often these stimulate theological reexamination and revision. To take but the most obvious recent example: were it not for the pressures exerted by a culture in which women are
reexamining their roles and identities, it is not likely that churches would
be scrambling back to the sources in the tradition with a view to ordain-
ing women—or finding bars against such ordination.

   Some opponents of change in ministry when these changes reflect
cultural change try to reject theological reexamination. The church should
be entirely inner-directed, according to this view. Such a hermetically sealed
approach to the tradition does not do justice to its own syncretic and culturally "open" roots in the Greco-Roman world. Today most Western Christian
churches are proud of their contribution to republican or democratic polities. They claim that the impetus for such polities and their freedoms are
integral to the Christian message and have been from the beginning. They
do well to listen first to Hannah Arendt, who, in effect, advises Christians
first to send a greeting card to whom it may concern in the Enlightenment
or to modernity, since that Christian political impetus had been only latent
for a millennium and a half. It needed nudges and climatic changes from
without. So it is with the clerical profession.

   For that reason it is good to see the ministerial profession in the context and sequence of the professions. The churches are still free to make
their moves in the light of their presumed lead-encased "inner norms." Yet
a historical study will show that Jewish and Christian concepts of clergy
are constantly shifting, often for the better, in the light of the cultural changes
that affect and afflict all the professions. The historians cannot tell religious
bodies what to do, but he or she can help free them to think about what

to do in the light of the fact that change has been a constant in the expression of ministry—and by no means always for the worse!

THE CONCEPT OF PROFESSION

The present concern is not, first of all, with the concept of a divine calling or call. A divine calling motivates people in lay vocations as well as clerical and is, in any case, not part of the present assignment. We simply do well to recall that this concept and reality often sustain people in the clergy when other sanctions give out and thus have at least an indirect but profound bearing on the profession.

Second, this is not an examination of the general concept of vocation, perceived personally, psychologically, or sociologically. I happen to believe that that concept can also inform and illumine ministry and the clerical profession. There is marvellous therapy for professionals in observations like José Ortega y Gasset's: "Strictly, a [person's] vocation must be his vocation for a perfectly concrete, individual, and integral life, not for the social schema of a career."[1] Vocation is not our subject; nor is career, however much it formalizes the idea of profession. By the nineteenth century, observes Burton Bledstein, "the new minister thought more in terms of a career which he actively made than a 'calling' into which he had been summoned."[2] It is simply more fruitful to cast glances at career in the light of professions than to let it dominate the inquiry into professions.

Fourth, needless to say, there is no present purpose to examine the clergy as a job. Of course, there is a crass side to this profession as to all others. One wishes to eat, to survive. As someone has said, "If we don't survive, we don't do anything else." Examination of the job concept informs professional inquiry; the "back to the treadmill," or "earn me this day my daily bread," or "another day, another dollar" approach may signal malaise or worse, but it has a pathological dimension not immediately germane.

We are left, then, with the assigned and central topic, the profession. Posthaste, let me propose a working definition, one of many, yet quoted so frequently that it has taken on the dimensions of classic. Louis Brandeis defined a profession as "an occupation for which the necessary preliminary training is intellectual in character, involving knowledge and to some extent learning, as distinguished from mere skill; which is pursued largely for others, and not merely for one's own self; and in which the financial return is not the accepted measure of success."[3]

The student of professions will find some qualifying nuances to that definition. Thus the Marxist critics would say that though Brandeis speaketh in the tongues of men and angels, he hath not realism. To the Marxists, the profession in our society is an invention of bourgeois entrepreneurs who devise jargon, symbols, arcane learning, and educational processes in order to keep the laity at a distance and to assure their income. Interview applicants to medical or law schools, they say, and see whether financial return is not the accepted measure of success and the essential goal.

Another subtle qualification comes from the theologically-minded capitalists, the George Gilders of the world. They would say people enter professions in order to find financial return, and that is good. Their search for financial return spreads altruism, since capitalist risk taking, of the sort known in professional preparation and life, is at heart altruism, and you can never get enough of that. Revise Brandeis in the opposite direction, they advise. Jewish and Christian "prophetic" critics of the clerical profession and professional*ism* sound more like the Marxists. Defenders of the clergy are free to sound rather noncapitalist since the clergy do not earn much in the first, or last, place. Thus they can rescue Talcott Parson's first characteristic of the professional. He or she is not "engaged in the pursuit of his personal profit, but in the performance of services to his patients or clients, or to impersonal values like the advancement of science."[4]

Nuances and subtleties behind us, we are free to focus on the clergy as a profession. The bibliography is enormous. In 1965, before the research boom, Robert J. Menges and James E. Dittes collated over 700 psychological studies of the clergy, most of them from the previous decade alone.[5] They could have found as many sociological or theological inquiries. Studies of professions also focus on professional training. A recent dissertation by Norman J. Kansfield builds on four major surveys of American ministerial training:[6] one was by Robert L. Kelly before 1914; a second was for the Institute of Social and Religious Research before 1934; in 1954 H. Richard Niebuhr, James M. Gustafson, and Daniel Day Williams issued an "epochal" study, which still determines many of the outlines for inquiry; in 1967 *Theological Education* undertook another inquiry. The Lilly Endowment in our time is the main agency sponsoring constant monitoring of the profession. Private enterprise in professional journals provides endless essays on the clergy as profession. Necessarily, we must speak and write in broad outlines, but they can serve provocative purposes.

I shall propose that three broad, chronologically sequential yet overlapping and not displacing forms of the clergy profession have emerged in the United States. First, from 1492 to the 1830s, the ministry can be seen chiefly as a *public* role in a congregational-territorial context, its soil being that of church establishment. The second period remembers the public dimension but produces a new professional context, the *congregational-denominational*. It remains strong and institutionally it even dominates, but cultural shifts have worked to produce a third model. This one took shape during the rise of the other professions in America, and builds on the congregational-denominational. The emergent accent for the past century at least has been toward the *private clientele* setting and expression.

THE PUBLIC PHASE

From 1492 to 1607 Roman Catholic "professed" clergy and religious had a virtual monopoly in the Americas. Whether Spanish, Portuguese, or, to a lesser extent, French—lesser because France was divided religiously and had a Protestant presence and some tiny Huguenot outposts in Florida for a moment—the clergy expressed established, territorial Christianity. In sense, they were—as they were in the minds of Queen Isabella and Christopher Columbus—latter-day crusaders against the infidel. Castile and Aragon hoped to gain gold and access to use for a stab in the back of the Muslims, and the clergy helped legitimate the enterprise. In the minds of the clerical professionals, fathers and brothers, they were missionaries of Christ and the church—*The* Church—on a mission of conversion and civilizing. The orders might practically compete. Theologically and ecclesiastically, however, the religious professions could conceive of themselves on a single crusade or mission. The chaplains to the *conquistadores* may often have had to—indeed, often did—protest the conquests in the names of Christian humaneness. Bartolomeo de Las Casas, one of the pioneer ordained clergy in the New World, made a career of doing so, but he had counterparts as well on the soil of today's Arizona and New Mexico. Theirs was a conflict of administration, psychology, and humane purpose, however, and they were not seen as private entrepreneurs in voluntary associational life. Las Casas used papal teaching and Thomistic argument that found a hearing in the court and among the old rich of Spain, who were threatened by the *nouveau riche* upstarts who lived off Indian slave labor in the New World. The professional clergy in this era were more likely missionaries and chaplains than "parish priests." In any case, however, because boundaries of church and state were congruent in New Spain, they were responsible in and for the larger public order.

That role disappeared, not in New France or the new Iberias, but

in New England, New Netherlands, New Sweden, and the Protestant do-
mains in the thirteen colonies that were to make up the United States. It
is hardly part of the reflexive consciousness of modern American Catholics.
The local archbishop may represent some political clout and bloc power
in city hall, but he knows, or is reluctantly learning, or had better learn,
that he has only persuasive, not coercive, power. He heads what the public
perceives as a voluntary organization competing with many others, religious
and secular. He must win, as must his priests and religious, whatever hearing they can on the basis of moral exemplarity, charisma, or persuasive
argument.

From 1607, with the arrival of Church of England clergy in Virginia
and southern colonies, and 1630, with the arrival of their Puritan and sometimes separatist colleagues and competitors in New England, the thirteen
colonies – nine of which had church establishments – came to be overwhelmingly Protestant. Some figure that by the end of the colonial era there were
only about 3,000 Jews and 30,000 Catholics among 3,000,000 and more
population, and almost all Catholics were in Maryland and southern Pennsylvania. During the two centuries before church disestablishment became
a national norm and before the large Catholic immigration, the study of
the profession of clergy is necessarily and advisedly Protestant. That makes
little difference: the model proposed or evolving in that period also was and
in many ways remained a norm for Catholicism. It adapted to the new styles
of flora and fauna that found their ecological niches and crannies in religiously free and voluntaristic America.

To see how this public style came to be displaced in Catholicism, one
need only look at the pioneering and still very useful study of *Religion as
an Occupation: A Study in the Sociology of Professions* by Joseph H. Fichter,
S.J.[7] I find no trace of a reminiscence of the public dimension that characterized the clerical profession in the theocratic contexts of European and
Latin American Christendom. It disappeared from view.

Ironically, the Protestants who always feared the Catholic theocratic
impulse and the public model of cleric perpetuated and refined it during
their two centuries of monopoly. Donald Scott, in an impressive work, *From
Office to Profession: The New England Ministry, 1750–1850*, summarizes the
public paradigm or expression:

> Eighteenth-century New England had possessed what might be
> termed a theocentric culture, in which the individual's relationship
> to God, the ordination of its institutions, the explanation of its his-

tory, and the norms governing manners, morals, and public obligations all derived from the word and will of God. . . . This theocentric communalism had given the eighteenth-century ministry its essential character as a public office. Public moneys had paid the minister, and the polity had taken part in his selection. Most importantly, however, the sacred office had defined and sustained the community as a public. The minister conducted what was referred to as "public worship," performing the rituals and delivering the Word that ordered the community as an organic whole. In this sense the minister belonged to the town.[8]

It is not important to romanticize this picture; indeed, it is important not to, and Scott does not. But it is valuable to understand the ways in which it expressed the intention of the ministerial profession. Of course, there were local variants. The Virginia clergy, agents of a bishop who remained 3,000 miles away and showed little care, were often inept, second-rate ordinands who had no place to go but Virginia and the Carolinas. They were often degraded by a lay vestry system which denied them tenure or security. They hardly set norms, though it may be observed that some were faithful to their sense of a divine calling in unattractive circumstances.

The New Englanders outside Rhode Island had the best opportunity to ground the public pattern in American life, and they did. They imported Cambridge graduates and then, at their own Cambridge and at New Haven, built Harvard College and Yale College—both as means of providing learned exemplars of public ministry. They displayed their public consciousness and had time to do so. Scott points to statistics that are incomprehensible to professional Protestant clerics in the subsequent two ages. In all, 71 percent of the Yale graduates who entered the ministry from 1702 to 1795 served one pulpit for their entire career. Only 7 percent had served three or more churches during their career. In contrast, of the 162 Yale graduates who entered ministry between 1795 and 1815, only 24 percent held one pastorate, and 29 percent had four or more positions.[9]

Several features of the professional role are noteworthy. First, in this public ministry era, the cleric was often the humanist in an era when the cleric (clerk) mattered. Of the modern cleric as humanist one must ask, as British philosopher Ernest Gellner does, "How seriously does one now take the *cognitive* equipment of the *clerk*?" He answers, "Alas: not very much." Scientific knowledge is taken seriously while the clerk, the cleric, the literate person whose literacy has led him or her to acquire good knowledge of the written word, "has lost much of his standing now as a source of *knowledge* about the world."

In the colonial and early national era, during the late stage theocracies, it was otherwise for the minister:

> The humanist intellectual is, essentially, an expert on the written word. One should not read this in a pejorative sense—as if to say, an expert on *nothing but* words. For words are a very great deal: the rules of their use are wound up with—though not in any simple and obvious way—the activities and the institutions of the societies in which they are employed. They embody the norms—or, indeed, the multiplicity of rival and incompatible norms—of those societies.
>
> Humanist intellectuals, as experts on words, and above all on *written* words, are the natural intermediators with the past and the future through records; with distant parts of the society; with the transcendent when the Word is held to contain the Message from it. . . .[10]

So it was in most of the colonies. The minister preached Fast Day and Election Day sermons, was an educator to the community at large, and monitored legal norms. There was a certain "signal-calling" role. Today we learn how lay colonists resisted their signals through what we may call "creative foot dragging," but they at least nominally accepted the ordering.

Along with this role came that of the minister as moral exemplar who must follow a certain decorum or etiquette in the profession. Yet this was a taken-for-granted element that went with the public role as such. One could attack the person, but not the post—while in the century to come, one could also challenge the post and seek the ministry of someone who held a different concept. Personal charism did not mean as much in the public era as it would later. In a battle over "sizing the common" and determining sheep-grazing rights in early Sudbury, Massachusetts, a layman named Ruddock rose to challenge Parson Brown: "Setting aside your office, I regard you no more than another man." The office demanded the decorum, but when it was not present, the office on its own terms commanded respect.[11]

THE CONGREGATIONAL-DENOMINATIONAL STYLE

The first great shift occurred in the early national period after the churches were disestablished and had become voluntary. By then church and state were "separated," the civil and religious authorities had circumscribed roles in respect to each other, the denominational pattern had become normative, and the vestiges of territorialism were disappearing as Baptists and Methodists ranged and grazed the pastures where earlier Anglicans and Congregationalists had held a monopoly. Roman Catholics in Maryland and Pennsylvania learned the new style, whatever legitimating theology issued to compete with their adaptations from headquarters in Rome. They were loyal to Rome theologically, and effective professionals in America practically.

If the change was complete by about 1830, the impetus for it was visible a century and more earlier, chiefly as a result of two circumstances. The first of these was the presence of nonestablished churches in four colonies and the rise of dissent in the establishmentarian colonies. In New Amsterdam the official Reformed church "connived" and "winked" to allow non-Reformed clergy, because New Netherlands was more an outpost than a colony, a trade center than a settlement, an inevitably pluralist center. In Pennsylvania the Quakers came with a very different concept of clergy, and their sylvan back country was home to many non-English speaking groups that met every classic definition of a sect—and hence were not even intentionally "public" minded. They tended their own flocks of what Benjamin Franklin called "Palatine Boors," and seemed to be at best bystanders and at worst obstructionists to the civil folk of Philadelphia. In Rhode Island from the first the Baptists, seekers, Quakers, antinomians, separatists, and others who fled to or found their original home in New England's *latrina* forced a new concept of professional ministry.

Alongside this world of mavericks, dissenters, and sectarians, there grew another world through the incident of the Great Awakenings, in the 1730s–40s and in the first decade of the new century. When an itinerant saddled his ass and rode into the shadow of the only steeple in town, only to dismount and preach a sermon questioning whether an "unconverted" ministry could be saved and could save others, the consequences were drastic. Soon there would be converts to the new way—America's revivalist "old-time religion" was, we remember, New School, New Light, New Side back then. Soon there would be a Second Congregational Church, or a First Separatist or First Baptist Church in each town, and established ministers, on the defensive, were hard pressed to defend their public role on legal terms. Often the newcomers possessed charisma and skills—notably in preaching and pastoral care—which the settled professionals did not have. They did not bother with "learned ministry," and the humanist and literary roles declined, to the expense of Harvard and Yale and the old credentialing system.

In the colonial pattern, clergy prepared for their profession chiefly by being apprenticed to established veterans. Now they either did not prepare at all, beyond responding to their call, or they issued from quick-fix and lively "Log Colleges" like the one the Tennents ran for revivalists in Philadelphia. Or, significantly, even the old established folks smelled a new era coming. They moved beyond the old Harvard/Yale College-plus-apprenticeship model to the more specialized seminary mold. The founding of Andover Seminary in 1808 is regarded by most historians as marking a change in epochs. By that time Catholics had established St. Mary's in Baltimore, recognizing that they could no longer be dependent upon the flow of maladapting Europeans who could not understand the American competitive and voluntary patterns.

The new seminary had an ecumenical dimension, but its graduates served the denominational world. As Kansfield pointed out, Andover knew it was in competition and had an elaborate public relations mission. The founders knew that the "parsonage" model was antique and inefficient; there had to be mass production. Standardized and specialized curricula began to develop. So did other seminaries — for the Presbyterians at Princeton in 1810, for the Reformed, on earlier foundations, at New Brunswick in 1812, and, later, for all the other groups.

The new seminaries proliferated along denominational and geographical lines. Roman Catholics chose to place theirs chiefly in rural settings, away from the distractions and competitions — until by 1964 there would be 571 places where one could prepare for professional clergy in Catholicism. The proliferation-in-isolation model had assets in that it trained people, men, for very specific locales and denominations. It had liabilities in that they lost the stimulus of centers of learning and urban pluralism. John L. McKenzie did some *ex post facto* moaning for them in 1964, using the language of Sirach 38:15: "How can the man become wise . . . whose discourse is with the sons of bulls?"[12]

The man "became wise" after the seminary fact by being plunged into the competitive pluralism of America's frontiers and cities. The Catholic professional was now anything but a public figure. He was seen as alienated, marginal — and very busy. Why? Because he was learning the American model. Jay Dolan in *Catholic Revivalism*[13] shows how the Catholic priest and brother quickly adapted to the modern resolution and style and freely borrowed from Protestants or instinctively invented, as they had, new approaches to charism in ministry, new uses of what Perry Miller called "the rhetoric of sensation," and new skills for commanding and retaining loyalties. All this atop the traditional demands made on priests.

Protestants were even busier inventing a profession as they lost the public context that provided meaning and power for their ancestors. Jews had to learn the new style. Isaac Leeser, an antecedent of the Conservative Jewish movement, by midcentury was already the equivalent of a circuit rider all over the Great Lakes shores, and Isaac Meyer Wise, leader of Reform, adopted liberal Protestant organizational styles. While historically the rabbi is a layperson, and may remain so in Jewish understanding, sociologically and functionally the rabbi became a professional cleric in America. Significantly, Hebrew Union College in Cincinnati and Jewish Theological Seminary in New York, centers for preparing professionals, also became the focus for coherence and congealing of the movements.

The transition from the public to the competitive congregational-denominational style was never complete. The heirs of establishment, Congregational-Presbyterian-Episcopal in ethos, retain a kind of privileged place on the public landscape. The Episcopalians get away with having "the National Cathedral" in Washington. A President Eisenhower can be baptized by a Presbyterian cleric after his election and the act looks so official it can go unnoticed; whereas it would have been unthinkable for his River Brethren or Jehovah's Witness leaders to take him to the river. But in the new era leadership was increasingly established by charisma, energy, effort, and success. Seminaries, where there were seminaries, existed to provide learning appropriate less for the public model—people doubted the cognitive equipment or value of the clergy of other churches—and applied the lore of their own tradition to their own tradition.

THE ERA OF PRIVATE RELIGION AND CLIENTELES

On the soil of modernity, even the inherited religious institutions on congregational-denominational lines came to be—come to be—called into question and bypassed by many. Publicly, Tom Paine and Thomas Jefferson in the eighteenth century were turning "private" in religion—"My own mind is my temple." A century later in psychology and philosophy William James and Alfred North Whitehead were defining religion as individual acts of solitary beings. Robert Bellah has said that it is a mark of religious modernity that people establish a direction for their spiritual journey; they find a satisfying trajectory. Then, to the degree that a particular religious institution effectively, even if only temporarily, enhances that direction and tendency, the modern will make use of it. Sometimes the pressures of choice force an almost fanatic loyalty, but it may be temporary. One is "into" renewal one year, being "born again" the next, pentecostalism the third, "encounter movements" the fourth, "Jesus" the fifth, "underground church" the sixth, and the like. Fanaticism does not necessarily mean durability in fidelity.

Modern, free, industrial, technological, media-dominated societies push religious institutions to the margins. They force specialization. In the modern contract, church and synagogue were assigned a place in private, personal, residential, and leisure life. Public life—economic, commercial, intellectual, cultural, and political—was seen to be a zone in which the clergy were intrusive and meddling. As Peter Berger has pointed out in *The Heretical Imperative*, reminding us that the root term *haeresis* means "choice," the essence of free modern religion is choice, the act of choosing. As one Cicero Catholic remarked on generational change when Pope John Paul II visited Chicago, the grandchildren "take their Catholicism a la carte."

Preparation of clergy for the professional role of ministering to congregations not as necessarily sacramental or ecclesial expressions but as clienteles—or ministering to individuals as clients!—was part of a revolution that began a century ago and crested in the 1960s. This was the era when professional preparation moved from the parsonages of pastors or the pastures of "sons of bulls" to or toward university centers. There the student candidate is formed in a setting of pluralism and secularity that does bear more resemblance to a "real world" than academics often are ready to recognize when commiserating with themselves.

The heart of the university, as opposed to the collegiate or isolated denominational seminary model, was its specialization. The city became a laboratory for preparation. The student was in range of denominational seminaries that also clustered near universities, and had access to university curricula, bewildering and adaptive as these may seem to be.

The new word was *specialize!* The congregation or parish may be the main agency of professional employment for the vast majority of clerics. There are theological, sacramental, political, and practical warrants for making it the focus—inside several ecclesiastical polities from episcopal through congregational. Yet the seminarian in this era has known that along with learning the basics it is wise to specialize. Increasingly theological educators have discerned reasons to help clerics "retool." The development of Clini-

cal Pastoral Education and the Doctor of Ministry degree are but two symbols of the need to specialize. The ease with which ordained professional
clerics move laterally into counselling firms or in several other professional
directions demonstrates that competencies in biblical interpretation, preaching, or administration of the sacraments are not the only earmarks or credentials in ministerial preparation and exercise.

The professional cleric today does not compete with Methodist, Baptist, Catholic or Jew. He or she competes with *Psychology Today* and Channel 38, the airport newsstand and the guru, the encounter group and the
classroom, the therapy of the season and the antiinstitutional ethos. The
minister who is settled in a congregation is uneasy. Two hundred fifty years
after Northamptonites dismissed notable cleric Jonathan Edwards the event
seems newsworthy. The Southern Baptist convention, conservative and
putatively committed to the congregational-denominational model, acknowledged recently that "clergy firings and forced resignations are at an all-time
high in the denomination." Within the year, 29 of 35 state Baptist newspapers had to carry editorials on the subject. North Carolina Baptists alone
discovered 100 of these.

> "In the past churches were reluctant to dismiss a pastor," said C. R.
> Daley, Kentucky Baptist Convention editor. "But now we find that
> methods used by the secular business world are more commonly be-
> ing used by the church. . . .
> Reasons for clergy firings included blaming the pastor for sag-
> ging church finances and attendance, general unstable conditions in
> the country that result in frustration among congregations and clergy,
> personality clashes, breakdowns in communications between congrega-
> tions and clergy and power struggles between the pastor and a faction
> within the congregation.[14]

Where local congregations are hugely successful, they are so as clienteles or constituencies, not as confessional expressions. Catholic charis-
matic priests and parishes compete with other Catholic parishes, not with
Protestants or secularists. It is hard to picture a member of the Crystal
Cathedral having chosen membership because its pastor and its official status are part of the Reformed Church in America. If a member leaves in
disaffection, it will not be because of that Reformed tie but because some
other minister or some other channel appeals more.

Even where the congregation-denomination remains the focus, the modern setting, with its differentiation, specificity, and universalization, has forced a diffusion on the theological student and minister. H. Richard Niebuhr quoted Mark A. May's 1934 study on *The Profession of the Ministry*: "Entering the ministry is . . . like entering the army, where one never knows where he will land or live or what specific work he will be called upon to perform. This lack of clear definition of the functions of the pastor that can be widely accepted influences theological education" in that it leads to diffusion.[15]

The reaction to diffusion is a renewed specificity. The Clinical Pastoral Education program thus helps prepare chaplains, many of whom lose interest in parish ministry. The parish minister is supposed to be a theologian, yet formal theology has moved out of the parsonage and pulpit and is the specialty of ministry in the academy. A study by Thor Hall in 1978 found that 38.06 percent of the 557 systematic theologians he studied had had pastoral ministry or other ecclesiastical posts, but only 14 of 558, or 2.51 percent, held nonacademic posts, one of which was "pastoral."[16]

Ralph Waldo Emerson, ever the trend spotter in himself, his culture, and his contemporaries, was a full epoch ahead of the game when he located the adaptive entrepreneur in the professions. In his *Journals* he scribbled: "The New Professions: The phrenologist; the railroad man; the landscape gardener; the lecturer; the sorcerer, rapper, mesmerizer, medium; the daguerreotypist. *Proposed*: The Naturalist, and the Social Undertaker." Burton Bledstein, in his study of professions, found the pressure to be entrepreneurs forced upon client-hunting ministers already in Emerson's day. Emerson did locate the mental equipment for the modern professional roles:

> . . . a new consciousness. . . . The young men were born with knives in their brain, a tendency to introversion, self-dissection, anatomizing of motives. . . . The key to the period appeared to be that the mind had become aware of itself. . . . It is the age of severance, of dissociation, of freedom, of analysis, of detachment. Every man for himself. . . . People grow philosophical about native land and parents and relations. There is an universal resistance to ties and ligaments once supposed essential to civil society.[17]

Ministers discovering clienteles from such a cohort matched up with them much more than a century before the Me Decade, the "I'll do it my way" way of salvation, but the latter decades of the twentieth century turned this avant-garde impulse into a norm for millions.

CONCLUSIONS: THE "LESSONS" OF HISTORY

Whenever fundamental changes in the context emerged, there were doomsayers. They are not joined this time by this observer of the changes. Marty's Law of the Professions reads that while some professions have split seconds of unquestioned prestige and effectiveness, overall they are all always in some sort of trouble. Attempts to diagnose them leads to moroseness and lugubriousness. Have stockbrokers today high morale? Or automakers? Savings and Loan executives? Have dentists the professional image they think others have? Will physicians and lawyers find happiness? Stay tuned. Admirals and clergy have always been adepts at self-commiseration, argued literary critic Richard Chase. Yet professional ministry endures, revives, finds new niches, attracts talent, enjoys support, for all its problems.

What about status, a constant question in the world of professions? Here the evidence is conflicting and even contradictory. Through three centuries of study about ministry one can find a strain of charts and graphs that shows constant decline in status and another strain that shows constant rise. Of course, Donald Scott is right: "In eighteenth-century New England, the ministry was the most highly esteemed of the 'learned professions.'"[18] But did the Reverend Mr. Brown of Sudbury have status and esteem to match that of Fulton Sheen or Billy Graham or Robert Schuller in the entrepreneurial era when each evoked awe because they had successfully scraped together a clientele? So much for the public model. As for the congregational-denominational model, ministerial status survived for the class of clergy in the competitive era because survivors in congregations had proven themselves effective and durable. The Roman Catholic pattern of clerical assignment protected the ineffective, but parishioners have ways of showing their esteem or lack of it toward the automatically durable. Joseph Fichter could write, "The Catholic priest tends to share in the relatively high status enjoyed generally by clergymen in America." He reported that in one national opinion poll ranking ninety occupations, the minister ranked fourteenth and the priest twenty-first.[19]

At almost the same time, Richard A. La Piere, "a sociologist," observed:

A hundred years ago the Protestant ministry was a profession of high prestige and equally high morale; it then drew to it men of intellectual vigor and strong ambition. Today the ministry is a profession as low in prestige as in income, and the general level of morale among ministers is lower still; today, therefore, the university training centers for the ministry gets the culls of the academic crop.

Yoshio Fukuyama, who quotes him, says that La Piere "did not provide empirical documentation for his conclusions, though his viewpoint is a persistent and popular one."[20] Then he presented empirical documentation from 1963 which showed ministers ranking with psychologists, below lawyers and architects, but ahead of civil engineers and—take that, La Piere—sociologists. Ministers then were ranked seventeenth among professions, while in 1947 they were thirteenth. Fukuyama concluded that the minister had lost status since colonial times, but the "profession is still esteemed in American society."[21]

What matters is not so much prestige or status but the argument over these in the light of religious standards. A "prophetic" school opposes professionalism of all sorts and carries this to the point of criticizing the concept of profession itself. The prophet looks for simplicity, unencumberedness, mobility—all of which the professional may easily lose. The diplomas, marks of office, institutional networks, and special languages are alienating. The poor and simple will be compromised. J. Roge called the French priest "the most institutionalized man of our time," and the prophet asks for an undercutting of institution and liberation from it.[22]

Ivan Illich typifies the prophetic critic in reference to all professions. The mark of the professional to him is not "income, long training, delicate tasks, or social standing. . . . Rather it is his authority to define a person as client, to determine that person's need, and to hand the person a prescription."[23]

We are not likely to hear—or to have ears to hear—too many prophets against professional*ism*, but the historian student of professions may find better things to say about them as conveyances of religious messages, services, meanings, and the like. Professions imply power, and power is a good biblical word, the capacity to effect intended results. The cleric therefore needs power. Walter Wagoner, in *Bachelor of Divinity*, quoted a study of *Professional People* by Roy Lewis and Angus Maude in 1952 to make this point:

> [Professional people] need to protect themselves and defend their ideals; they need to understand and uphold their personal attainments . . . they are an aristocracy of a sort. They certainly need the humility which self-knowledge demands, and should discard the dangerous false modesty of pretending to be "ordinary people . . . only an expert in this or that." On the contrary it is important that their differences from other people should be emphasized . . . let professional people empha-

size the hierarchy of professions, of education, of esteem. Let them not shirk the truth expressed by Matthew Arnold: "the highly instructed few, and not the scantily instructed many, will ever be the organ to the human race of knowledge and truth."[24]

I would not let that paragraph stand in isolation from Illich's, but, taken together, they represent poles either of which polemicists or professionals can neglect or reject.

The clerical figure in the age of clienteles often does seem bereft of traditional supports. Professional ministers in Christianity must often have analogous experiences to those that motivated the outcry of Rabbi Arthur Hertzberg, a cry that conjoins pathos and defiance:

> In the contemporary situation, the rabbi has only his biography, nothing else. He no longer has anti-Semitism to "keep the Jews down on the farm," he does not have an organized community, he has competition. With only himself, and what he is, he feels terribly cold and terribly lonely, and he would like to be able to say like Moses, the very first rabbi and the greatest of them all, "Go send somebody else." But here *we* are. *We* are sent. We cannot avoid it. . . . We Modern rabbis choose some values to affirm and to fight for and some to ignore. . . . And so we are, if we are honest with ourselves, in the most difficult and loneliest situation in Jewish history. We are rabbis who have nothing going for us except our own passion, our own conviction, our own lives, and what we are willing to put them on the line for.[25]

Still, three out of five Americans, in the face of all contrary lures, bother to affiliate with religious institutions, and two out of five attend worship weekly. There must be vestigial communalism behind the clienteles and a reminiscent public behind the congregationalism. Many professional clergy are not merely passive in the face of change. They have located the enemy — not so much the pervasive secularism but the perduring private religiosity. They are calling their clienteles to a *ressourcement*, a tradition born in, positing, and generating community. There is some awareness again of a clerical role in the public arena. The congregation is a plausible arena for professional enactments and service.

Should the clerical profession disappear, as some prophets seek? Adaptive as it is, it is more likely to find new ways to survive and be of service than to disappear. Historians are experts at recounting how people live in

the midst of ambiguity and brokenness. I have no empirical documentation, but I doubt whether many of them would join the romantics who
claim to support Christian community but foresee its survival entirely in
the hands of nonprofessional lay people. It has been tried. The worker priests
became workers, not priests. The underground church when priestless dis-
solved and disappeared. Lay Christians seem to have done best when they
have been equipped to work alongside clergy who have never lost sight of
the needs of persons—while demonstrating that in the good sense of the
term they can also be "real pros."

NOTES

1. Quoted in Robert McClintock, *Man and His Circumstances: Ortega as
Educator* (New York, 1971), p. 118.

2. Burton Bledstein, *The Culture of Professionalism: The Middle Class and
the Development of Higher Education in America* (New York, 1976). p. 176.

3. Quoted by Paul Pigors and Charles Myers, *Personnel Administration* (New
York, 1947), p. 308.

4. Talcott Parsons, *Essays in Sociological Theory Pure and Applied* (Glencoe,
Ill., 1949), p. 186.

5. Robert J. Menges and James E. Dittes, *Psychological Studies of Clergymen*
(New York, 1965).

6. Norman J. Kansfield, "Study the Most Approved Authors" (Ph.D. dissertation, University of Chicago, 1981).

7. Joseph H. Fichter, S.J., *Religion as Occupation: A Study in the Sociology
of Professions* (Notre Dame, Ind., 1961).

8. Donald M. Scott, *From Office to Profession: The New England Ministry,
1750–1850* (Philadelphia, 1978), p. 148.

9. Ibid., p. 74.

10. Ernest Gellner, "The Crisis in the Humanities and the Mainstream of
Philosophy," in J. H. Plumb, *Crisis in the Humanities* (Baltimore, 1964), pp. 71, 72.

11. Sumner Chilton Powell, *Puritan Village: The Formation of a New England
Town* (Garden City, N.Y., 1965), p. 164.

12. Quoted in James Michael Lee and Louis J. Putz, *Seminary Education
in a Time of Change* (Notre Dame, Ind., 1965), p. 407.

13. Jay Dolan, *Catholic Revivalism: The American Experience 1830–1900* (Notre
Dame, Ind., 1978).

14. News item in *The Lutheran* 17 March 1982, p. 19.

15. See the comment on May in Yoshio Fukuyama, *The Ministry in Transition: A Case Study of Theological Education* (University Park, Pa., 1972), pp. 3, 19.

16. Thor Hall, *Systematic Theology Today: The State of the Art in North America Part I* (Washington, 1978), pp. 38–42.

17. Quoted by Bledstein, *Culture of Professionalism*, pp. 175, 177.

18. Scott, *From Office to Profession*, p. xi.

19. Fichter, *Religion as Occupation*, p. 125.

20. Quoted by Fukuyama, *Ministry in Transition*, p. 19.

21. Ibid., pp. 20, 21.

22. Quoted by Hervé Carrier, *The Sociology of Religious Belonging* (New York, 1965), p. 197.

23. Ivan Illich, *Disabling Professions* (London, 1977), p. 17.

24. Roy Lewis and Angus Maude, *Professional People* (London, 1952), p. 173.

25. Arthur Hertzberg. *Being Jewish in America: The Modern Experience in America* (New York, 1979), pp. 123–24.

THE CLERGY: SUGGESTIONS FOR FURTHER READING

Bellah, Robert N., et al. *Habits of the Heart: Individualism and Commitment in American Life.* Berkeley, Calif., 1985.

Calhoun, Daniel H. *Professional Lives in America: Structure and Aspiration, 1750–1850.* Cambridge, Mass., 1965.

Fukuyama, Yoshio. *The Ministry in Transition: A Case Study of Theological Education.* University Park, Pa., 1972.

Haig, Alan. *The Victorian Clergy.* London, 1984.

Heeney, Brian. *A Different Kind of Gentleman: Parish Clergy as Professional Men in Early and Mid-Victorian England.* Hamden, Conn., 1976.

Hertzberg, Arthur. *Being Jewish in America: The Modern Experience.* New York, 1979.

Holifield, E. Brooks. *The Gentlemen Theologians: American Theology in Southern Culture, 1795–1865.* Durham, N.C., 1978.

Hutchinson, William R. *The Modernist Impulse in American Protestantism.* New York, 1976.

Marsden, George M. *Fundamentalism and American Culture: The Shaping of Twentieth-Century Evangelicalism, 1870–1925.* New York, 1980.

Marty, Martin E. *Modern American Religion.* Vol. 1: *The Irony of It All, 1893–1919.* Chicago, 1986.

Moore, R. Laurence. *Religious Outsiders and the Making of Americans.* New York, 1986.

Scott, Donald M. *From Office to Profession: The New England Ministry, 1750–1850.* Philadelphia, 1978.

5. THE AMERICAN MILITARY PROFESSION

John Shy

The Impossible Profession is the subtitle of a recent, fascinating, best-selling book. Alas, it does not deal with my own subject—the military—but with the profession of psychoanalysis. Had Janet Malcolm not preempted the label, I would have used it to describe the *military* profession in American society, a profession where frustration and failure are so built into the status and purpose of the profession that it often, indeed, appears impossible.

Deprived of what seems the obvious label for this lecture, let me fall back on two less familiar, more academic adjectives, two words that have the virtue of specifying how and why this peculiar profession is, if not truly impossible, at least close to impossible. The two words are *truncated* and *inchoate*. By *truncated* (a word first encountered in high school geometry) I mean "cut off"; the military profession is, and has been, cut off in various ways from what, in other professions—including psychoanalysis—would be a normal professional life and normal professional development. The other word (not learned until graduate school) is *inchoate*—fuzzy, blurry, unclear, jumbled, confused. Largely because it is a uniquely *truncated* profession, the military profession is—unlike law, medicine, science, or business—*inchoate*, not clear about its boundaries, its proper work, its responsibilities, or even the criteria by which its performance will be evaluated.

All this might sound surprising. After all, the military seems especially well defined by law, even by the special clothes it wears, more clearly defined, for example, than the clergy which has gradually discarded or deemphasized its professional uniform. And the military has one special, awful task: war, and preparation for war. What could be clearer than a uniformed specialist in warfare? But if we look more closely at the actual situation, we see that this clarity of status and task is an illusion, and that the professional soldier lives and works in a world of strange expectations, foggy criteria, and ill-defined tasks—a world, above all, cut off from professional reality.

Some of you may have expected another kind of introduction to this subject. After all, for the last decade, book after book has told us that the American military profession is in crisis, that somehow it must be reformed or reform itself. And if you have missed the books, news magazines and television specials have hammered the same theme. Covering up My Lai, lying about air attacks in Vietnam, giving up the USS *Pueblo*, losing control of its troops, and, above all, failing to win the war in Vietnam, have cost the military the confidence of the American people, and especially the confidence of the American military in itself. Isn't this contemporary crisis of the profession the proper place to begin? Without denying that the American military profession is today in serious trouble, my answer to the question is no, because the American military profession, itself an extreme case of the modern military profession as it had emerged by the eighteenth century in Western civilization, has *always* had serious troubles, troubles historically rooted in the nature of democratic American society, and in the peculiar nature of the professional military role.

Success in war, and more often simple lack of attention, have tended to conceal just how deep, and deeply rooted, are the troubles of this peculiar profession. It is, and has long been a profession cut off—

—cut off from the actual practice of its real professional work. Wars, thank God, are very infrequent, and only fragments of warfare can be simulated, so that military professionals—unlike doctors, lawyers, business executives, or even teachers—exist in a professional never-never land of guesswork, memory, and prediction.

—cut off from a healthy political and psychological relationship with its own clients, government and the general public. Soldiers, like lawyers, doctors, business executives, and even teachers, are mistrusted and disliked, but more so because the soldier's job deals with deliberate killing by a coercively run organization, so at odds with the ideals and usual practice of modern civilized society, especially in America. At the same time soldiers are often praised extravagantly and seem to be loved, by the same people who dislike and mistrust them, because the uniformed soldier is a visible, evocative, and—particularly in wartime—emotionally powerful symbol of the mystical, intangible nation that binds us together, a symbol so strong that it transmutes the mass murder of war into holy crusade. Here, too, the *American* situation pushes the problem several notches up the scale of difficulty, leaving the American soldier even more in limbo, cut off from a healthy, supportive, rational environment within which to live and work.

—and, finally, cut off in two other ways that developments during the last century have made acute. Soldiers are cut off by modern technology from the basic tools of their profession, the weapons, communications, and transportation systems that even before 1900 were the work of engineers and other technicians, *not* of professional soldiers. Only a very few soldiers (e.g., a rare Rickover) could begin to comprehend the new technology and thus they fell more and more into the role of passive, even impotent consumers of what *other* kinds of professionals designed and produced. Just as modern technology has cut soldiers off from their own tools, so modern organization has cut them off at their most vital point—it has destroyed their concentration, their dedication, their very professional life by pushing them, typically, *out* of the military when still in their forties, in the very prime, when presumably professional soldiers have at last learned their business after a long apprenticeship and should have the most to contribute to the profession of arms. Soldiers are pushed out because modern organization, with its pyramidal hierarchy of rank and pay, will not tolerate the slower promotion among the *younger* members in their twenties and thirties and the lower rate of intake of *new* members. A different kind of organization would use fully the experience, education, and wisdom of people in their fifties, sixties, and seventies—just the kind of older people who, of course, the modern medical profession has helped to make more active, productive, and numerous.

To sum up: American professional soldiers are cut off:
  —from their real work by the infrequency of war,
  —from a healthy environment for their work by the strange mixture of emotions aroused by both the role and that work,
  —from the tools of their work by modern, ever more complex technology,
  —and from a truly professional, lifetime commitment by the organization's need to attract and motivate younger members, as well as by its pyramidal structure of rank.

Cut off, truncated, in these ways, the American military profession is indeed in trouble, and at the center of the trouble has been our inability to see the various symptoms as a syndrome. The professional troubles of the soldier are baffling because the profession itself is so inchoate. We, soldiers or civilians, cannot diagnose and prescribe because we cannot see the trouble whole: what is new, what is old, what can be fixed, what can only be mitigated, and what is hopeless—the tragic that must be endured, but at least can be understood.

What I have said so far is not the diagnosis, much less the prescription, but only sketches a way of attacking the problem, as a whole. A sketch, a skeleton, it needs filling out, illustrating, testing against the evidence—contemporary and historical—before trying to say something about the future of the American military profession. So let me, briefly, shift the level of this discussion from sweeping generalization down to the level of gritty facts at least giving some better idea of where and how, in my historical knowledge and personal experiences, these generalizations are coming from. Let me begin with one of the simpler parts of our problem—the role and status of the military profession in American society.

*   *   *   *   *

The Virginia habit of using military rank—Colonel Byrd, Major Washington, Captain Lee—even when the rank was merely honorific, is well known and has its origins in the earliest history of the South. Equally well known is the tendency of Georgians, Kentuckians, and Texans to imitate colonial Virginians in their fondness for military titles. Much less well known is that the same habit appears in colonial New England, allegedly a hotbed of anti-military attitudes. In fact, it was not unusual for an early New England town to have each of its six or seven selectmen styled "captain" or "lieutenant," and to send a "major" or a "colonel" to represent it in the provincial assembly. As in the southern colonies, these New England officers were either holders of militia ranks or, occasionally, the veteran officers of some war against the Indians, French, or Spanish. This is not a trivial matter of words; rather, it reveals a colonial American perception of the world that attaches prestige and even a certain glamor to military titles, although the neighbors may know that Colonel X or Captain Y has never heard a shot fired in anger. In a society with few and hazy social distinctions except those of wealth, sex, and race, a military rank may have been so attractive because it was legally established and ostensibly earned, and at least suggested that its holder had certain virtues.

George Washington became, as in so many other respects, the role model for American military professionalism. Compared to many of his contemporaries among the Virginia aristocracy, young Washington was not well educated. Intelligent and literate, he was not learned in the way that Jefferson or Madison were, nor did he have the formal education needed to compete in the law courts and House of Burgesses with men like Edmund Pendleton or Patrick Henry. Not disposed to gamble and drink his life away, as a few great planters like William Byrd III were doing, the young Washington found in the profession of arms what he wanted—a chance to exploit his impressive physical and moral qualities while minimizing the weakness of his formal education—above all, the chance to distinguish himself in public life. His military career began badly, with mistakes, defeat, and humiliation. But he swallowed defeat, learned from his mistakes, and persevered. Professional success, however, required more than a provincial, wartime title; only a regular commission in his Majesty's Army could give Washington the permanent, respected position that his ambition demanded. For various reasons political and accidental, this British regular commission eluded him, and Colonel Washington seemed destined to remain a civilian, a provincial planter, and only a sometime semiprofessional soldier.

Washington wore his Virginia colonel's uniform to the Continental Congress. If a smaller, less awesome man had done that, it might have seemed ludicrous. But slick New England politicians, like John Adams, saw how valuable a Virginia commander for what was still a New England army would be. John Hancock, who loved to parade at the head of his Boston cadets, wanted the job; but only Washington, one of the few candidates with any real military experience, could transform a regional conflict into a national cause, and he did. As commander of the Continental Army, Washington looked to the European model of military professionalism, in which officers were gentlemen, distant from their troops, suspicious of politicians, and quietly contemptuous in their attitude toward all civilians. It was the enlightened, late eighteenth-century version of an ancient ideal in Western civilization, that of the warrior-aristocrat, the Christian knight who did not live by labor, commerce, or pen, but whose privileges and leisure were justified by his exquisite sense of honor and, behind honor, his courage. Washington played this role, encouraged his junior officers to imitate him, and frowned on those who neglected to do so.

Washington, with his tremendous balance and strength of character, never let the role carry him too far or lost sight of the higher values of the new American Republic. But younger, lesser men were not so clear-headed or self-disciplined. Many Continental officers, by the later years of the Revolutionary War, were touchy, arrogant caricatures of the European gentleman-officer, damning politicians and cowardly civilians, demanding their privileges, duelling at the drop of an insult, and in general behaving like so many uniformed fools, out of touch with the realities and the goals of the democratic revolution that they had volunteered to join and defend. Washington deserves our gratitude for moderating the worst excesses of these aspiring American warriors, especially for his insistence at critical moments that the military must subordinate itself to legitimate civil authority, however badly the civilians might misuse that authority. But Washington was also chiefly responsible for the way in which this original nucleus of American professional soldiers cut themselves off from their own native roots and instead looked outside, to England and Europe, for their understanding of military manners, attitudes, and standards. Cut off during the colonial era by the absence of any specialized American military organization, the American military profession that emerged from the Revolution had cut itself off, more or less deliberately, from the chance to work out a tradition better adapted to the peculiar needs and conditions of American life.

From the Revolutionary War, through the nineteenth century, and into the twentieth century, there is a discernible, continuous pattern of American experience with the military profession. There are three parts to the pattern, each related to the other two. First, most of the tiny minority of career soldiers in American society continue to ape the European gentleman-officer at his worst, with all his pompous self-importance. This was—and is—unfortunate. Whether the fuss-and-feathers of Winfield Scott, the Napoleonic posturing of George B. McClellan, or Adjutant General Fred Ainsworth's defiance of Secretary of War Henry Stimson, American military professionals' ingrained sense of themselves as more worthy than the people they serve is a sad story. Exciting hostility and suspicion from fellow Americans, soldiers explain these feelings as the predictable ingratitude and ignorance of people who lack the martial virtues. In private, the former Secretary of State, Alexander Haig, a professional soldier to the core, was said to use especially ugly words to describe his critics in Congress and the press, words that question both their integrity and their manhood. If true, it is not a new story, but an old pattern of behavior with deep historic roots.

But there are the other two parts of the pattern. One is a continuing American susceptibility to those who win wars or are simply brave in battle. Presidents and members of Congress, from Andrew Jackson to John Kennedy, are only the most prominent of hundreds, thousands of ambitious Americans who have converted good military records into political success.

Most of these warrior-politicians were not professional soldiers, but it is clear that nothing stopped professionals Zachary Taylor and Dwight Eisenhower from exploiting the American political magic latent in military heroism. Surely, somehow, American readiness to see special virtue in the Cincinnatus figure, turning the soldier's hand to the political plow, has helped to feed the sensitive, inflated ego of the professional military officer.

But there is one more part: antimilitarism and hostility toward military professionals, especially at their arrogant worst, is an element of this part, though clearly not all. Soldiers as military as Andrew Jackson have been able to play off this third part, exploiting the slightly comic figure of the spit-and-polish professional, and, appealing to the untidy, balky, democratic side of American life. Even some professional soldiers themselves, like Grant, Mahan, Omar Bradley, and Creighton Abrams, won respect and affection by refusing to conform to the stereotypical martinet who seemed to characterize their own profession. What to label this third part? It is certainly not pacifism, or even antimilitarism, but more a healthy skepticism that tight, bright uniforms, short hair, and shoes polished to a mirrorlike shine have much to do with the rough and dirty business of warfare. General Abrams, like General Grant, looked as if he had slept in his ill-fitting uniform, and for some mysterious reason we thought more of him for being so unkempt. Alexander Haig, on the other hand, even in pin stripes and rep tie, always seemed a little too natty, the soldier ready for Saturday inspection and parade; a little too much oversize ID bracelet on his right wrist clanking lightly as he signed the treaty; a little too-too, a tense, hostile martinet behind the televised smile. Surely some of his troubles as Secretary of State came from what seems to his skeptical American audience as the image of the stereotypical "soldier," the same self-inflicted image that blighted the political ambitions of Douglas MacArthur (though not those of the more Washingtonian George Marshall and Dwight Eisenhower).

William Tecumseh Sherman in his memoirs says almost nothing about what drew him to the military profession. In contrast with his detailed and interesting narrative of army service in Florida and California, his four years at West Point are passed by with little comment; and it appears that the lure of a free education for the son of a numerous family whose father had recently died, but whose political friends were eager to help, was the reason for his choice of the profession. When economic opportunity beckoned, after the Mexican War, he seems to have had no qualms about giving up his uniform for the clothes and profession of a banker in San Francisco.

At only one point in his account of army life before the Civil War does Sherman reveal some deeper sense of military professionalism. During the confused period of military government in California, Colonel (and Governor) Richard Mason ordered a local commander, Captain John Brackett, to remove from civil office a Mr. Nash, who had been elected by recent immigrants to the Sonoma Valley. Captain Brackett declined the order, on the grounds that the situation was dangerous, that Nash was popular, and that he—Brackett—intended to leave the army soon and settle in the Sonoma Valley. Lieutenant Sherman, on Mason's staff, immediately offered to arrest Nash, and he did so. "Brackett . . . by-the-way," writes Sherman, "was a West Point graduate, and *ought to have known better*." Despite Sherman's cold, unsentimental view of the profession, he concedes, in his few words about this minor incident, that there is a distinct professional ethic, which anyone who has had professional training ought not only to *know*, but to *regard* as superior to the democratic, individualistic ethic typical of antebellum America.

Attitudes toward things military in America are less evident.in the great, historic event or person than in a thousand little incidents, the revealing minutiae of everyday routine. One last example from this revealing minutiae: Thomas Wentworth Higginson was a nineteenth century Boston aristocrat, a Harvard prodigy, a writer, an intellectual, a friend of Emerson and Thoreau, a progressive clergyman, and a radical crusader against slavery and for women's rights and a host of other causes. During the Civil War, for about a year and a half, he had led a Negro regiment of ex-slaves, the first in the Union Army, on active operations along the southeastern coast. No professional soldier, Higginson, like his black soldiers, performed well; Higginson was wounded in 1864 and left the army. Sixteen years later we find his wife still referring to her eminent husband, not as "Wentworth" or "Doctor Higginson," but as "the Colonel." Higginson himself, upon re-reading his published memoir, *Army Life in a Black Regiment*, said that he was seized "with a sort of despair at the emptiness of all other life after that," and felt that "those times [in the army] are ever fresh and were perhaps the flower of our lives." Higginson lived almost a half century, busy and productive decades, after his brief military service, but never ceased being "the Colonel" or escaped the haunting memory of war. It is not that such incidents are peculiar to America; they are certainly not. Rather, it is that such incidents pervade the almost four centuries of American history, and that each is a node of unresolved tension in what we imagine to be the American way of life.

Between the Civil War and the Vietnam War, the American military profession at least maintained, and after 1945 certainly strengthened, its position within the society. Three great, victorious wars—the Civil War and the two world wars—gave the military profession new levels of attention and prestige, even as the traditional suspicion and dislike toward the military persisted. This is no contradiction; two opposed attitudes simply coexisted, often in the same mind. Sherman and Grant, even Lee, were national heroes, but public opinion still looked askance at the American military.

During this same century, key members of the American military profession developed several very important national strategies: Mahan's concept of sea power, the concept of strategic bombing, and—after Hiroshima —the concept of limited war. In each case, these strategies, or strategic ideas, were remarkable for their intellectual qualities; they were clear, persuasive, and quite radical. Each of these new American strategies rejected traditional, common-sense strategic thinking. Mahan turned the dispersed, defensive notion of sea power into a concentrated, offensive, imperialist doctrine. Billy Mitchell and like-minded enthusiasts argued that airplanes were not simply flying artillery and airborne observation posts but were potentially ultimate weapons that would make surface warfare secondary, even irrelevant. And the limited-war strategy, evolved by army officers like Maxwell Taylor with much help from civilian think tanks, argued that warfare could be deliberately limited in scope and intensity despite the existence of weapons of incredible destructive power. These are radical military ideas, make no mistake, because each—as I have said—challenged conventional military wisdom. Let me repeat myself: sea power, said the Mahanites, was *not* essentially defensive and dependent on dispersion of naval force over the waters of the world. Air power, said the true believers in bombing, was *not* just another weapon, making navies more mobile and more powerful. And war in the nuclear age, said the "limited warriors" (or "flexible responders") would *not* escalate uncontrollably to global holocaust but might be managed *better than ever* as an instrument of national policy.

Doubtless I exaggerate and simplify in ascribing credit for these radical new strategies wholly to the American military profession. But not much. Each idea, if it did not originate in the profession, quickly took root in some corner of it—navy, air corps, or army—and there gained the strength and force to push influentially into the realm of national policy and international relations. No other national military profession, not even the vaunted German General Staff, has such a history of creative strategic thinking. This is impressive, important, and surprising, considering the peculiar historic position of American soldiers, dominated as they have been by civilians, usually made to feel unappreciated, occasionally praised as national heroes, but always uneasy in pursuing such a profession in an individualistic, democratic society. Yet the ideas and the environment are not unrelated. The ideas, impressive as they are, have caused the nation some real grief: aggressive, imperialistic behavior in the early twentieth century in the Caribbean and East Asia continues to haunt us; so does the memory of city-busting air attacks on Germany and Japan; and the *Pentagon Papers* amply document how the confidence of General Taylor and other "limited warriors" made the step-by-step entry into the Vietnam War seem reasonable and responsible. Cut off from a healthier relation to state and society, the American military has been susceptible to radical ideas about strategy, which then feed back, filling the vacuum of serious thinking about war and peace in the society itself. Perhaps I should state all this more cautiously, as a set of hypotheses or questions, because none of it is easily proved. Yet in trying to make sense of what I learned through experience and study of this profession since my first direct encounter with it, in 1947, I offer these thoughts on its history for your consideration.

*   *   *   *   *

How, if at all, can the history of the American military profession, from colonial New England towns calling their elected officials by military titles to U.S. Army officers with graduate degrees in the 1960s developing a doctrine of limited warfare, be related? No one can be honestly certain. But there appear to be important links between the present, past, and probably future of this peculiar profession, links that should provide some guidance in our current confusion. Always there appears the exaggerated tension of the love-hate relationship: the military as patriotic and public-spirited; the military as corrupt, corrupting, and dangerous. From Yankee selectmen posing as captains, to modern soldiers inventing simplistic doctrines for the integration of war and diplomacy, there is something here strange and extreme. Even the intelligent, unmilitarized, coldly pragmatic Sherman believed that a normal young American, after four years of West Point, should know enough never to question an order from his commander. Very strange. Victors in the Second World War, professional soldiers—Marshall, MacArthur, Eisenhower—are godlike figures. Frustrated in Vietnam, Taylor, Harkins, and Westmoreland are professional incompetents, or worse. If the American military profession appears unstable in its relationship to the society, and inchoate at its professional center, then a large part of the explanation surely lies in this long history of contradictory extremes. We expect too much; we permit too much. Lack of respect coexists unstably with excessive admiration.

Reform of any large institution, with traditions impressed upon it by generations of time, is extremely difficult. Billy Mitchell thought that nothing less than disaster could bring real change. Whether Vietnam was such a disaster is debatable. Chances are that nothing much will change, despite the criticism and prescriptions of authors like Cincinnatus, James Fallow, and so many others, and that the American military profession will soldier on more or less as it has since the Second World War.

But if reform is to be undertaken—reform that makes things better and not worse—what guidance does the historical perspective suggest? Above all, it suggests that there is no easy or obvious resolution to the deep contradiction built into the profession, and especially built into its American version, that the business is highly abnormal and yet is seen to be the ultimate guarantor of normal life. In less abstract terms, the efforts, notably of Robert McNamara, to normalize the profession, to bring its norms and habits more into line with the normal civilian world, were mostly disastrous because they struck so often at the emotional heart of the profession, at just those appeals of tradition, duty, and loyalty which attract grown-up little boys (and now girls) into the profession, and which actually motivate mature professional soldiers to extraordinary efforts and sacrifice. *Tradition* of course is the last refuge of hard-pressed vested interests, but at the same time we need to learn from the mistake of the brilliant McNamara. For example, James Fallow thinks we should follow what he believes to be Prussian practice, requiring every future officer to serve a year in the ranks before attending a short officer-training course, with more sustained schooling postponed for the more able young officers until about age thirty. It is not enough to debate the obvious pros and cons of such a change; we had better be sure we know *why* teen-age boys apply to the service academies and enter ROTC programs before we make this, or any other, reform in the way military professionals are recruited.

Again, years before the actual end of selective service, McNamara was pushing for an all-volunteer army as professionally better at a lower economic, social, and political cost. Critics and doubters were less articulate than McNamara and his supporters, and made their case in mainly negative, slightly fuzzy, frequently historical terms—much like this essay. But I think that experience is bearing out the doubters and is exposing the argument to end any form of military obligation as superficial, simplistic, and unhistorical. If you think this means that I favor, on historical grounds, reinstituting the draft, let me try to clarify the point. It was a terrible mistake to end the draft when and as we did; historical experience argues that now we are in a worse mess than ever, having first perverted (through Selective Service as administered in the 1950s and 1960s), then shattered, the fragile ties between citizenship and military service. To believe that rebuilding those ties can be easy is simply to ignore the historical dimensions of the problem. Easy answers do not exist; if they did, they would have been adopted, because we are not talking about people less intelligent than ourselves, peculiar as they may be in some respects.

Can anything more positive be suggested? Certainly one of the most troubling features of the profession, one not so deeply rooted, is the hemorrhage of middle-aged talent and experience, the forced retirement of colonels in their forties, so that there will be promotion for the captains, space for the new second lieutenants, and no more of a glut in the general officer ranks than already exists. This "up or out" situation—and it is "out" even for many of the best officers—contributes to two serious, widely recognized vices in the profession. One is the notorious ticket-punching system, in which terrific competition for promotion causes ambitious officers to compile an ideal, flawless record of service at any price. The six-month combat commander in Vietnam was the extreme to which this pressure carried, not simply individual officers, but the Army itself. The other vice, not quite so notorious but no less serious, is the weakening commitment of many senior officers, usually with children in or near college, to the military profession. Even with their pensions, they—and often their spouses—must quickly find another remunerative life when military careers are, more or less abruptly, terminated. This is a debilitating situation, and I suspect that it begins to affect many officers as early as their mid-thirties.

Here again, the solution is not as simple as it looks. The pyramid of rank is near the heart of the professional tradition, and near the top of the pyramid are those few command and general staff positions which are the goal of most ambitious junior officers. Only by deemphasizing military rank as such, and by finding or creating more military functions in which rank is irrelevant but experience and ability may be utilized, can the problem be solved. The best answer might be in the educational side of the profession, the armed forces being, among other things, a vast school for their members. But then we must seriously consider whether fifty- or sixty-year-old professionals, who might once have led battalions or squadrons into battle, could work easily and equally with former platoon sergeants as colleagues, and young captains and majors as their clients. To some extent this is already happening in the staff and war colleges, but only on a small scale, and the concepts of rank and tour of duty still have a blighting effect on any serious efforts to incorporate that large majority of colonels who will *not* make general into *another* way of remaining a part of the profession.

This is only an example, intended to show that reform is both urgent and feasible, but also that reform needs to consider all elements of the professional situation, especially the less tangible and less rational factors so easily overlooked or brushed aside as trivial. Any forceful argument for this change or that, from me who only observes the profession, sympathetically if critically but from a distance, would be out of place, certainly out of tune with all that I have been trying to say. To reduce it to a last few words: the deep, inner life of this thing "American military" is fascinating, complex, and poorly understood, by its busy, present-minded young members as well as by an inattentive public, who is repelled more than attracted by things military. There are problems buried in this profession's history that are chronic and still with us. Because some of those problems cannot be solved, we would all do well to know and think about this important matter, to argue less, to have a little more humility about what we think we believe, and to try harder to combine some sympathy for the professional soldiers (who, after all, are human beings too) with a more critical, realistic set of expectations about what the military profession can actually do.

MILITARY: SUGGESTIONS FOR FURTHER READING

I. GENERAL

Ambrose, Stephen E. *Duty, Honor, Country: A History of West Point.* Baltimore, 1966.
Gray, J. Glenn. *The Warriors.* New York, 1959.
Huntington, Samuel P. *The Soldier and the State.* Cambridge, Mass., 1957.
Janowitz, Morris. *The Professional Soldier.* Glencoe, Ill., 1960.
Karsten, Peter. *The Naval Aristocracy.* New York, 1972.
Karsten, Peter, ed. *The Military in America.* New York, 1980.
Millis, Walter. *Arms and Men.* New York, 1956.
Weigley, Russell F. *The American Way of War.* New York, 1973.
Weigley, Russell F. *History of the United States Army.* New York, 1967.

II. Wars & Periods

Catton, Bruce. *A Stillness at Appomattox*. Garden City, N.Y., 1956.

Coffman, Edward M. *The War to End All Wars: The American Military Experience in World War I*. New York, 1968.

Cunliffe, Marcus. *Soldiers and Civilians: The Martial Spirit in America, 1775–1865*. Boston, 1968.

Greenfield, Kent Roberts, ed. *Command Decisions*. New York, 1959.

Kinnard, Douglas. *The War Managers*. Hanover, N.H., 1977

Leonard, Thomas C. *Above the Battle: War-Making in America from Appomattox to Versailles*. New York, 1978.

Lovell, John P. *Neither Athens nor Sparta: The American Service Academies in Transition*. Bloomington, Ind., 1979.

Marshall, S. L. A. *The River and the Gauntlet*. New York, 1953.

Morison, Samuel E. *The Two-Ocean War*. Boston, 1963.

Royster, Charles. *A Revolutionary People at War*. Chapel Hill, N.C., 1979.

Shy, John. *A People Numerous and Armed*. New York, 1976.

III. Biographies & Autobiographies

Blumenson, Martin. *The Patton Papers*. 2 vols. Boston, 1972.

Buell, Thomas B. *The Quiet Warrior: A Biography of Admiral Raymond A. Spruance*. Boston, 1974.

Connelly, Thomas L. *The Marble Man: Robert E. Lee and His Image in American Society*. Baton Rouge, 1977.

Cunliffe, Marcus. *George Washington, Man and Monument*. Rev. ed. New York, 1982.

Grant, U. S. *Personal Memoirs*. 2 vols. New York, 1885.

Hurley, Alfred F. *Billy Mitchell*. New York, 1964.

Hurley, Elting F. *Admiral Sims and the Modern American Navy*. Boston, 1942.

James, D. Clayton. *The Years of MacArthur*. 2 vols. to date. Boston, 1970–75.

Pogue, Forrest C. *George C. Marshall*. 3 vols. to date. New York, 1963–73.

Sherman, William T. *Memoirs*. 2 vols. Rev. ed. New York, 1886.

Taylor, Maxwell D. *Swords and Ploughshares*. New York, 1972.

Weigley, Russell F. *Eisenhower's Lieutenants*. Bloomington, Ind., 1981.

IV. Novels

Bunting, Josiah, III. *The Lionheads*. New York, 1972.

Cozzens, James Gould. *Guard of Honor*. New York, 1948.

Myrer, Anton. *Once an Eagle*. New York, 1968.

Shaara, Richard. *The Killer Angels*. New York, 1974.

Wouk, Herman. *The Caine Mutiny*. Garden City, N.Y., 1952.

6. AMERICAN SCIENCE

Daniel J. Kevles

The professionalization of American science is in significant and often over-looked respects a product of the history of democracy in the United States. It is a commonplace of Western belief that science is an ally of democracy. And in many respects it has been, from the Enlightenment to our own day. We Americans still operate under the Enlightenment propensity, fostered by science, for an empirical adventurousness at once corrosive and construc-tive. Combined with an appeal to natural law, reasoned empiricism under-mined monarchical and ecclesiastical authority and promised, through the understanding and control of nature, broad-based material advancement. Yet for all its alliance with antiauthoritarianism and material wealth, science has always been marked by contrary tendencies. The life of science pivots on the exercise of authority and in a special sense it glows with a spiritual fire akin to religion.

The tendency to authority in science derives from the simple fact that all students of nature are not equal in preparation or ability. At the one extreme is the ignorant layperson, at the other the esoterically knowledge-able specialist. Even among specialists there is a spectrum of talent. Some scientists have always been better than others, not only in productivity but in quality and judgment. One Newton, Darwin, or Einstein is worth thou-sands of lesser natural philosophers. Thus science, democratic in its toler-ance of diverse opinions, is usually not democratic in the formation of judgments. The validity of the law of gravity can hardly be determined by majority vote. In science, as Joseph Henry, physicist and secretary of the Smithsonian Institution, once said, opinions must be "weighed, not counted."[1]

Through the nineteenth century many scientists were religious per-sons who understood the world to be God's creation. To lay flora and fauna away in specimen cabinets or to record the position of the stars and planets was to accumulate a factual variorum of the Creator's imprint on the universe. To study nature was to know God. Then, too, many scientists insisted as an article of secular faith that the universe was worth knowing for its own sake, apart from the material benefits that might proceed from the enterprise. In the nineteenth century such scientists distinguished between abstract and practical science just as later generations would distinguish between basic and applied research or between science and technology. Henry A. Rowland, the Johns Hopkins University physicist, evoked widespread applause among his fellow students of nature when in 1883 he asked in a public address "what must be done to create a science of physics in this country, rather than to call telegraphs, electric lights, and such conveniences by the name of science. . . . The cook who invents a new and palatable dish for the table benefits the world to a certain degree," Rowland observed; "yet we do not dignify him by the name of chemist."[2]

If Rowland manifested a certain dissatisfaction with his country, his predecessors of the late eighteenth century felt more at home in their America. Benjamin Franklin happily combined practical invention with philosophizing upon the nature of electricity. Thomas Jefferson was interested in the flora and fauna found by Lewis and Clark, no less for their own sake than for their implications for westward expansion. At the turn of the nineteenth century, American society was comparatively stratified, its churches generally pervaded with the tolerant spirit of the Enlightenment. The higher learning was generally free of untoward pressure from religious concerns on the one side or from materialist demands on the other. Natural philosophers of the day were able to maintain a happy balance between God and knowledge, between the abstract and the practical.

Yet as the nineteenth century progressed, the balance grew precarious. For as the common people demanded and increasingly won their just rights, they worked a social, religious, and political change in American society that the scientific community perceived to threaten the pursuit of knowledge for its own sake and its accustomed insulation from lay interference. Joseph Henry complained in the 1840s: "Our newspapers are filled with puffs of quackery and every man who can . . . exhibit a few experiments to a class of young ladies is called a man of science."[3] Any dabbler who collected natural specimens or fiddled with an electrical battery might expect to deliver the results before a scientific meeting or publish them in one of the scores of local scientific journals. Even the principal organ of research in the country, the *American Journal of Science*, depended upon subscriptions from numerous amateurs, its editor aptly observed. To a significant extent for the sake of protecting science against the invasion of a vulgar democracy, natural philosophers in America turned to professionalization. It was no accident that the professionalization of science in the United States began with the Jacksonian period, with its democratic assault upon traditional secular and religious authority, and that it came to flourish in the era of Ulysses S. Grant, with its celebrations of material progress so annoying to Henry Rowland.

According to the model advanced by the historian George Daniels, the professionalization of American science occurred in four overlapping stages: preemption, institutionalization, legitimation, and, finally, professional autonomy. Daniels's is a useful model that helps formalize the antidemocratic tendencies in the professionalization of science. The preemptive stage is provoked by the increasingly esoteric quality of natural knowledge, of the march of learning beyond mere fact gathering to complex relationships, to systematics, to theory. In botany, for example, preemption followed on the spread of the Linnaean system, with its categories of species, genus, and type. Only specialists, not the mere Sunday naturalist, could classify new specimens. The point in time of preemption may have varied with discipline, but in all disciplines it worked a similar effect—the exclusion of the lay amateur from scientific discourse.

The institutionalization of exclusiveness was no mean task in democratic America. There were numerous local scientific societies in the United States. Most, Rowland ruefully observed, were "dignified by high-sounding names," and each had "its local celebrity, to whom the privilege of describing some crab with an extra claw . . . is inestimable."[4] At the national level in 1844, professionally-minded scientists formed the American Association for the Advancement of Science. To be sure, membership was open to any interested layperson willing to pay the dues, but the constitution of the AAAS virtually guaranteed the election of professional scientists to the governing offices, including a standing committee whose approval was required for the presentation of a paper at the meetings or its publication under AAAS auspices. Narrowing matters still further, in 1874 the constitution was revamped to restrict officeholders to a new, special class of members, or "Fellows," accomplished in research. Still more exclusive was the National Academy of Sciences, founded in 1863, admission to which required distinction in research and election by the existing, limited membership.

Amid the proliferation of specialized knowledge, no single society or association could expect to accommodate the interests of the diverse groups of scientists that steadily sprang up in the United States. If scientists wished to insulate themselves from the laity, so chemists wanted to protect themselves from entomologists, physicists from natural historians, etc. Pursuing professionalization to its logical end, specialists in various fields began after the Civil War to organize special societies. The first in science was the American Chemical Society, founded in 1876. Soon following suit were geologists, astrophysicists, botanists, physicists, and mathematicians. Like the AAAS, most of these professional societies opened their membership rolls to the general, interested public, but they also restricted control of the organization —of its offices, budget, journal, and meetings—to an elite accomplished in research.

After the Civil War, the trend to professionalization in science spread to institutions of higher learning. Recent scholarship has made clear that the *antebellum* colleges by no means ignored science. Physics, mathematics, natural history, and often more were standard parts of the required curriculum. But the courses were taught largely by rote rather than with laboratory experience. Hardly any college taught them beyond the elementary level. And there was no graduate training to speak of in science or any other subject. But in the post–Civil War decades, a new generation of college presidents revolutionized higher learning in America. They fostered the introduction of laboratory work in scientific courses and created the elective system, which, liberating students from the constraints of a required general education, permitted them to pursue courses in a given specialty to an advanced level even as undergraduates. And, following the lead of Daniel Coit Gilman at the Johns Hopkins University, they established graduate schools devoted to training students in research.

American scientists were gladdened by the creation of the university system. Not only did it advance their self-interest through the institutionalization of their professional aims. It also helped accommodate the exclusiveness of professional culture to democratic aims and assumptions. For if professionalism meant exclusion, the new higher education meant accessibility. Scientific training, both undergraduate and graduate, would make for a continuing supply of new knowledgeable talent, while the process of certification inherent in graduate work would restrict entrance into science to people qualified to pursue professional work.

The wiser leaders of American science recognized that in the United States, which, unlike Europe, had no monarchy or formal aristocracy to supply the patronage of learning, it might be dangerous to carry the exclusiveness inherent in professionalization too far. And if they insisted upon independence and autonomy for science, they recognized that the larger society would expect a return for allowing them such privileges. The return they promised, what Daniels has called the legitimation of professional science, took the form—in part and for a while—of calling continued attention to the way that the study of nature would fortify religion by revealing God's handiwork in the universe. But the natural theological content of scientific legitimation fell rapidly away after Darwin unleashed his theory of evolution and society grew more secularized.

The more long-lasting claims of legitimation—they remain with us today—centered on three points: first, that the study of science fostered disinterested, even moral, habits of thinking, that science, in the words of Charles William Eliot, the onetime chemist who headed Harvard for forty years, "enables and purifies the mind";[5] second, that scientists, at once expert and morally objective, could be counted upon to supply the nation with indispensable disinterested advice and guidance as it plunged irrevocably into the modern urban, technological age; and third, that the pursuit of abstract, or what by the 1880s was called "pure," science would eventually pay rich dividends, in the technology of material wealth, better health, and, to anticipate a key legitimation of a later day, national defense.

Yet in the late nineteenth century American scientists were more successful in pursuing professionalization than in convincing their compatriots to respect such claims of legitimation. The symbolic proprietor of the burgeoning electrical industry was of course not a physicist but Thomas Alva Edison, who once gibed; "Oh these mathematicians make me tired! When you ask them to work out a sum they take a piece of paper, cover it with rows of A's B's and X's Y's . . . scatter a mess of flyspecks over them, and then give you an answer that's all wrong."[6] Geologists from the National Academy of Sciences recommended that the government reform the homestead system, since it was inappropriate to the arid lands west of the hundredth meridian. Theorists had pronounced the homestead system dead before, cried Representative Martin Maginnis from the Montana Territory. Yet settlers had gone west and, "practical men" all, had "seen the capabilities of this land which had escaped the notice of our scientists and statesmen." In the end, the Congress left the public land system intact. Congressman Dudley C. Haskell of Lawrence, Kansas expressed the pervasive evaluation at the time of scientific advice for public policy. "Now . . . if you want a lot of astronomical figures, if you want a lot of scientific material, then authorize them to get out there and dig and hunt bugs and investigate fossils and discover the rotundity of the earth and take astronomical investigations. But if you please, while you are there acting in the interest of science and in the interest of professional bug-hunting, leave the settlers upon our frontier alone."[7]

Federal policy toward pure research was even less tolerant than Haskell made it sound. In the 1880s the federal government was perhaps the largest single employer of scientists in the United States. Yet Washington was hardly a haven for abstract research. Every federal scientist, beleaguered before the governmental apostles of utility, could understand the defense offered before a Congressional investigating committee: "We are not fomenting science. We are doing practical work for practical purposes."[8] The principal American arena for pure science was the universities, but there pure science was handicapped, even after the pro-science revolution worked by people such as Charles William Eliot and Daniel Coit Gilman. In the late nineteenth century university presidents exercised virtually autocratic power over their institutions, and, with the exception of Gilman at Hopkins, tended to use that power to foster teaching over research. Eliot and his fellow college presidents had reformed higher education principally for cultural purposes. They respected scholarship more than their old-time predecessors; they believed with the president of MIT that "Our aim should be: *the mind of the student*, not scientific discovery, not professional accomplishment."[9] In the late nineteenth century, the main object of the university was to develop character by diffusing science and its way of thinking, not by stressing its advancement.

Thus, by the late nineteenth century American scientists may have succeeded in professionalizing themselves, but they had not accomplished the similarly important task of accommodating their particular profession to the values and culture of the American democracy. And the points of tension between themselves and their society centered precisely on their principal claims of legitimation. If they considered pure superior to applied science, most Americans preferred the gadgets and machinery that made for material wealth and comfort. If they thought themselves valuable public counselors, advisors upon technical matters of public interest, the public viewed them as impractically abstract. If they claimed a special virtue, if they insisted that, as scientists, they were suffused with a moral disinterestedness, many Americans could agree with the opinion of the editors of the influential *Scientific Monthly*, who remarked that, like other people, scientists were "self-seeking, ambitious, and have their personal ends to gain. Can we assume that morally they are any better than their neighbors; or that, if they get possession of place and power, they will not use and pervert them to the promotion of their selfish objects? It is to be hoped that in the future science will become so developed as to react upon character and give us men morally as well as intellectually superior; but we are far from any such happy result as yet."[10]

In the post–Civil War decades, amid the disrespect and lack of opportunities for careers in basic research, there was no general democratization of access to the profession of science. Only a handful of secondary schools provided any scientific preparation whatever, especially in the laboratory sciences of the day. In higher education, the number of scholarships and fellowships was minute; most young people could not afford an undergraduate education, let alone graduate school or study in Europe. Then, too, as a Cornell scientist aptly expressed a widespread belief: "In this country, men devoted to science purely for the sake of science are and must be few in number. Few *can* devote their lives to work that promises no return except the satisfaction of adding to the sum of human knowledge. Very few have both the means and inclination to do this."[11] As a result, American scientists of the day tended to come from a narrow, upper-crust fragment of society. Most were the sons—or married the daughters—of well-to-do merchants, gentry, lawyers, ministers, or teachers. Almost all were white Anglo-Saxon Protestants. Almost all were male.

By the late 1880s the American scientific community totaled no more than a few thousand people. Although Edison hired a few physicists, the typical industrial scientist of the day tended to be a consulting or entrepreneurial chemist or geologist, and such people in any case amounted to only a small fraction of the scientific community. By far a more significant scientific employer was the federal government. (In the late nineteenth century, in fact, one budget-cutting member of Congress complained that the United States government was spending more for scientific research than all the nations of western Europe combined.) About half the membership of the National Academy of Sciences in the 1880s consisted of federal scientists. But federal science was differentially important with respect to discipline. With the practical purposefulness of government science, Washington was a center of those disciplines understood to be relevant to the government's practical tasks of the day—exploration and settlement. Thus Washington was a center mainly of the earth, rather than of the physical, sciences. Geologists, geodesists, or meteorologists were more likely to be found in federal agencies than physicists or chemists. Yet whether involved with the earth or physical disciplines, almost all scientists were employed in the sector of society that only upper-crust Americans seemed to consider important, the academic world.

It was with considerable justification that Henry Rowland lamented in 1883 that American science was a thing "of the future, and not of the present or past."[12]

Not long after Rowland's lament, in the 1890s, the scientific community started demonstrating, with growing persuasiveness and at a steadily increasing rate, the validity of at least some of its claims to legitimation. Scientifically trained people—some from American colleges and universities and others from abroad—trickled into industry, often as entrepreneurs. Bringing with them a knowledge of basic science, they gradually introduced a higher degree of technical complexity into chemicals, petroleum, mining, pharmaceuticals, and the like. Typically, they fostered the use of alternating current in the electrical industry, which had hitherto relied on direct current. In DC circuits, simple algebra and an elementary knowledge of electrical phenomena would suffice the engineer. AC circuit analysis required calculus and training in electromagnetic theory. Symbolically, in the early 1890s Thomas A. Edison sold his firm to a new combine called General Electric and left the light and power business for good. The principal figure in the GE technical works was Charles Proteus Steinmetz, a German immigrant with advanced training in physics. As early as the 1890s, Andrew Carnegie, apostle of the self-made man, announced that the "trained mechanic of the past . . . is now to meet a rival in the scientifically educated youth, who will push him hard indeed."[13]

The scientifically trained who entered industry arrived with an important piece of attitudinal luggage, drawn from their teachers' claims to legitimation—that the pursuit of basic knowledge would eventually lead to practical and profitable results. Circumstances in the more technologically intensive industries ratified the claim. The chemical industry drew upon basic organic chemistry in such areas as dyestuffs and fertilizers, while the electrical communications industry was compelled, once it began to exploit the vacuum tube, to consider such phenomena as the behavior of electrons in gases. Hungry for the development of basic knowledge in areas of particular interest to their firms, the rising scientifically trained managers adventurously urged their companies in the decade or so before World War I to establish their own research laboratories. Typical of them were Frank B. Jewett, a Ph.D. in physics from the University of Chicago, who inaugurated what became the Bell Telephone Laboratories, and Willis R. Whitney, a product of advanced training in physical chemistry at MIT, who started the research laboratory of General Electric. Many of the scientists hired by Jewett, Whitney, and others were duty-bound to engage in reasonably practical research, but a few were permitted the freedom to roam in areas more remote from the firm's practical interest.

Among them, at General Electric, was Irving Langmuir, a physical chemist and Ph.D. who had studied in Europe. For some years at GE, Langmuir explored the behavior of gases in the neighborhood of hot filaments. He contributed tellingly to the fundamental field of surface chemistry, but his research also, virtually by serendipity, pointed to a valuable technological innovation. Electric light bulbs of the day tended to blacken after comparatively short use. The cause tended to be attributed to the air in the bulb, and much effort had gone into attempting to manufacture evacuated bulbs. Langmuir's research revealed that the blackening occurred as a result of interactions between the oxygen in the air and the filament. The key to a more long-lived bulb? Not to evacuate the lamp but to fill it entirely with nitrogen, which did not interact with the filament. With the advent of the nitrogen-filled lamp, General Electric's investment in the ostensibly impractical work of Langmuir was demonstrated to pay enormous dividends, a lesson that was not lost on business executives in other firms and fields.

Early in the century, professional scientists continued to urge the economic utility of science upon the federal government. Particularly active now were physical scientists, who insisted that, just as Washington had sponsored work in the earth sciences in the era of westward settlement, so in the new century it should facilitate the growing use of the physical sciences, notably physics and chemistry, in the national economy. At the turn of the century, the University of Chicago physicist Samuel Wesley Stratton lobbied for and almost singlehandedly persuaded the federal government to create the National Bureau of Standards, the first scientific agency in Washington devoted entirely to the laboratory disciplines. As its title suggests, the bureau was created to provide authoritative standards and measures for the diverse materials and physical constants essential to the burgeoning industrial machine. Following in the tradition of his predecessors in federal science, Stratton interpreted his mandate broadly, so that the bureau became a major center of research in those areas of the physical sciences which underlay the establishment of reliable measures. For many years, in fact, the bureau employed more physicists than any other institution in the United States.

Yet early twentieth-century scientists were alive to more than the economic utility of knowledge. Like their nineteenth-century predecessors, many of them advanced the claim to legitimation that professional scientists could provide expert disinterested advice upon the problems of a technological age. Amid the steady growth in the role of government in the nation's increasingly urban and technological life, the claim acquired ever more solidity. In the early twentieth century, geologists, heirs of the great public resources reformer John Wesley Powell, became enmeshed in the formation of federal policy for public lands and conservation; Samuel Wesley Stratton threw the Bureau of Standards into consumer campaigns for honesty in weights and measures. At the Bureau of Chemistry in the Department of Agriculture, the chemist Harvey Wiley helped spark the public debate over questions related to purity in foods and drugs that led in 1906 to the creation of the Food and Drug Administration. In the early twentieth century, professional scientists came to form an indispensable cadre within the government's expanding regulatory army.

The more the nation's scientific professions seemed to validate their claims to legitimation, the more they grew and flourished. The growth dated from the 1890s, with the appearance of industrial demand for technically trained workers. American college enrollments started to climb exponentially, and after the turn of the century, despite setbacks in war and depression, they continued to climb in the same fashion. Technical enrollments, particularly in engineering, but also in the sciences, followed a similar pattern. Often students who entered college intent upon careers in industry or medicine discovered that they liked science as such. Their ambitions came to focus on the professoriat, and not unrealistically, for in all fields the increase in undergraduate enrollments stimulated a steady increase in the demand for college and university teachers of science. After the turn of the century, graduate enrollments in science also rose exponentially. In 1920, American universities produced 280 Ph.D.'s in science outside of engineering; in 1939, almost 1,400.

During the period 1920 to 1939, the professions of science turned into an avenue of social mobility. While they did not draw from the bottom of American society, they did provide a means by which the children of middle- to lower-middle-class families, often from rural areas, migrated to the urban upper middle class, both in income and in social status. To be sure, the American scientific professions remained overwhelmingly white, Anglo-Saxon, Protestant, and male, but between the two world wars they also became an avenue of mobility for one minority group, American Jews.

The Jewish entrance into science turned in part on their group's cultural attachment to learning, in part on their long-standing belief that professional careers, which depended on the unconfiscatable properties of the mind, would better insulate them against the hazards of anti-Semitism, which could lead to the deprivation of property in land or business. (The refugee physicist Abraham Pais once remarked: "The Jew has the tradition of the book first because so it was in the ghetto, but secondly . . . because the contents of the book are inalienable—even if the book itself is not.")[14] By the end of the 1930s, Jews were represented in American physics at least in proportion to their weight in the overall population. The combined presence of both natives and refugees from Hitler's Europe starred American Jewish physicists with a disproportionately significant role in the leadership of their discipline.

Discrimination did a good deal to keep blacks, Catholics, and women comparatively underrepresented in the scientific professions. But the record of Jewish Americans, who also suffered from discrimination, suggests that discrimination was not the whole story. For obvious reasons, black Americans had no tradition of learning or professional aspiration. National cultural standards discouraged most young women from thinking about careers at all, and careers in science were considered particularly unwomanly. Women who turned to the physical sciences had always to expect the ambivalent salute that Voltaire rendered his mistress, the brilliant Madame du Chatelet: "A woman who has translated and illuminated Newton . . . [is] in short a very great man."[15] Women with a bent for technical subjects turned to "womanly" pursuits—schoolteaching, nursing, the practice of medicine, or, perhaps, the study of animate, organic nature. During the interwar years, well over half the women scientists in America were in psychology, botany, and zoology, and more than three times as many women took doctorates in the biological and social as in the physical sciences.

Neither academic discrimination nor church doctrine played a telling role in producing the low representation of Catholics in the American scientific professions. More important were the pre–World War II poverty of Catholic higher education and of the American Catholic community in general. Still, the Notre Dame biochemist Julian Pleasants once observed: "Ours is not an abject but a discriminating poverty; it lays bare our scale of values by indicating what we feel we can do without." The modern American Catholic, Pleasants noted, placed "a very low value on . . . scientific research."[16] Clannish in the face of the majority's hostility, young Catholics who could afford college preferred to prepare for work among their own group, frequently in the law. Besides, whether they had come from Ireland or the nations of central and southern Europe, American Catholics generally derived from peasant cultures. In the old country, learning as such had been left to the priests; in the new, as an observer who understood his fellow Irish pointed out, "intellectual curiosity . . . was taboo because it was lazy and nonutilitarian." But, he added, "a 'good head for business'—ah, that was a gift from heaven, indeed!"[17] During the interwar years, more Catholics went to college not only because they could afford it but because it had become an accepted and advantageous way to get into the most admired and financially rewarding of American occupations. But few Catholic students had any taste for careers in pure science, and few actually joined their Protestant and now Jewish peers in the scientific professions.

From the turn of the century through the 1930s, those professions grew at roughly comparable rates in all scientific disciplines, including the physical, the earth, and the biological sciences. All had strong contingents in the academic world. Some, notably chemistry and then physics, carved out solid sectors of employment in industry. For, following the examples of Whitney and Jewett at Bell Telephone and GE, business leaders and philanthropists increasingly embraced the economic legitimation of science. The circumstances of international trade were enough to convince them that, if the United States were to compete economically in the world, industry had to support research, including pure research. From the 1920s on, industry and industrial philanthropists donated considerable funds to the enterprise of basic science. Part of the money went into the academic world. A great deal of it was invested in industrial research laboratories, some of which devoted at least part of their effort to pure science. A few of these laboratories—the Bell Telephone Laboratory is an outstanding example—achieved world rank in their fundamental areas. Indeed, by the 1930s, in most fields the United States had taken its place among the leading scientific nations.

The ascendancy occurred without significant federal support of science as we know it. For from the turn of the century through the 1930s federal science tended overwhelmingly to consist, in the nineteenth-century vein, almost entirely of research related to the practical concerns of the economy or of regulation. The FDA, for example, in order to carry out its statutory responsibilities of assuring the safety of what we eat and drink, had to sponsor an ongoing research program into the hazards of ingestible market products. And most federally supported research was carried out in federal laboratories like the National Bureau of Standards. To be sure, the federal government did begin in 1887 to fund research at agricultural experiment stations located at state or land-grant universities, and did enlarge support for both early in the 1930s. Still agriculture was an exception.

Before World War II there was no significant federal funding of scientific research, pure or applied, in the academic world.

The reason, in part, was that American scientists were decidedly ambivalent toward the idea of federal patronage. On the one hand, they came increasingly to want the money, particularly in the 1930s, when academic science, like most other areas of American life, was undermined by the depression. On the other hand, they feared federal support because with it might come federal control. The fear was sometimes expressed in terms of Galileo's battle with the church—that politics would determine what scientists could think and publish. But the more common and profound fear centered on what had helped provoke American scientists to professionalize in the first place; apprehension that, through the instrument of political power, nonscientists might set the subjects and direction of research.

Whenever the nation's scientific leadership had brushed up against the possibility of federal support for academic science, they had sought to reconcile what they wanted with what they feared. As the means of reconciliation, they usually advanced administrative mechanisms that would permit the flow of federal money into academic research in a way that insulated the flow from direct political control. They justified the demand on grounds of their requirement of professional autonomy, and by insisting that, as moral, disinterested persons, they could be expected to spend public funds in the public interest. Again and again, their proposals failed. Politically responsible officials would not go along with such a mixture of public support without public accountability. Unlike other interest groups, which commanded millions of votes or dollars or both, the nation's scientists lacked sufficient political power to force an accommodation with the government on their own terms. Or at least they lacked it until in World War II they validated their most powerful claim to legitimation—their utility to the national defense.

American scientists, mainly chemists and physicists, had been involved in defense work before, particularly in World War I. They had worked on chemical weapons, aircraft, submarine detection, radio, and the like. For a number of reasons, not least among them the retreat into isolationism, there was no postwar commitment to research for national defense. During the interwar years, defense research was carried out in military or industrial contract laboratories and, for the most part, did not utilize scientists in the academic world. Yet the experience of World War I had sensitized a number of those scientists involved in it to the necessity and the possibilities of science for military purposes, and, as the specter of war rose over Europe in the late 1930s, they decided to act. An exaggerated importance has been attached to the letter that Albert Einstein sent to Franklin D. Roosevelt in 1939, calling his attention to the military potential of the recent discovery of nuclear fission. Einstein's letter was not terribly critical, either for the launching of the ultimate Manhattan Project that produced the atomic bomb or for the wartime mobilization of science in general. Of central significance to both efforts was Vannevar Bush, a veteran of the submarine detection work in World War I, and a small group of similarly experienced scientists around him, who in 1940 prevailed upon President Roosevelt to establish what soon turned into the spectacularly successful Office of Scientific Research and Development, or OSRD.

Headquartered at Bush's office in the Carnegie Institution of Washington, OSRD established no laboratories of its own. It operated primarily by contract, with industrial and with academic laboratories. Among its largest facilities was the Radiation Laboratory at MIT, which consisted of some four thousand staff members at its height. Many of the Rad Lab staff were professional physicists, often mere fledglings not yet out of graduate school. The lab had an academic flavor to it. OSRD contractors successfully developed not only numerous radars but also solid fuel rockets, proximity fuses, and myriad other devices that played effective, and often decisive, roles in the war effort. The atomic bomb work was originally conducted under a special section of OSRD until, when it was sufficiently well along, it was transferred to the Manhattan District of the Army Engineers. After the war ended, Rad Lab workers liked to say, "Radar won the war. The atomic bomb only ended it."[18]

Both radar and the atomic bomb drew upon advanced physics and required physicists well versed in the intricacies of their discipline. The success of OSRD and the Manhattan Project convinced millions of Americans, ordinary citizens and high policy makers alike, that basic scientists were indispensable to the national defense because they were essential to the advisory system of national security and because they produced the new fundamental knowledge upon which the technology of modern military power rested. The nation's basic scientists thus acquired a degree of political power in America that hitherto they had not possessed. Not based on votes or dollars, their power resided in their command of an esoteric knowledge. They had become a strategic elite in American life, and they exploited their power to construct the postwar system of federal support for science to a considerable extent on their long-standing terms of professional autonomy. They helped create a system of granting agencies that supplied a rich level of funds to academic science with only a loose degree of accountability or control. And they forged an advisory system for federal science, culminating in the establishment of the President's Science Advisory Committee in 1957, that carried them to the center of power while maintaining their independent academic and industrial bases.

In the quarter century after World War II, the professions of science flourished in the United States far beyond the dreams of their pre–World War II, let alone nineteenth-century, leadership. The exponential increase in the number of scientists continued. In 1970 American universities produced more than ten thousand doctorates in science outside of engineering, and there were almost a half million scientists practicing in the United States. The federal budget for research and development burgeoned, reaching some $15 billion per year by 1967. Academic, industrial, and governmental science departments expanded steadily, and American scientists commanded the world, winning the lion's share of Nobel Prizes of the period. Yet, despite the apparent ratification of their traditional claims to legitimation, the American scientific professions lived in an uneasy tension with the larger society.

In part, the tension derived from the very success of professional science. Rich, immense, and powerful, it was a salient target for dissatisfaction with wealth, size, and power, particularly on the part of those groups—women, blacks, and Catholics—whom it tended not to include. In part, the tension lay in the content of the legitimation, in the strong identification of science with industry and the military. During the depression science had been charged with responsibility for undercutting humanistic values, for making possible a technology that robbed people of their jobs. In the late 1960s these themes were revived and new charges added, all with the virulence that pervaded the dissent from the war in Vietnam. People, the critic John Leonard observed, tended to blame the perversions of modern technological society on single causes; but the cause most prevalently blamed, and with special animosity among those of a humanist or literary sensibility, was science—"science," which in Leonard's itemization, "brought you technology . . . ; science, which has steadily reduced the number of things for which God can be held accountable and, thereby, pinned the rap on man . . . that *science*. And those scientists."[19]

Scientists may have proudly claimed legitimation by identifying their works with technological progress. They may have happily accepted the patronage that came with such legitimation from industry and the military. In the era of Vietnam not only exponents of the New Left but many liberals, too, indicted scientists for contributing to the degradation of the environment and the destructiveness of the military, and for advancing a barbarous industrial and military power. Scientists may have taken a certain satisfaction from their involvement in the post-1945 governmental advisory structure. They were considered suspect merely by virtue of association with the military. No matter that some of them had fought to slow the strategic arms race. According to Fred Bramfman, the head of an antiwar research group, such efforts merely meant that the scientists involved in them were "lesser, rather than greater, war criminals. They are dramatic examples of how it is possible to be a moderate, well-meaning, decent war criminal."[20]

Yet in more profound part, the tension between the nation's professional scientists and their society lay in the inevitable conflict between the demands of professional autonomy and the requirements of democratic accountability. Through most of the post–World War II era, the government's scientific advisers had tended to avoid the normal political process of open pressure, advocacy, and debate. "The overwhelming majority had never wanted any part of this," John Fischer, the editor of *Harper's*, wrote with dismay. "Typically, they regard the political process as something sinister if not dirty; often they treat politicians . . . and sometimes the ordinary voter as well with scarcely veiled contempt."[21] If such attitudes displeased Americans, so increasingly did a salient product of the generally closed-door politics of science—the penchant of governmental research and development policy for stressing, outside of industrially and militarily relevant work, research in esoteric areas of pure science. How could enormous expenditures for particle accelerators be justified, critics asked vociferously, when the cities were clogged in traffic, slums, and pollution? By 1970 a growing number of Americans were asking with the respected journalist Meg Greenfield: "As presiders over the national science purse, are the scientists speaking in the interests of science . . . government or . . . their own institutions? Is their policy advice . . . offered in furtherance of national objectives—or agency objectives—or their own objectives?"[22]

As a result of the rebellion of the Vietnam era, the scientific professions in America suffered a degree of disestablishment. Among the salient characteristics of the change have been a shaping of federal scientific programs in a way more reponsive to social needs, a greater role for nonscientists in determining research objectives, and a drop in the rate of real growth —in a number of years it fell to zero or below—in federal scientific support. But the prestige of the scientific professions, if not the same as in the heady quarter century after Hiroshima, remains at an enviably high level. So does federal funding for research and development. So does the power that the professions of science wield in American life. If Americans are uncomfortable with, and at times rebellious towards, insistently autonomous groups, they also recognize the considerable merits in the claims of legitimation advanced by professional scientists for the last century and a half. Suspected yet respected, esoteric yet indispensable, the nation's professional scientists are bound to operate in tension with their society indefinitely.

NOTES

1. Joseph Henry to C. Dewey, November 7, 1859, quoted in Robert V. Bruce, "Democracy and American Scientific Organizations in the Mid-Nineteenth Century," unpublished manuscript, pp. 13–14.

2. Henry A. Rowland, "A Plea for Pure Science," in *The Physical Papers of Henry Augustus Rowland* (Baltimore, 1901), p. 594.

3. Joseph Henry to_____?, February 27, 1846, quoted in Howard S. Miller, *Dollars for Research: Science and Its Patrons in Nineteenth-Century America* (Seattle, 1970), p. 7.

4. Rowland, "A Plea for Pure Science," p. 610.

5. Quoted in Henry James, *Charles W. Eliot: President of Harvard University, 1869–1909*, 2 vols. (London, 1930) 1:64.

6. Quoted in Matthew Josephson, *Edison* (New York, 1959), p. 283.

7. U.S. Congress, House, *Congressional Record*, 45th Cong., 3d Sess. (18 February 1879), pp. 1202, 1211.

8. Julius E. Hilgard, in U.S. Congress, Joint Commission to Consider the Present Organization of the Signal Service, Geological Survey, Coast and Geodetic Survey, and the Hydrographic Office of the Navy Department, with a View to Secure Greater Efficiency and Economy of Administration of the Public Service . . . , *Testimony*, 49th Cong., 1st Sess., Sen. Misc. Doc. 82 (16 March 1884) Series 2345, p. 54.

9. Francis A. Walker to Alpheus Hyatt, August 29, 1889, Alfred M. Mayer –Alfred G. Mayer–Alpheus Hyatt Papers, Rare Book Room, Princeton University, Princeton, N.J.

10. *Popular Science Monthly* 27 (October 1885): 846.

11. William A. Anthony, in *Proceedings of the American Academy for the Advancement of Science, 1887*, p. 70.

12. Rowland, "A Plea for Pure Science," p. 594.

13. Quoted in Irving G. Wyllie, *The Self-Made Man in America* (New Brunswick, N.J., 1954), p. 112.

14. Abraham Pais to Oswald Vablen, August 19 [1957], Oswald Veblen Papers, Library of Congress, Washington, D.C.

15. Voltaire to Francois Thomas Marie de Baculard d'Arnuaud, October 14, 1749, in Theodore Besterman et al., eds., *The Complete Works of Voltaire* (Geneva, 1970) 95: 178–79.

16. Julian Pleasants, "Catholics and Science," *Commonweal* 58 (28 August 1953): 511, 512.

17. Harry McGuire, letter to the editor, *Commonweal* 9 (1 May 1929): 748.

18. Interview with Lee A. DuBridge.

19. John Leonard, "The Last Word: Should Science Be Shot?" *New York Times Book Review*, 18 July 1971, p. 31.

20. Quoted in "Jason Division . . . ," *Science* 179 (2 February 1973): 460.

21. John Fischer, "Why Our Scientists Are About to Be Dragged, Moaning, into Politics," *Harper's*, September 1966, p. 22.

22. Meg Greenfield, "Science Goes to Washington," *The Reporter*, 26 September 1963, p. 26.

AMERICAN SCIENCE: SUGGESTIONS FOR FURTHER READING

Beardsley, E. H. *The Rise of the American Chemical Profession, 1850–1900*. Gainesville, Fla., 1964.

Bledstein, Burton J. *The Culture of Professionalism: The Middle Class and the Development of Higher Education in America*. New York, 1976.

Bruce, Robert V. *The Launching of Modern American Science, 1846–1876*. New York, 1987.

Cole, Jonathan R. *Fair Science: Women in the Scientific Community*. New York, 1979.

Cole, Jonathan R., and Cole, Stephen. *Social Stratification in Science*. Chicago, 1973.

Cravens, Hamilton. "The Role of Universities in the Rise of Experimental Biology." *Science Teacher* 44 (January 1977).

Daniels, George H. "The Process of Professionalization in American Science: The Emergent Period, 1840–1860." *Isis* 58 (1967): 151–66.

David, Joseph Ben. *The Scientist's Role in Society: A Comparative Study*. Princeton, N.J., 1971.

Dupree, A. Hunter. *Science in the Federal Government: A History of Policy and Activities to 1940*. Cambridge, Mass., 1957.

Goetzmann, William H. *Exploration and Empire: The Explorer and the Scientist in the Winning of the American West*. New York, 1966.

Kevles, Daniel J., "The National Science Foundation and the Debate Over Postwar Research Policy, 1942–1945: A Political Interpretation of Science—The Endless Frontier." *Isis* 68 (1977): 5–26.

Kevles, Daniel J. *The Physicists: The History of a Scientific Community in Modern America*. New York, 1979.

Kevles, Daniel J., Sturchio, Jeffrey L., and Carroll, P. Thomas. "The Sciences in America, circa 1880." *Science* 209 (4 July 1980).

Klaw, Spencer. *The New Brahmins: Scientific Life in America.* New York, 1968.

Kohlstedt, Sally Gregory. *The Formation of the American Scientific Community: The American Association for the Advancement of Science, 1848–1860.* Champaign, Ill., 1976.

Mason, Karen Oppenheim. Review of *Fair Science. Science* 208 (18 April 1980): 277–78.

Oleson, Alexandra, and Brown, Sanborn C., eds. *The Pursuit of Knowledge in the Early American Republic: American Learned and Scientific Societies from Colonial Times to the Civil War.* Baltimore, 1976.

Oleson, Alexandra, and Voss, John, eds. *The Organization of Knowledge in Modern America, 1860–1920.* Baltimore, 1979.

Reingold, Nathan, ed. *Science in Nineteenth-Century America: A Documentary History.* New York, 1964.

Reingold, Nathan, ed. *The Sciences in the American Context: New Perspectives.* Washington, D.C., 1979.

Rosenberg, Charles E. *No Other Gods: On American Science and Social Thought.* Baltimore, paperback, 1976.

Rosenfeld, Albert. "The Quintessence of Irving Langmuir." In *The Collected Works of Irving Langmuir,* ed. G. Guy Suits and Harold E. Way, 12:3–232. Elmsford, N.Y., 1960–62.

Rossiter, Margaret. "Women Scientists in America before 1920." *American Scientist* 62 (May-June 1974): 312–23.

Rossiter, Margaret. "Women's Work in Science, 1880–1910." *Isis* 71 (September 1980): 381–98.

Rudolph, Frederick. *The American College and University: A History.* New York, 1965.

Smith, Alice K. *A Peril and a Hope: The Scientists' Movement in America, 1945–1947.* Chicago, 1965.

Weiner, Charles. "A New Site for the Seminar: The Refugees and American Physics in the Thirties." In *The Intellectual Migration,* ed. Donald Fleming and Bernard Bailyn. Cambridge, Mass., 1969.

7. EPISODES IN THE HISTORY OF THE AMERICAN ENGINEERING PROFESSION

Bruce Sinclair

Even though the images lie deep in the more remote recesses of my memory, I can still recall fragments of a movie of my childhood titled *Trail of the Lonesome Pine,* which incidentally was the first outdoor movie made in technicolor. Produced in 1936, it starred Fred MacMurray, Sylvia Sidney, and Henry Fonda. MacMurray was a civil engineer, dressed the way one imagined a civil engineer should be—khaki shirt, riding trousers, and wearing those tall, laced-up leather field boots. Manly and straightforward, he surely represented modern progress. Sylvia Sidney played a backcountry woman of the Blue Ridge Mountains where his railroad was to be built. A lovely person of rustic simplicity, she found herself attracted to MacMurray and then caught between his ambitions and her brother's opposition to the project. Henry Fonda played that part, a dark moody role which wrapped up primitive fears of technology with the sensitive realization that the railroad would destroy the mountain people's way of life. An audience today might react differently, but in those bygone times we wanted MacMurray's railroad to be built and, of course, we wanted him to win Sylvia Sidney. I don't recollect much more about that movie, but the central image, that American style civilization came in the person of a tall, handsome, vigorous, clean-shaven, outdoorsman-engineer proved memorable: Hollywood was always good at showing us our most romantic ideas.

For at least a hundred years before that film, before there was an engineering profession, Americans already believed that technical skill was a fundamental element of the nation's historic destiny. They thought of themselves as an ingenious people, almost by birth or instinct handy at fixing

127

things or thinking up new ways to do old jobs. As a Bostonian claimed in 1826, "The quick invention and skillful application of practical principles in the arts" was so commonplace as to be a native talent.[1] Yankee ingenuity seemed the most obvious ingredient of the national character, and European visitors to the United States in the nineteenth century recognized the same things. Technology, as one of them suggested, was the American's natural artistic medium.[2]

Yet that was not a self-image born simply of the frontier experience. In one of history's most stunning coincidences, the American Revolution and the Industrial Revolution came at the same time (if one thinks of Watt's steam engine signalling the latter event), and by the early nineteenth century Americans explicitly and frequently proclaimed a close connection between technology and the country's future. Listen, for instance, to the enthusiasm of the Phi Beta Kappa lecturer at Yale in 1825, when he told his audience:

> The present is, pre-eminently, an age of inquiry, and of enterprise, of discovery, of invention, and of universal improvement. It is an age, full of destiny; and, if we are just to ourselves, of most auspicious augury to our country.[3]

Americans also firmly believed, even from the early days of the republic, that in exporting the nation's technology they sent out to the world the democratic ideals of the Declaration of Independence.[4] The vitality of the engineering would prove the rightness of the politics. Or, to put it another way, the mechanic arts—what engineering was called in the early nineteenth century—flourished best in a free society, where education was easily available and useful knowledge was not scorned. And in a nice sort of reciprocity, that open access to practical learning eliminated economic and social privilege based only on birth, thus guaranteeing the success of the democratic experiment. What is important about these ideals, as the first steps towards professionalism were taken, is that from the very outset engineering in America was solidly connected to great national goals. By the 1830s, the tasks of engineers were already defined; they were to create a prosperity for the mass of citizens such as the world had never known and by that abundance demonstrate the wisdom of the country's political system. This national agenda infused the rhetoric of the profession for decades afterwards, though in practice it often found itself in tension with that earlier democratic ideology.

What I want to talk about, then, is the way the engineering profession emerged and then evolved from those days of youthful faith. I see the profession as an institution and my analysis flows from that viewpoint. Thus, I will not deal with the many and remarkable accomplishments of engineers acting in their technical capacity, noteworthy as they are, but rather with engineers as inventors and managers of institutions. That approach inevitably leads one to focus on the problems—the differences, as it were, between what people say and what they do. That may seem a negative method, but as all engineers know, it's when something doesn't work properly that it really becomes interesting.

Besides its practitioners, with their specialized education, a profession consists of organizations which hold meetings, publish transactions, define intellectual style as well as norms of conduct, and generally act to promote the interests of their members.[5] For engineering, that sort of full-blown institutional development only came after 1870. But the preprofessional phase, a time of highly creative institutional experimentation beginning in the early nineteenth century, settled such important points as the nature of the occupation—how, for example, it differed from a career in science or from work as a skilled craftsperson—the sort of training the new occupation required, and as I have already claimed, the relation of engineering to national concerns. And those issues were resolved in organizations which prefigured the ones of the post–Civil War years.

The first step, however, was the emergence of the occupation itself. Canal construction, making and using steam engines, and building machine tools were the kinds of pursuits which created engineering as an occupational specialty in America.[6] These new technologies were usually beyond the abilities of someone who might have learned surveying or something of Isaac Newton's physics, just as they were also beyond most skilled artisans, and the initial work in these fields was often done by emigré European engineers. But beginning in the 1820s, in a period of extraordinary institutional inventiveness, Americans began to establish village lyceums, mechanics' institutes, scientific libraries, and special schools—literally hundreds of such institutions scattered throughout the country—all of which exemplified the dawning awareness that technical advance required different social structures than existing schools or craft associations.

Most of these agencies, begun in the heady idealism of Jacksonian America, incorporated egalitarian ambitions. Although now a famous engineering school, Rensselaer Polytechnic Institute in Troy, New York, was founded in 1824 to teach the sons and daughters of ordinary people "the applications of science to the common purposes of life."[7] The Maryland

Mechanics' Institute established in Baltimore the same year avowed that its educational program in applied science aimed "to establish that equality so particularly recognized in our Bill of Rights."[8] And it was the ideology which spawned a novel plan to create a new kind of artisan, better equipped to deal with an increasingly sophisticated technology. Marvellous in its simplicity, the idea was to teach workers the principles of science. Its projectors imagined that if one practiced in the mechanic arts understood the scientific principles which underlay one's work, one could escape the intellectual limitations of an older craft training to become capable of integrating both theory and practice.

But that hope to graft a better educated technician onto the old working-class stock withered after only a few years. There were two basic problems. One was that in a context of evening lectures and occasional magazine articles—a relatively informal and casual educational system—science had to be taught at such an elementary level that it lost any utility. The other and more serious difficulty was that the principles of science were not really of much use to workers. What technology required for its advancement, as Edwin Layton has pointed out, was not the principles of science, but its methods.[9] And it was precisely in adopting the methods of science that engineering emerged in a self-conscious way. Furthermore, the most active centers of experimentation in egalitarian education were the first to realize that engineering was something different than science or the crafts, and that it needed its own institutional forms.

Thus, the Franklin Institute in Philadelphia, which pioneered in efforts to educate artisans in science, shifted its emphasis in the 1830s explicitly to point out some of the elements of engineering professionalism. The *Journal of the Franklin Institute*, for instance, was reorganized in 1836, and its new format included a section entitled "Civil Engineering," for the publication of original research in that field, plus another section called "Progress in Civil Engineering," which presented abstracts and translations from the current British and European technical journals.[10] Research, publication, and keeping up with the literature of one's field became in this fashion the marks of engineering professionalism. The model was taken from science, but the objectives belonged to engineering.

Ellwood Morris's efforts to introduce Fourneyron's water turbine into the United States demonstrate the new style in action. Morris had learned of French improvements in reaction water wheels and perceived their value as prime movers in a country where industry still depended largely on water power. He translated French experiments with the Fourneyron turbine for the *Journal of the Franklin Institute*, drew up plans for a turbine that was built and installed in a Philadelphia plant, conducted his own tests of its efficiency, and then published those results, too. Morris thought of himself as a member of a technical community, with an obligation to the intellectual standards of that group, doing work that would enhance his own reputation for expertise while simultaneously serving national interests. In that ideal role, the engineer employed specialized knowledge in an independent, dignified, objective manner, to the benefit of career and the country's technological progress.

A similar concern to discover the proper educational format for engineering led the Franklin Institute's leaders in 1838 to propose a tax-supported state technical university. The school was to be organized into departments corresponding to civil, mechanical, mining, and chemical engineering, mathematics, and agriculture. Besides subject matter, the proposed School of Arts was distinguished from the University of Pennsylvania's traditional orientation to the classics by laboratory work and field practice. Its objectives were shorn of that rhetoric which had infused democratic experiments of the previous decade. Instead, the emphasis was on systematic analysis and the most efficient exploitation of the state's natural resources in order to secure that bounty "abundantly and at least expense."[11]

What the school's advocates described then, as they put it themselves, was a "professional education," specialized just the way the education of doctors and lawyers was, and they confidently expected an equivalent social status for its graduates. When the bill to establish the school failed by a narrow margin in the Pennsylvania legislature, those who had been behind the idea pressured the University of Pennsylvania subsequently to create a similar if somewhat less developed program of applied science instruction. Ever afterwards, Americans thought of engineering education in terms of a formally organized, full-time, university level curriculum. Its students would not be apprentices or artisans seeking self-improvement in their spare time, but young men — no one expected young women to follow such course — of the background and intellectual abilities for advanced study who wished to pursue a technical career rather than to follow one of the other professions. That approach was adopted by all the privately funded educational institutions that began to offer programs in engineering in the years before the Civil War, just as the Morrill Act of 1862 provided public money for agricultural and mechanical colleges like the one Philadelphians had argued for in 1838.[12]

The same kind of historical process links the mechanics' institutes, technical periodicals, and related institutions of the pre–Civil War era with those of the later nineteenth century. There is a tendency to think that the profession did not exist until the formation of national societies. But in fact all of what are called the "founder societies," in civil, mining, mechanical, and electrical engineering, grew out of a rich institutional matrix, and most of the ideas surrounding what might be called the first stage of engineering professionalism existed before there were associations to express them in national terms.

What one might reasonably expect, therefore, is that national societies were called into being to pursue objectives already fairly well agreed upon. To the degree that is true, useful chronological distinctions in the history of these groups do not necessarily hinge on their founding dates. Not that such milestones are historically unimportant. It is rather that they provide occasions clearly to recognize an agenda the profession has already ratified. Ceremonials of institutional beginnings are written in the rhetoric of aspiration, but the organization is based upon a set of preexisting economic, social, and political relations.

This theory of institutional history helps us to understand why it is that engineering, the single largest professional occupation for men in the United States and one which has always incorporated some of America's most cherished cultural images, has nonetheless been historically characterized by troubled institutions and a level of public appreciation that seldom met the expectations of its practitioners. The institutions of mechanical engineering, a field which seemingly best expressed American notions of native ingenuity, reflect just such contrasts, and their experiences were much like those of the other major branches of engineering.

When organizations like the Franklin Institute, whose main interest was in mechanical engineering, shifted the emphasis of their program away from the education of artisans to identify instead a method the more effectively to bring the fruits of systematic technical analysis to industry's benefit, it was because the Institute's leadership had been taken over by a coalition of scientists and industrialist-entrepreneurs. In a sort of partnership paralleled in Boston, New York, and elsewhere, that group perceived a set of common interests in industrial research projects, in a scholarly style of technical journalism, and in the kind of training that would produce experts able to assume managerial roles in mechanical industry. At the most obvious level of interest, the scientists saw career opportunities in teaching, research, and publication, while the entrepreneurs visualized greater profits from an applied-science-based industry, though each side of the partnership described the value of the relationship in terms of the rise of America's scientific and technical capability to equal that of the Old World.

Industry's interests gave a distinctive character to American products, which Europeans with technical skills who visited the United States before the Civil War were quick to recognize. Joseph Whitworth, the most celebrated English engineer of the time, best known for a uniform system of screw threads, toured the United States in 1853, along with George Wallis, a prominent English technical educator; and their report described, as they put it, the "eager resort to machinery" they saw everywhere in America. Another feature that characterized American industry was its attraction to uniformity. Wallis discovered in the Philadelphia Gas Works, celebrated, he said, for the "scientific principles" on which it was erected, a unique system of standardized fittings, to permit repair of any part with the least possible time and trouble.[13] New England's arms industry carried the idea even farther; an array of special purpose machine tools made possible the rapid production of thousands of rifles, each one identical to any other. By the 1860s advocates of America's mechanical industry were arguing for a nationwide level of attention to those techniques, the most essential point of which was that they saved labor. William Sellers, the most celebrated American mechanical engineer of his day, who in 1863 had devised a standard system for American screw thread practice, argued, indeed, that the central task of mechanical engineers was to devote their knowledge to the perfection of machines "to utilize unskilled labor."[14]

Thus, when the American Society of Mechanical Engineers was established in 1880, the field of mechanical engineering had a remarkably coherent sense of mission. Its founders were Sellers and others who commanded large industrial enterprises, or those who had emerged as the first generation of specially educated professional engineers. As direct participants in the creation of the new organization, they wanted to endow the moment with particular significance. Robert Henry Thurston, the society's first president and its chief theoretician, achieved the right effect in his presidential address, drawing upon ideas familiar to his audience but putting them in a way freshly to suggest their great future importance as a profession. Thurston began his speech by applying Herbert Spencer's philosophy to their field. It was "scientifically correct conduct," he told his fellow engineers, to pursue self-interest in a context which also promoted the interests and happiness of others.[15] That viewpoint not only gave professionals great scope for their special abilities, as well as enhanced social status, but also carried with it the idea that the professional engineer's work simultaneously forwarded larger social benefits.

The proof of the argument, Thurston indicated, was in the great material prosperity their labors had already generated. He expressed their contributions to labor's wages, the creation of capital, the value of raw material consumed and manufactured goods produced in the billions of dollars. Besides those staggering sums of money, their expertise had given the United States a universal reputation for ingenious machinery and had made it the refuge for the ambitious and hard-working of other lands. The lesson America had taught the Old World, with its ancient prejudices against the mechanic arts, was, Thurston claimed, the happy outcome when a society educated its people in "mind and hand together." Only on that basis could a people achieve an equitable distribution of wealth, stable government, and national prosperity.

But in addition to these assurances of their centrality in the creation of modern civilization, Thurston outlined a future role for mechanical engineers which remained unchallenged until the twentieth century. Thurston saw professionalism in both intellectual and social terms. In the first case, the principal duty of engineers was to process information—to generate technical knowledge through experimentation, research, and practice and then to convert that information into industrial knowledge through applications. As Thurston explained it, the problem was to organize facts "in the most accurate possible manner, and so systematically and completely that they shall be readily and conveniently available, and in such shape that their values and mutual relations shall be most easily detected and quantitatively measured."[16]

Because he saw engineering primarily in terms of its intellectual functions, as the creation and utilization of specialized insights into materials and processes, Thurston believed engineers should enjoy a special social status, too. So he sketched a partnership much like that which had been formed in America's most active centers of mechanical industry half a century earlier, but more explicitly drawn. He described two interconnected spheres of interest. One was made up of what he called "men of the world" who were primarily concerned with the creation of wealth, while the other consisted of "men of science" who were devoted to the creation of knowledge. It should be ASME's most important business, Thurston argued, "to narrow the gulf which has separated men of business from men engaged in study, in experiment and in diffusing useful knowledge."[17]

The partnership Thurston imagined was symmetrical, harmonious, and fruitful. The production of wealth in modern history depended on a continuing search for new knowledge and on his translation into practice. On the other hand, the acquisition of that knowledge, whether in experimental research, teaching, publication, or other forms of study, required financial support. But the relation between men of science and men of the world involved more in Thurston's mind than a simple monetary *quid pro quo*. He thought of engineers and industrialists united to press for political action across a broad front, from government funding for materials testing or legislation to provide better facilities for technical education, to tariff protection for industries in which knowledge and profits were undeveloped. The scenario Thurston outlined for the profession, then, was that of an elite group of engineers in an active alliance with industrial capitalism to generate wealth by the creation and skillful manipulation of technical knowledge. The objective was still America's democratizing mission to the world, but Thurston expected engineers to enjoy a special status in it because of their own unique contributions to that goal.

In practice, during the first two decades of its existence, the ASME reflected Thurston's program for it remarkably well. For instance, the most important of the new projects the society initiated, framing standardized dimensions for the building materials of mechanical engineering, constituted the arrangement of data to make it most readily available, in a form convenient for wide usage. And those most eager to extend that work to include, as one of them put it, standardizing everything from shop drawing symbols to nut bevels to mechanical dictionaries, thought of it as a problem of information storage and retrieval. Similarly, developing a uniform practice for tests of steam boilers involved assembling data from practice and experimentation, then compiling it in such a balanced way as to insure that the standard would prove usable "by every engineer of ordinary information and attainment."[18] In this world of standardized and codified knowledge, engineers themselves were neatly fitted into an industrial system.

The social style and institutional policies of ASME seemed also to embody Thurston's concepts. All its early leading figures were the owners of firms: Henry Towne, of Yale and Towne, for example, whose application of standardized techniques to lock manufacturing had made him a wealthy man indeed; or men like Thurston himself—head of Cornell University's Sibley College of Engineering—outstanding in the field for their intellectual attainment. They were all white, Protestant males, who placed a high value on free enterprise, individualism, hard work, ambition, and success.[19] These men made up the society's council, which met privately and without interference from the membership to make policy, handle finances, and admit new members. By common agreement, papers sensitive to the interests of a council member were not accepted for presentation at meetings, while papers which in presentation proved sensitive were not published in the society's transactions. And in the early years there were very few members who objected to such an arbitrary manner of proceeding. Engineers generally worked in industrial firms organized on strict hierarchical lines and they also tended to believe that men who had achieved success in business should play the leading roles in their professional societies.

The social style of the society's meetings reflected the sense that engineers comprised a group of men that had important interests confided to them. Their meetings featured dress balls of the sort Mr. and Mrs. George Westinghouse hosted in Washington, with two orchestras playing in an orchid-filled ballroom. Most satisfying of all, however, to the feeling that the profession represented a compelling new force in the world, was the 1889 trip of American engineers to Europe. Many of ASME's leading personalities had been there before. Ambrose Swasey, of the Warner & Swasey Machine Company in Cleveland, and George Babcock, of Babcock and Wilcox, regularly vacationed in Europe. But the plans for a trip, which had originated in the ASME and then were expanded to include the other founder societies, came to be seen as an official tour of the American engineering profession. A steamship was chartered for the occasion and refitted to make all accommodations first class. And their reception abroad was everything the engineers might have hoped. Their travel was entirely complimentary and special trains and carriages swept them from one dazzling party to another. They received the same treatment in France, crossing the Channel in a chartered boat and going to Paris in a special train for more elegant soireés in that city. But besides the gustatory and celebratory pleasures of the excursion, it gave American engineers the sense that they had arrived on the world stage of engineering professionalism.

These early years of ASME, like those of other American engineering societies, had a comfortable, men's club quality to them. And besides the comfort, there was a robust side to their profession. Joseph Holloway once described what members liked to think was a typical meeting:

> It has been our practice . . . to seek some spot abounding in smoke chimneys and dusty thoroughfares, where, surrounded with rumbling wheels, roaring blast and hissing steam-pipes, we proceed to enjoy our-

selves by climbing up and down cinder-heaps, tumbling over scrap-heaps and piles of pig-iron or rails, half blinded with the glare of roaring furnaces, and nearly melted by their heat. We come to the close of the day, begrimed with our surroundings, wilted as to our attire, but full of the conviction that we have been having a delightful picnic.[20]

Robert Thurston expressed that same sense of the organization's style when he described ASME members as "good mechanics by instinct, good men by original construction, good fellows by nature and habit and training."[21]

This self-image of hard workers and hard players lives on in the profession, as does an echo of the camaraderie engendered in a small organization when its members have similar backgrounds and interests as well as equivalent social and economic status. But by the end of the nineteenth century, important structural changes in mechanical engineering and in the profession rendered that old style increasingly obsolete, to the disruption not only of ASME's internal harmony but also to the notion of a consensus about the society's objectives.

In the nineteenth century engineers thought of professionalism as the application of specialized knowledge in the interest of one's employer. That was certainly the understanding of the majority of American engineers, since whatever their specialty they generally worked for large firms. A higher percentage of civil engineers worked as independent consultants—the ideal of engineering professionalism—and ASCE liked to take upon itself the mantle of objectivity, though in fact, most civil engineers were employees, too. When the number of engineers was relatively small and when the growth of transportation systems, of resource development, and of manufacturing industry insured jobs and the prospect of career advancement, that earlier definition of engineering proved reasonably satisfactory. But beginning around 1880, the profession began suddenly to grow, quadrupling in size by 1900, and the annual rate of increase was itself going up each year. That dramatic alteration in the nature of the profession was matched by a simultaneous set of changes in industry with implications just as profound. Partnerships and owner-manager firms in the mechanical industries, the kind of enterprises that had set the style of professionalism, were increasingly being replaced by corporate structures. Instead of a manager engineer intimately familiar with the shop floor, these new corporations featured engineering departments separated not only from the shop floor but from the firm's financial administration, too. And in those larger organizations the drive for system and order which Alfred Chandler has so well described tended increasingly to make engineers, especially junior ones, identical units in the corporate machine.[22] So, just as mechanical engineering was losing its nineteenth-century forms of identification, great numbers of recent graduates from those new technical schools and universities came flooding onto the job market.

Some dates are instructive at this point. While a national society of civil engineers was established in 1867, it did not begin to function effectively until the early 1870s. The American Institute of Mining Engineers was founded in 1871, ASME in 1880, and the American Institute of Electrical Engineers in 1884. Those societies only began the process of institutional specialization, soon to be followed by organizations for chemical engineers, heating and ventilating engineers, industrial engineers, and a host of others within the next decade or so. And just as these societies were being formed, so were new technical schools being established. Case Institute of Technology was founded in 1880, Georgia Tech at about the same time, and, in a list almost as long as that of new engineering societies, large numbers of other specialized technical schools sprang into existence across the country during the following ten years.[23] Graduates from those new institutions, coming into a field of rapidly increasing size and specialization, were not part of mechanical engineering's old aristocracy, nor was admission to it open to them. Yet, more than any previous generation of engineers, they wanted a professional identification for themselves.

These changes in mechanical engineering, furthermore, came during a time in American history of considerable reform ferment called the Progressive Era, which had interesting implications for professionalism in engineering. The Progressive movement began in a wave of reaction against urban corruption, which was particularly rampant in cities that had also grown at extraordinary rates in the closing decades of the nineteenth century, and its remedy was to bring objective expertise to the city's ills. Instead, for instance, of city hall bosses ruling through patronage, Progressives advocated the new city manager form of government in which professional political scientists applied their special knowledge to urban administration. Since much of the graft that sullied America's cities flowed from urban engineering projects—street paving and lighting, sewer construction, and urban transit systems—it was only natural that newly emerged experts in that kind of work would also see in the application of their knowledge to public service a new level of professionalism.

There is yet another element that figured in what Edwin Layton has called "the revolt of the engineers."[24] A centrifugal force characterizes the profession's organizations and it acts, even to the present, in two ways. One is from the effect of specialization. In the seventeenth century the only distinction in engineering was whether it was directed toward civil or military purposes. In an effort to defend its institutional territory, the ASCE often argued that old definition to claim that it represented all nonmilitary engineers. And in an exactly analogous fashion, ASME continually fought to keep those of its members whose particular focus led them to group together from splitting off into separate organizations. The problem was, however, that the technical subspecialties were engaged in competition with each other for a share of the society's resources, and some subspecialties proved more successful at that than others. Engineers concerned with the generation of electric energy, for instance, had by the first world war become one of the most politically powerful groups within ASME, a position they continued to enjoy for years afterwards. But besides the tensions that specialization created within engineering's institutions, it acted also to prevent the profession from agreement upon a common set of ethics. Just at a time, in other words, when the national political climate most encouraged a new definition of the engineer's social responsibilities, specialization splintered the profession into increasingly divergent groups.

A similar centrifugal force acted, and still does, at a geographical level. As the headquarters city for most American firms that employ significant numbers of engineers, New York appeared the logical place for the professions to locate their own head offices. Yet, particularly when travel was less convenient, it was difficult at best for the societies to represent distant members. As a result, many engineers found a more hospitable professional connection with local municipal engineering societies in Chicago, Saint Louis, Cleveland, Boston, and elsewhere, all of which enjoyed an active prosperity during the Progressive era. For reform-minded engineers, moreover, what made the geographical bias of the national societies especially troublesome was that New York–based interests seemed easily able to control institutional policy and practice.

All these factors—large numbers of younger engineers looking for careers, the decline of older professional styles, a rising tide of political reform spirit, and certain features in the organization of national engineering societies—came together in the first two decades of the twentieth century to create a time of great turmoil, that also marked out the principal issues which still trouble America's technical institutions.

Just as no war ever started from a single event, there was no single trauma to trigger the rebellion that occurred within each of the founder societies, to speak only of them. It was fought with varying intensity in each, but the battles essentially pitted young ambitious engineers against older members of the engineering establishment, municipal engineering associations against national organizations, and, frequently, scientific management-oriented engineers against corporate engineers, especially those from the utilities.

In the ASME, for instance, the most vocal of the reformers was Morris L. Cooke, a Lehigh University graduate in mechanical engineering and a scientific management disciple. He was hired by Frederick Winslow Taylor, ASME president in 1904, to help reorganize the society's headquarters procedures as part of a general administrative shake-up. Taylor himself was already famous for his time and motion studies; and scientific management, as he called it, promised a new objectivity for engineers, lifting them above the warfare between capital and labor—a different relation than Thurston had proposed—but giving them a rational basis for the solution of that vexing problem. Many younger engineers, attracted both by the supposedly factual nature of scientific management and by its potential application to a wide variety of social as well as industrial problems, saw in it a more appealing, broader, immediately applicable kind of professionalism, and Cooke was one of those. But in his own efforts to bring the engineering profession to the reform of America's cities, Cooke was led to a campaign to reform the engineering profession itself.

One of the things Cooke discovered while working as Philadelphia's city engineer was how difficult it was for municipalities to get expert advice. Engineers with the best reputations for knowledge of street-paving materials, for instance, or on the costs of electric power generation, were already consultants for those industries. Here, in his mind, was an ideal role for the professional engineering society; it could provide unbiased information for the public good.

Cooke consequently organized a session for the 1909 annual meeting on the subject of air pollution, a serious problem in all of America's major cities. From his experience in ASME's headquarters he knew there would be opposition to his program, so he supported his appeal to the committee on meetings with a petition signed by many of the ASME's prominent men. The committee turned his proposal down flat, however, and in the ensuing debate it is clear that New York Edison and the New York Central Railroad had proved powerful enemies to the idea. Cooke's crusade to swing the engineering profession over to the public's side touched sensitive nerves, since many of the society's leaders worked for private utilities; and when, ruthless in his zeal, he attacked them by name in a Harvard speech for colluding to keep utility rates high, they brought a motion of censure before ASME's council.

The details of that particular fight are not especially relevant here, but the pamphlets Cooke published at the time and circulated to the ASME's membership are worth notice. In them he connected the disproportionate power of utility engineers in the society with its own undemocratic procedures and thus posed several important questions. Did engineering professionalism have any deeper ethical principles than loyalty to one's employer? That in turn raised another interesting issue, namely, what were the purposes of a professional engineering society? Or, perhaps to phrase that matter in a more fundamental way: what was the role of expertise in a democracy?

The ideal of engineering professionalism is occupational independence, the freedom achieved when specialized knowledge is applied to socially important goals. In that spirit professionals apply to the best of their ability their expertise and judgment to their client's problems. The client is not obliged to take their advice, but the pure professional/client relation imagines a direct positive connection between the recommendations and the professional's own integrity. Doctors and lawyers appeared best to embody that vision of professionalism, and engineers often expressed the hope that their profession might enjoy the same social status as those older specialties. But technical men were generally not independent consultants, their professionalization came at a later point in history, and their institutional structures were necessarily different. All the national engineering societies of the nineteenth century were established in the conviction that the engineers' best interests were identical with those of the firms for which they worked—a conception which suited an era when the profession's leaders owned the firms. But, by the twentieth century, engineering had developed a large rank and file membership. What their professional ideals should be and how engineering institutions should serve such a membership were also questions that arose from Cooke's analysis of engineering's social responsibilities.

Because its institutional style discourages public discussion of the profession's internal politics—never mind the private business arrangements of its leaders—Cooke may seem an especially flamboyant critic. But he was merely the most outspoken of those early twentieth-century engineers who sought to redefine Thurston's program for the ASME in the light of more modern realities. Furthermore, the concerns Cooke and others addressed at that time continued to perplex engineers because they spring from fundamentally conflicting elements in the profession and its institutions. Many engineers during the Great Depression of the 1930s also felt that special interests were unduly influential in society affairs, that the concerns of New York headquarters were often not those of the ordinary member, and that because of an imperfect professional image the public failed to appreciate their contributions to modern civilization. Nor, indeed, have times changed much since then. Anyone familiar with the movement against nuclear power knows that these same kinds of issues are very much alive.

These episodes, so often disturbing to engineers, may be taken as examples of the failure of idealism, instances of the gulf between virtues the profession claimed for itself and the practices in which it has actually engaged. In my mind, however, times of conflict and dissent serve rather as occasions to understand the real nature of the profession in American history. One of its salient characteristics has long been an attachment to established national goals and to a kind of American self-image. The space race is simply the most recent evidence of that old historical truth; Americans have always expected there to be a powerful connection between their technology and their political ideals. That is why Fred MacMurray's characterization of the civil engineer struck such a resonant note. But it is also true that Cooke was right in his accusation of collusion. The profession, after all, was called into existence to serve private interests. Its past has been and presumably its future will be shaped by the often creative tension between these two essential features of the engineering profession.

NOTES

1. *American Journal of Education* (March 1826): 180.
2. It was a *London Times* correspondent to the Philadelphia Centennial Exhibition of 1876 who reported, "the American mechanizes as an old Greek sculptured, as the Venetian painted." Quoted in John A. Kouwenhoven, *Made in America* (New York, 1962), p. 25.
3. James Gould, *An Oration, Pronounced at New Haven, before the Connecticut Alpha of the Phi Beta Kappa Society, September 13, 1825* (New Haven, Conn., 1825), p. 29.
4. As the editor of the Philadelphia *Mechanics' Register* put it, "Wherever our ingenuity and enterprise extend into foreign countries, an evidence and conviction of our greatness goes with them" (February 1837) p. 15. See also Eugene S. Ferguson, "The American-ness of American Technology," *Technology and Culture* 20 (January 1979): 14.
5. For a sociological analysis of the profession, see Joel E. Gerstl and Rob-

ert Perrucci, *Profession Without Community: Engineers in American Society* (New York, 1969). See also Joel E. Gerstl and Robert Perrucci, eds., *The Engineers and the Social System* (New York, 1969).

6. Daniel H. Calhoun, in *The American Civil Engineer: Origins and Conflicts* (Cambridge, 1960), describes the creation of a civil engineering profession in the United States.

7. Samuel Resneck, *Education for a Technological Society: A Sesquicentennial History of Rensselaer Polytechnic Institute* (Troy, N.Y., 1968).

8. *The Mechanics' Press* (Baltimore), 19 November 1825.

9. Edwin T. Layton, "Mirror-Image Twins: The Communities of Science and Technology in Nineteenth-Century America," *Technology and Culture* 12 (October 1971): 562–80.

10. Bruce Sinclair, *Philadelphia's Philosopher Mechanics: A History of the Franklin Institute, 1824–1865* (Baltimore, 1974), p. 212.

11. *For the Establishment of a School of Arts: Memorial of the Franklin Institute, of the State of Pennsylvania, for the Promotion of the Mechanic Arts, to the Legislature of Pennsylvania* (Philadelphia, 1837), p. 8.

12. The widespread interest in technical education in pre–Civil War America is described in Earle D. Ross, *Democracy's College: The Land Grant Movement in the Formative Stage* (Ames, Iowa, 1942).

13. Nathan Rosenberg, ed., *The American System of Manufactures: The Report of the Committee on the Machinery of the United States, 1855, and the Special Reports of George Wallis and Joseph Whitworth, 1854* (Edinburgh, 1969), p. 276.

14. Bruce Sinclair, "At the Turn of a Screw: William Sellers, the Franklin Institute, and a Standard American Thread," *Technology and Culture* 10 (January 1969): 26.

15. Robert Henry Thurston, "President's Inaugural Address," *American Society of Mechanical Engineers Transactions* 1 (1880): 15. For more information on the society, see Bruce Sinclair, *A Centennial History of the American Society of Mechanical Engineers* (Toronto, 1980).

16. Thurston, "President's Inaugural Address," p. 15.

17. Ibid.

18. *ASME Transactions* 8 (1887): 972.

19. That group is described in Monte A. Calvert, *The Mechanical Engineer in America, 1830–1910* (Baltimore, 1967), pp. 110–20.

20. *ASME Transactions* 6 (1885): 356.

21. *ASME Transactions* 14 (1893): 497.

22. Alfred D. Chandler, *The Visible Hand: The Managerial Revolution in American Business* (Cambridge, 1977).

23. The forces behind the efflorescence of specialized schools and associations in late nineteenth-century America are analyzed in Burton J. Bledstein, *The Culture of Professionalism* (New York, 1976).

24. Edwin T. Layton, *The Revolt of the Engineers: Social Responsibility and the American Engineering Profession* (Cleveland, 1971).

ENGINEERING: SUGGESTIONS FOR FURTHER READING

Calhoun, Daniel H. *The American Civil Engineer: Origins and Conflict.* Cambridge, Mass., 1960.
Calvert, Monte. *The Mechanical Engineer in America, 1830–1910.* Baltimore, 1967.
Layton, Edwin T. *The Revolt of the Engineers.* Cleveland, 1971.
Noble, David. *America by Design.* New York, 1977.
Sinclair, Bruce. *A Centennial History of the American Society of Mechanical Engineers, 1880–1980.* Toronto, 1980.

8. THE PROFESSION OF JOURNALISM IN THE UNITED STATES

Michael Schudson

Journalism is not one of the venerable professions. Certainly it was not well established when Ben Franklin's older brother James began printing the second newspaper in the colonies in 1720. James Franklin's friends tried to dissuade him, saying they thought the paper not likely to succeed, "one newspaper being in their judgment enough for America."[1]

Journalism is better established now but it is still not among the respected professions. While journalists in France, England, Germany, the United States, and elsewhere have associated with the wealthy and the powerful, they have never been respected among them. As Max Weber pointed out, the journalist "belongs to a sort of pariah caste, which is always estimated by 'society' in terms of its ethically lowest representative."[2] The most recent instance is the Pulitzer Prize scandal of 1981. The Pulitzer award for feature writing went to Janet Cooke of the *Washington Post*, but the prize was revoked when it turned out that Cooke had invented the character of the 8-year-old heroin addict who was the center of the story. A deluge of criticism of the press followed. An Omaha editor reported, "My dentist talks to me about Janet Cooke" and a Houston editor complained of an attorney friend who, pointing to Janet Cooke, insisted, "You make things up all the time." People seemed eager to focus their hostility toward the press on a clear transgression and so they took Janet Cooke as representative of the class of journalists.[3]

What leads a profession to be highly esteemed? There is no single or simple reason. Yet it seems that the professions taken most seriously and regarded as most honorable are those with some evident connection to matters of ultimate concern—medicine treats life and death, law considers liberty and justice, the clergy deals with transcendent meaning. Respected professions are also those which deal with what the culture considers important and dignified subjects. Until cats are taken as seriously as children, veterinarians will not enjoy the same respect as pediatricians. Among physicians, the ear, nose, and throat specialist will not be taken as seriously as the internist and the urologist will not command as much respect as the cardiologist.[4]

Most of journalism is irrelevant to matters of ultimate concern. The comics, the ads, the sports page, the fashion and entertainment and feature sections of the paper may be enjoyable. They may be useful. But few people regard them as touching on ultimately important issues. The only part of journalism that consistently commands the serious attention of the public is political journalism. The symbolic center of the news media is politics. And that's the rub: politics itself is not dignified. In American culture, at least, people believe there is something vulgar about it. People respect the politician who is "above politics," but not a judge "above the law" or a physician "above medicine."

Still, politics has its moments of dignity, ceremony, and sacral significance. We may speak of politics derisively, but we still take it for granted that government is housed in buildings with stately Greek columns. Journalists may treat politics humorously and they sometimes reduce reporting on politics to sports stories—but they cannot long escape criticism for doing so. In political reporting, there are high ideals and there is something vital, of ultimate concern, at stake: our citizenship itself.

Americans rely on journalists to provide the information and views that link us to the governance of our cities, states, and nation. If journalism is to be taken seriously as a profession, this is the one task it must handle with expertise, independence, and a continuing concern for the public interest. At the same time that we expect professional services from journalists, however, we do not grant most journalists the authority to express their political convictions. We are more comfortable, as a culture, with the position that journalists are, or should be, a transmission belt of neutral facts about events in the world. Their only passion should be dispassion.

Thus the pride journalists are expected to take in their work is not the pride in advocacy, writing for one side or another, but the pride in being attacked by both sides for "writing down the middle."[5] This is what is sometimes called objectivity or fairness. This is the indication that the journalist is deserving of the public trust. Writing it down the middle has some critics, of course. Lyndon Johnson used to tell a story of an unemployed teacher who applied for a job in a small town in Texas in the depths of the depression. One old rancher on the school board asked him, "Do you teach that the world is round or that the world is flat?" The desperate young man, not able to read the faces of the school board members, allowed how he could teach it either way.[6]

Still, today we rely on journalists for political knowledge and we insist that they keep their political views to themselves. We deny that they may speak authoritatively in personal voices, but we grant them enormous authority so long as they agree to report on the objective realities in the world and refuse to comment on them.

This view of the journalist would be practically unrecognizable to Americans of the eighteenth century. It would be not much more familiar to nineteenth-century journalists. The history of journalism in America has often been celebrated as a continuous growth toward more and more freedom of the press, faster and better coverage of the news. I think it wiser to suggest that the past is not a well-paved and unbroken road. If history is a road, it is one with deep potholes, with bridges washed out, and with large chasms across which one can hardly imagine movement. I want to discuss two revolutions in the American press that laid the groundwork for the kind of authority, powerful yet circumscribed, which American journalists exercise today. The first of these revolutions took place in the 1830s; the second, early in our own century. The first made news, rather than political opinion, the heart of the newspaper. The second defined the authority of the journalist in relation to news, making objectivity the defense and pride of the reporter. These revolutions made it possible for journalism to emerge as a serious, independent, and self-conscious occupation. At the same time, I want to suggest, they placed a wedge between the journalist and politics in a way that expresses and keeps alive American ambivalence about politics and our doubts about taking the journalistic enterprise seriously.

The modern American newspaper first emerged in the 1830s in the seaport towns of New York, Baltimore, Boston, and Philadelphia.[7] Before that time, newspapers were relatively expensive, they could be bought only by subscription, and they were not sold on the street. Their circulations were very small and they had a readership largely among political and commercial elites. They were media for advertising but they did not normally make profits from commercial advertising. More commonly, newspapers were just one part of a printers' business, and profits came from other job printing assignments. Newspapers were subsidized by political parties or factions within political parties. Editors might get rich if they backed a winning party and then garnered government printing contracts when that party took office. There was no such thing as a profession of journalism. The editor was also printer, business manager, sometimes bookseller or post-master, all in one.

And there was little we could properly call reporting. Certainly no one was hired as a reporter. The early nineteenth-century American news-paper centered on the expression of political opinion. The editorial column was the heart of the paper. It appeared on page 2 of what was generally a 4-page paper. Page 2 also included assorted items of news; page 3 was financial news and financial advertising; page 4 was advertising; page 1 was advertising and sometimes long news stories. The newspaper was not read in those days from page 1 on. Pages 1 and 4 were something like the covers of a magazine, and readers turned inside for the substance of things. In 1829, for instance, the *Morning Courier and New-York Enquirer*, one of the city's leading dailies, apologized for putting important stories on page 1. "A num-ber of articles omitted yesterday will be found on the outside of this day's paper. We must request our readers at all times to look at our first page, where necessity compels us to put much which we would be pleased to have appear on the inside of our sheet."[8]

But in the 1830s, a revolution took place in American journalism. The newspaper became a self-supporting, commercial institution. A new kind of paper called the "penny paper" began. Penny papers sold for one cent, not six cents like conventional papers. The penny papers were hawked on the street by newsboys. They sought large circulations and the advertis-ing dollars large readership would attract. The penny press featured news rather than political commentary, and it focused on local news, not on items reprinted from London papers. Until the 1830s, a reader in New York could expect to learn more of London than of Manhattan from the local paper. Midwestern journals, in turn, reprinted from the New York press instead of gathering their own news.[9] But the penny press changed that. In the penny papers, for the first time, news focused on local government, crime, society, and scandal, and the papers hired reporters to seek out the news. The point of competition between papers shifted from the editorial column to the news columns. While papers remained political, they were less par-tisan than before and the new papers frequently made claims which shocked the conventional press—claims to political independence. One penny editor wrote of politics, "We trust our readers will pardon us when we declare, that in common acceptation of the term, *we have none*."[10]

This was not modern professionalism. The revolution of the penny press was prerequisite to the emergence of a belief in objectivity among journalists. It was crucial for the newspaper to come to depend on a source of financial support other than the political party; it was critical for the newspaper to develop a marketable product, news, separate from political commentary. But in the 1830s the newspaper was still an editor's organ, not a reporter's institution, and there was no well-defined sense that there is a barrier between facts and values and that special steps need to be taken to preserve the facts from distortion. The penny papers' world view was in keeping with other cultural currents of the day. In science, there was a passion for fact gathering, and it is not surprising that geology and the descriptive aspects of botany and zoology should have been popular at the time. There was a strong sense of the democracy of research. Any ordinary citizen could add to scientific knowledge by identifying local plants and animals and sending the information on to the academies. Journalism's view of the facts was similar: facts are things in the world to be gathered.[11]

The commercialization of the press was part of a movement to wider democracy, the inclusion of the growing middle class in the body politic. Mass-based political parties began to supplant legislative caucuses for the selection of political candidates. Economic expansion was fueled by new means of financing, including the stock market and lotteries, that enabled families of relatively modest means to become investors. The passion for equality that Tocqueville noted on his visit to America expressed itself in aggressive opposition to elites and cliques of all sorts. In the 1830s and 1840s, for instance, licensing requirements for physicians and lawyers were reduced, or abolished altogether, in many of the states.[12]

The penny press took advantage of this spirit and, proud and smart-alecky, shouted its superiority to the conventional six-penny papers. It took pride in its nonexclusive readership, in what *New York Herald* editor James Gordon Bennett called his "nonsubscriber plan" of selling papers daily on the streets. Only the penny press could be free, he wrote, "simply because it is subservient to none of its readers—known to none of its readers—and entirely ignorant who are its readers and who are not."[13] In aim and in image, the penny paper was to the conventional paper what a street poster is to a lithograph in a gallery—an open invitation to look, not an exclusive showing. Indeed, the street posters that were springing up in Paris in these same decades have been defined as "pictures meant to be seen by people who did not mean to see them."[14] The same can be said of the penny press: they were newspapers meant to be read by people who did not mean to read them. The older papers were small circulation newsletters designed for people already part of a group and already in-the-know. The penny papers aimed at a wider public, at once enlarging democratic society and enriching themselves.

So, in the 1830s, journalism became a business. It became a full-time occupation. Reporters, with no responsibility for printing, business, or editorial functions, were hired to gather news. But the degree of professionalism of these early journalists was slight. They cared about accuracy of reporting—reporters good with shorthand ridiculed those who were not so skilled. And they cared about the speed of getting the news into the paper and the paper into the streets. But the business of politics, the center of the journalistic enterprise, was still in the hands of editors. The reporters had little or no political presence.

Journalism grew in the late nineteenth century. The newspaper became more and more important as a vehicle for advertising, especially as advertising itself became more central in an expanding economy. In the 1880s and after, department stores became centers of retailing and, along with patent medicines, they were the mainstay of newspaper advertising columns. Want ads became more important. Nationally advertised brand-name products—soaps and baking powders and others—began to take to the newspaper columns. Newspaper circulations boomed. The number of journalists employed increased and clubs for journalists were established in the larger cities. These were social clubs rather than professional associations—indeed, this remains true of American press clubs. The clubs were, at any rate, the first institutionalized signs that journalism was becoming a self-conscious occupational group.

But until the turn of the century, reporting tended to be a rote task, especially with regard to politics. Some star reporters at the larger papers became relatively autonomous in their work, but most remained under the thumb of editors. The editors, in turn, were well aware of the tone their publishers wanted the papers to have (often, of course, editor and publisher were the same person). The ethics of journalism in 1900 would make Janet Cooke look like a saint. Reporters were at once hobbled by allegiance to the point of view and tone of their own papers and, at the same time, unleashed to improvise in a story to make it more entertaining. Even journalism textbooks coming into use in the fledgling courses in journalism advised students to improvise upon the facts to offer readers not just "facts" but "color." One text of the 1880s urged writers not to put editorial opinion in news stories, but then turned around to warn that this advice should not be taken strictly. Put in opinions to keep the story entertaining, the text suggested, and be wary only of including opinions that might be libelous or that "might differ from the 'policy' of the paper."[15]

Despite the continued importance of the editor, the news page was becoming more important than the editorial page. Teddy Roosevelt fully recognized, and was the first president to do so, that if he could dominate the columns of the front page in the news he need not fret about what the editorial writers were saying. He curried favor with reporters and was the first president to provide a room in the White House for correspondents. The attention that powerful people were beginning to pay to lowly reporters was flattering and it urged on the second transformation in the press.

The second revolution in the press began with an institution outside journalism: public relations. As late as 1908 Congress could still insist in an agriculture appropriations bill that "no part of this appropriation shall be paid for the preparation of any newspaper or magazine article," and in 1913 Congress passed a law denying the use of appropriations for payment of "publicity experts" unless specifically designated by Congress. But the law was a dead letter, washed away by the flood of government propaganda bureaus in World War I. The war enlisted journalists in a propaganda machine both in Europe and at home. The domestic experience was especially notable. President Wilson created the Committee on Public Information in 1917. This Committee employed dozens of journalists writing, collecting, and distributing information favorable to the American war policy. It was America's contribution to making World War I "the first modern effort at systematic, nationwide manipulation of collective passions."[16]

The war experience provided a model for business public relations during the 1920s. As early as 1919 journalists complained that they were suddenly outnumbered by publicity agents; by the early 1930s an editor observed that schools of journalism produced more public relations agents than newspeople and that half or more of the news items in the daily press originated in publicity work. Editor Don Seitz observed, "I venture the guess that the Pulitzer School of Journalism turns out far more of these parasites than it does reporters."[17]

By the 1920s, then, there was an entirely new occupation catering to the power of journalists. Reporters in the nineteenth century could naively believe that reporting consisted in gathering facts, chipping them away from the mountainside of reality like geologists gathering samples. But now they could see that the facts rained down upon them—and not from "reality" but from interested parties. The job of the press seemed to be changing from reporting the news to reprinting interested parties' definitions of the news.

It is no wonder that Walter Lippmann and John Dewey both saw the rise of public relations as the most significant change in the political life of the twentieth century. Nor is it any wonder that dramatic changes began to take place in journalism.

In the 1920s, journalism openly acknowledged what public relations was making all too apparent: the subjectivity of facts. Bylines appeared much more frequently, tacitly acknowledging individual human responsibility even for "facts." Bylines appeared even in wire service stories. Interpretive reporting emerged and was hotly debated, just as it would be debated all over again in the late sixties. Part of the justification for interpretive reporting was simply that *all* reporting is interpretive in any case, and one might as well make conscientious and self-conscious efforts to present facts analytically. When news on radio began, news commentators led the way. H. V. Kaltenborn and others pioneered a form of personal and opinionated news commentary that remained in vogue until World War II.[18]

The most visible and important change was the appearance of the political column. Until the 1920s, the only regular newspaper columnists were humorists. In the twenties, the political column developed with the work of David Lawrence, Mark Sullivan, Heywood Hale Broun, Walter Lippmann, and others. These columns were syndicated and reached people all over the country. When Robert and Helen Lynd studied Muncie, Indiana, in 1925, the local papers carried two columnists. Ten years later the morning paper alone had five columnists and the afternoon paper four. *The New Republic* noted in 1937 what is in most respects still true, that "much of the influence once attached to the editorial page has passed over to the columnists."[19]

A more subtle change came in the style of writing basic political news stories. If one examines the way the president's State of the Union message was reported in the nineteenth century, the pattern is very simple. All commentary was reserved to the editorial page. The news story simply noted, in an account of a day's congressional proceedings, that the message of the president was read—the full message was then printed verbatim elsewhere in the paper. Sometimes the reaction of senators and representatives to the message was also noted—whether they slept or seemed interested, whether they grimaced or smiled. But not until the twentieth century did journalists take it upon themselves to highlight and summarize the main points of the presidential message itself. Of course, this is a necessarily selective task, one in which the reporters must make some political judgments. This was not part of the nineteenth-century Washington correspondent's responsibilities, but twentieth-century correspondents take it for granted. In the twenties, journalists not only summarized what they believed to be the most important points of presidential messages—they would even note what the message omitted. The *New York Times* story in 1924 opened, "President Coolidge's annual message . . . was notable for its lack of specific recommendations." In 1928 the *Times* reporter wrote, "Perfunctory and colorless as it may have seemed to most of those who heard it read in the Senate and the House this afternoon, President Coolidge's last annual message to Congress contained certain suggestions *between the lines* calculated to disarrange legislative plans for the session which was begun yesterday."[20]

That is a more interpretive style of writing than can be found in almost any nineteenth-century account of presidential messages. The world of journalism was changing to recognize a need to interpret the complex world that national politics had become and to accommodate a growing autonomy among reporters.

The belief that news reporting is subjective and that "interpretive" writing is desirable reached into the most conservative branches of journalism. As early as 1913, the managers of the Associated Press and the United Press met at a university symposium where the AP defended unbiased reporting and the UP claimed that there is no such thing. Will Irwin wrote of this meeting:

> The old and the new in journalism met on the same platform, and held debate—the old generation, clinging to the fallacy that news can be written from a god-like height of abstract truth, biased and knowing it not; the younger generation, perceiving that humanity sees truth only from a point of view, honestly biased and knowing it well.[21]

It was a sign of things to come. By 1934 the American Society of Newspaper Editors resolved to devote more space to interpretive news because of the increasing complexity of world events and the growing interest of citizens in public affairs.[22]

With bylines, political columnists, and interpretive reporting, journalism accommodated a world where facts could not be trusted. Newspapers institutionalized these forms of subjectivity. Ironically, journalism also resisted the recognition of the shadowiness of facts by developing an ideal of objectivity. Again, the influence of public relations played a role in this. One of the founders of public relations and long-time publicity man for John D. Rockefeller, Ivy Lee, declared in 1924 that facts did not exist: "The effort to state an absolute fact is simply an attempt to achieve what is humanly impossible; all I can do is to give you my interpretation of the facts." For Lee, there was no such thing as disinterestedness. "All of us are apt to try to think that what serves our own interests is also in the general interest. We are very prone to look at everything through glasses colored by our own interests and prejudices."[23] Reporters of the 1890s would not have known what Lee was talking about; reporters of the 1920s accepted much of what Lee said as true. At the same time, this very understanding made them ready to believe that in a world of subjectivity one must toe the line of established rules and procedures for reporting. As Walter Lippmann put it, "As our minds become more deeply aware of their own subjectivism, we find a zest in objective method that is not otherwise there." Lippmann argued that in the modern world almost all news comes at second-hand. People no longer act directly on the environment but on a pseudoenvironment of reports, rumors, and guesses. In a world of such diversity and uncertainty, the only kind of unity would lie in science, "a unity of method, rather than of aim; the unity of a disciplined experiment."[24] Thus, at the same time that journalism responded to subjectivity by institutionalizing it in the political column, it reacted against subjectivity by pronouncing objectivity its ideal and by setting up rules and routines of reporting to embody the ideal.

It is important to see how original this was. Nineteenth-century journalism was certainly concerned that newspapers might not tell the truth. But the nineteenth-century worry was exclusively about *intentional* shadings of the truth for *partisan* ends. The concern was about the danger of partisan views. The twentieth century added the danger of *partial* views, the inevitable selectivity of facts, the inevitable exercise of judgment in interpreting the real world. The nineteenth century worried about journalists' *intentions* and what they wanted to do. In the twentieth century, there is an additional concern about journalists' *attentions* and what they are able to see and do. In the nineteenth century, there was fear that journalists would not simply record the world but would think about it and promote their own thinking. In the twentieth century there is the new worry that journalists *will* simply record and will not think, thereby promoting someone else's thinking, namely that of the government and other powerful interests.

The nineteenth-century concern that the news media will be intentionally partisan persists, and for good reason, in our own time. But the twentieth century's novel concern, that the news media will be partial, without exercising self-conscious intention, is an insight that the nineteenth century did not have.

Now, the danger in that insight is that it can lead to the kind of juvenile relativism Ivy Lee expressed. It became all too fashionable in the past decade to say that objectivity is impossible, a myth, mere ideology designed to cover up the essentially conservative or essentially liberal coloring of the press, depending on the critic's view. This has become a familiar common sense: that there are no facts, only interpretations, that we see everything through the glasses of our own interests and prejudices.

But there is an equal and opposite common sense that some institutions are more objective than others, some people more objective than others, and the same person more objective in some situations than in others. Of institutions, think of the judiciary versus the legislature: the judiciary is clearly subject to political pressure but *less* so than the legislature. It therefore has fewer impediments to rational judgment and can be called, in Alexander Bickel's phrase, "the least dangerous branch" of government.[25] Or think of people with whom one discusses a personal problem. Not all people are equally good prospects for making a dispassionate judgment about another person's problem; some people listen better than others and can keep their own problems in check as they respond to someone else. Or think of individuals: do they always give in to their own interests and prejudices? Are there not occasions when they guard against their own preconceptions, expose them intentionally to the judgment and criticism of others, or bend over backwards to put their own inclinations aside?

Obviously, people's ideas do tend to coincide with their backgrounds, interests, pocketbooks, experiences, and associates. But if there is a social determination of ideas, there is also a social determination of the extent to which ideas are socially determined. Some institutions and conditions are designed to screen out the biases of personal background. For instance, science is distinguished from other pursuits in part because it is a social institution set up in a certain way, a community of inquiring scholars with a set of tools, organizations, values, and patterns of association designed in some measure to protect against both prejudicial intentions and selective attentions. It is not complete and does not always work and is always subject to error. But it is organized and patterned and provides for restraint on bias and the correction of errors.

Journalism is not in the position of science. Still, reporters have some safeguards against seeing the world simply according to their own untutored lights. There is the safeguard of the marketplace—competition between media leads to a premium upon accuracy. There is the restraint of the legal system —the threat of libel hangs over the press and leads editors to insist upon conscientious work in their reporters. There is the safeguard of occupational rivalry. Even within the same newspaper, reporters vie to gain reputations for reliability and sparkle. And there is the protection professional pride offers—journalists seek the respect of their colleagues, the recognition of professional organizations, and the self-respect that comes with doing quality work.

Despite these protections, journalism remains highly vulnerable to the dangers of both intention and attention. Some of these dangers, ironically, come from the same sources as the protections of journalism. The competitive spirit in journalism, for instance, is a spur to quality but also a call to cut corners. There are other dangers endemic to daily journalism, especially the fact that the reporter cannot wait until "all the data is in." Decisions must be made quickly. And journalism is vulnerable to its data in ways science rarely is. Stars do not talk back to astronomers nor guinea pigs to biologists nor, for the most part, human subjects to social scientists. The journalist, in contrast, has an ongoing relationship with sources and must play stories in ways that, short of lying, do not deeply offend. I. F. Stone was unique among Washington reporters in eschewing interviews with sources. He worked only from documents and, in that sense, is the only uncorrupted journalist in America. Most Washington reporters avoid documents whenever possible and seek the more accessible and dramatic, but entangling, information from sources.[26]

In journalism, there is also a danger that, as reporters gain greater independence from the partisan views of their publishers, they will turn increasingly dependent upon the partial views of their colleagues. The very professionalism that has increasingly provided journalists, especially at elite news institutions, some freedom from editorial supervision and some authority to interpret politics, has centralized political analysis in the hands of a relatively small group of reporters and columnists who see the world from much the same vantage. This leads to a familiar dilemma. From within the occupational group, professionalism is viewed as a great goal, and has been promoted from early on in the twentieth century as a liberation from publisher and editor. From the outside, professionalism in journalism may be seen as a conspiracy against the public.

Let me illustrate what this might mean in journalism. There was an incident in the 1980 presidential campaign that drew some attention. At a Kennedy rally in San Antonio, the Kennedy press corps arrived wearing big tourist sombreros. One reporter said, "My God, it was like bringing a watermelon into Harlem. And afterwards, two of them leaned up against

a wall and pulled their sombreros down to look like sleeping Mexicans."
Roger Simon of the *Chicago Sun-Times* commented:

> Candidates sometimes put on exotic hats, but only when they are
> presented with them as a sign of solidarity and support. The press
> did it as a goof, a lark, a joke. They did it because they have become
> a small world unto themselves and they don't care anymore about the
> world outside. The people in the crowds have become props to them,
> just furniture to fill up the hall while the candidate speaks. The people
> are outsiders and are not part of their tight, little world.

Simon concludes: "After traveling day after day on the road, it is easy for reporters to develop a certain disdain for politics. It is easier still to develop disdain for politicians. But when reporters start developing disdain for people,
maybe it is time for them to rethink what they became reporters for."[27]
  What Simon points to is a pathology of success, not failure. He is
writing not about an isolated reporter who takes to invention but about
the *shared attitudes* of some of the most successful journalists in the country,
shared views that may not reflect very much outside their own small world.
The critics of journalism, on one side, are those who attack the reporters
who do not live up to the mottos of objectivity, journalists who do not
tell the truth because they are intentionally partisan or consciously inventing. But a second set of critics looks precisely to the journalists who *do* live
up to the professional ideals. These critics ask not about the moral pluses
or minuses of individual reporters but about the moral climate in which
journalism itself exists. These critics would say that we have relatively little
to fear from the Janet Cookes of the world. Their inventions are a mere
scratch on the surface of public faith in the press. The deeper gouges have
been made by the Rupert Murdochs, who see their businesses exclusively
as public entertainments, not public services, and by the narrow conventions of the respectable press corps itself, which favor officials over dissidents
(except in reporting on communist countries) and reproduce the outlook of
a moderately liberal, procapitalist, pro–welfare state upper middle class.[28]
  While there is no defending what Janet Cooke did, publishers and
editors seemed all too eager to jump on the bandwagon and talk about how
wrong she was. They seemed too ready to turn the question of journalistic
ethics into one of individual morals. But hers was a petty fraud. The real
issues in journalism ethics are much larger. How can we have a responsible
journalism when the news media are intent primarily and sometimes ex-

clusively on making money, not providing service? How can we have a responsible journalism when our leading media professionals share a narrow conventionality of the liberal upper middle class? These are the elements of the moral climate of journalism today, and they are elements the media establishment has not shown great interest in discussing. Janet Cooke has been as much a smokescreen as a scandal.

The further problem with professionalism in the news media is that it asks journalists to stand outside politics as analytic or descriptive observers. The ability of American journalism to do this has been, in some respects, its glory. At the same time, it begins to undermine the passionate connection between journalism and politics that alone allows us to take journalism seriously as a profession. From the distance of cocktail parties and magazine columns, the neoconservatives harp at the liberal politics of the press corps. But social scientists who actually interview journalists find something more troubling—not that reporters are liberal but that they are astonishingly apolitical. David Halberstam's view of Ben Bradlee as being interested in politics for the sport of it corresponds to the findings of Herbert Gans and Stephen Hess that our leading journalists tend to be without political conviction, spurred on by a passion for the chase of politics, not for the quest.[29]

It may be, as Henry Fairlie has written, that politics is so central to the identity of the press that reporting on politics is not enough:

> The task of the political journalist—and of the newspapers or television companies which employ him—is to strengthen . . . the determination of the political world to assert itself. He may criticize an individual politician; he has no right to diminish the political function. He has no more right to do so than an art critic, in criticizing an individual artist, has the right to diminish the function of art, or a music critic, in criticizing an individual composer, has the right to diminish the function of music.[30]

I think it is important to assert, in an age of professionalism where professionalism too often becomes its own justification, that journalism is about politics. There is much else in journalism, but none of it matters without the political. Several years ago a Polish social scientist and member of Solidarity came to San Diego and gave a talk about events in her country. People in the audience were hushed because we felt in touch with something not wiser or better but more alive than ourselves in our daily lives. She was impassioned as she discussed the Polish situation and her hopes that a new day would be coming. A student, moved by the talk, asked her if there was anything he could do to help. She replied quickly, "Send paper."

Send paper, send the materials which allow political communication to take place. That is still the chief responsibility of the profession of journalism—to provide the materials that allow political communication to take place and to champion the cause of politics itself. That is not easy to do, especially in a culture with such ambivalence toward the state and toward political functions and functionaries. It is difficult to avoid falling into cynicism, on the one hand, or righteous self-importance, on the other. But it is the task that needs doing, if journalism is to be the profession, the calling, it can and should be.

NOTES

1. Benjamin Franklin, *Autobiography* (New York: New American Library, Signet Classic, 1961), p. 32.

2. Max Weber, "Politics as a Vocation," in *From Max Weber: Essays in Sociology*, ed. Hans Gerth and C. Wright Mills (New York, 1946), p. 96.

3. *New York Times*, 25 May 1981, and *Newsweek*, 4 May 1981.

4. The literature on the sociology of the professions is vast. For particularly insightful discussion of the sources of "honor" among professions, see Everett C. Hughes, "The Study of Occupations," in *Sociology Today*, ed. Robert K. Merton, Leonard Broom, and Leonard S. Cottrell (New York, 1959). For a review of the literature, see Michael Schudson, "A Discussion of Magali Sarfatti Larson's *The Rise of Professionalism*," *Theory and Society* 9 (1980): 215–29.

5. David Broder, "Political Reporters in Presidential Politics," in *Inside the System*, ed. Charles Peters and John Rothchild (New York, 1973), p. 23.

6. Quoted in Daniel P. Moynihan, *Coping* (New York, 1973), p. 185.

7. The following discussion of American newspaper history draws heavily on my book, *Discovering the News* (New York, 1978).

8. *Morning Courier and New-York Enquirer*, 16 September 1829. A few years later the *New York Herald* experimented with putting the main editorial and news columns on page 1. Editor James Gordon Bennett defended the practice as similar to the Paris press: "The most important part of a paper—its eyes, face, and features—is its editorial head—and why should not this head begin under the general head on the first page?" But the practice was abandoned. See the *Herald*, 9 February 1836.

9. On the practices of early Midwestern papers, see Franklin W. Scott, *Newspapers and Periodicals of Illinois 1814–1879* (Springfield, Ill., 1910), p. xxxiii.

10. New York *Evening Transcript*, 10 March 1834, quoted in Willard G. Bleyer, *Main Currents in the History of American Journalism* (Boston, 1927), p. 167.

11. On science in the Jacksonian era, see George Daniels, *Science in American Society: A Social History* (New York, 1971); George H. Daniels, "The Process of Professionalization in American Science: The Emergent Period, 1840–1860," *Isis* 58 (1967): 151–66, and Hyman Kuritz, "The Popularization of Science in Nineteenth-Century America," *History of Education Quarterly* 21 (Fall 1981): 259–74.

12. On law, see Alfred Z. Reed, *Training for the Public Profession of the Law* (New York: Carnegie Foundation for the Advancement of Teaching, Bulletin No. 15, 1921). On medicine, see Magali Sarfatti Larson, *The Rise of Professionalism* (Berkeley, Calif., 1977).

13. *New York Herald*, 21 November 1837.

14. A. Hyatt Mayor, *Prints and People* (New York, 1971), p. 640.

15. Robert Luce, *Writing for the Press* (Boston, 1891). There were earlier editions in 1886, 1888, and 1889.

16. Jack J. Roth, *World War I: A Turning Point in Modern History* (New York, 1967), p. 109.

17. Don Seitz, "The American Press: Self-Surrender," *Outlook*, 10 February 1926, p. 210. It was probably not quite so bad as Seitz feared. In a survey of Columbia School of Journalism's first ten years of graduates, 95 worked on newspapers, 37 in advertising and publicity, 25 on magazines, and 23 in positions outside journalism. See Ernest Gruening, "Can Journalism Be a Profession?" *Century* 108 (September, 1924), p. 702.

18. Erik Barnouw, *The Golden Web: A History of Broadcasting in the United States, vol. 2, 1933–1953* (New York, 1968), pp. 74–78, 135–37.

19. "The Press and the Public," *New Republic* 90 (17 March 1937): 188.

20. *New York Times*, 4 December 1924 and 5 December 1928. My italics.

21. Will Irwin, "The United Press," *Harper's Weekly*, 25 April 1914, p. 6.

22. See Curtis D. MacDougall, *Newsroom Problems and Policies* (New York, 1941), p. 193.

23. Ivy Lee, *Publicity* (New York, 1925), p. 38.

24. Walter Lippmann, *Liberty and the News* (New York, 1920), p. 67.

25. Alexander Bickel, *The Least Dangerous Branch* (Indianapolis, 1962).

26. On Washington journalists' distaste for written documents, see Stephen Hess, *The Washington Reporters* (Washington, D.C., 1981), p. 52.

27. *Chicago Sun-Times*, 2 May 1980.

28. See Herbert Gans, *Deciding What's News* (New York, 1979), pp. 39–69.

29. David Halberstam, *The Powers That Be* (New York, 1979), p. 531; Hess, *Washington Reporters*, pp. 78, 89, 115; Gans, *Deciding What's News*, p. 184.

30. Henry Fairlie, "Press Against Politics," *New Republic*, 13 November 1976, p. 14.

JOURNALISM: SUGGESTIONS FOR FURTHER READING

I. HISTORY OF JOURNALISM IN THE UNITED STATES

Some of the most interesting material is in original sources. See especially Benjamin Franklin, *Autobiography* and Lincoln Steffens, *Autobiography*. The most comprehensive surveys are Frank Luther Mott, *American Journalism*, and Edwin and Michael Emery, *The Press and America*. The most provocative treatment, focusing on the development of journalism as a profession, is Michael Schudson, *Discovering the News*.

Emery, Edwin, and Emery, Michael. *The Press and America*. Englewood Cliffs, N.J., 1984.

Franklin, Benjamin. *Autobiography*. (Many editions.)

Mott, Frank Luther. *American Journalism*. New York, 1962.

Schudson, Michael. *Discovering the News*. New York, 1978.

Steffens, Lincoln. *The Autobiography*. San Diego, Calif., 1968.

II. JOURNALISM IN THE UNITED STATES TODAY

Studies of journalism have flourished in the past ten years. Among the best are Todd Gitlin, *The Whole World Is Watching*, a study of media coverage of the New Left; Herbert Gans, *Deciding What's News*, a study of *Time*, *Newsweek*, and the national news; Leon Sigal, *Reporters and Officials*, a study of the *New York Times* and the *Washington Post*. An unusually good journalistic account of journalism is Timothy Crouse's study of journalists covering the 1972 presidential campaign, *The Boys on the Bus*. Also important is Bob Woodward and Carl Bernstein's own account of Watergate, *All the President's Men*. David Halberstam's *The Powers That Be* is seemingly endless, but it is a storehouse of information and anecdote on CBS, *Time*, the *Washington Post*, and the *Los Angeles Times*.

Crouse, Timothy. *The Boys on the Bus*. New York, 1973.

Gans, Herbert. *Deciding What's News*. New York, 1979.

Gitlin, Todd. *The Whole World Is Watching*. Berkeley, Calif., 1980.

Halberstam, David. *The Powers That Be*. New York, 1979.

Sigal, Leon. *Reporters and Officials*. Lexington, Mass., 1973.

Woodward, Bob, and Bernstein, Carl. *All the President's Men*. New York, 1974.

9. THE PROFESSION OF GOVERNMENT SERVICE

Don K. Price

Is government service a profession? Since I signed on to write this essay, I should not deny that it is. Since I have been for some years in a so-called professional school for the advanced education of those in government service, I am committed to defend the proposition that it is. And I am not alone; in the American university world, the fastest growing field of graduate education in the past decade may well be the field of public administration and public policy: the National Association of Schools of Public Affairs and Administration started about twenty years ago with about twenty members, and now has 185.

Yet I would have to express some reservations about the proposition, indeed to deny vigorously that government service can be—in a complete sense—a true profession, for two main reasons.

The first is that it cannot stake out an exclusive domain for itself as against rival professions, all of which muscle in on its territory. Service in government involves all the occupational skills and all of the professional specialties that exist in private life. A medical doctor in the largest hospital system in the country, the Veterans Administration, should conform to the same professional standards which apply in a private hospital. The engineer for a state highway system deals with the same professional problems as those of a private construction company. And the hundreds of thousands of attorneys in all levels of government probably think of their calling not as that of bureaucrats but as the ancient and honorable profession of the law.

The second reason is that it cannot meet one of the main tests by which a profession is defined. There are various erudite definitions of a profession, but they seem to me to include three main criteria. First, a pro-

163

fession deals with a definable body of organized knowledge, and to communicate that knowledge it adds to the proficiency acquired by practical experience some system of formal training. Second, it involves a moral commitment of service to the public that goes beyond the test of the market or the desire for personal profit. On these two tests, government qualifies as a profession.

But the third criterion is that the profession is recognized as deserving at least a measure of self-government, the right as a separate entity in society to regulate its own affairs and define its own standards. Here is the issue of political status that sets the field of public administration or public policy, as a career system, apart from the traditional established professions.

If we want to think about the professional status of government service, however, this difference gives us a clue to the definition of our field of interest. If those in the total range of government service cannot assert any right to become a partially self-governing profession, it is because much of their work comes more directly into contact, and potentially into conflict, with political authority.

This distinction gives me a basis for defining what I propose to discuss in this paper. There are lawyers and engineers and doctors in government who, by preference or formal assignment, are confined to their specific professional fields. They try to exclude from their scope of responsibility those issues—usually the issues involving value judgments of a general kind, or policy or political conflicts—which are not covered by their professional expertise. These are the issues that are involved in *general* administration. Some government officials are completely generalists: their training and range of duties deal mainly with these policy-ridden areas. And there are also many professional specialists who move into such areas, especially in the higher ranks of government service, and thus become general administrators as well as professional specialists—often without realizing that they have done so.

So for this discussion I propose to limit my view of the profession of government service to those concerned with general administration of public policy. And I would like to consider how the desirable qualities of a profession—the development of a useful body of knowledge, and the acceptance of a moral obligation to public service—have been or can be developed for those government employees whose work deals in whole or in part with issues that are deeply involved in policy or political conflicts.

This has been a slow development, for reasons that are deep in American history, and because of prejudices that applied to the traditional professions as well as to government service.

My grandfather began to practice law just a century ago in Rensselaer, Indiana. When he did so, and for a half-century longer, the formal status of the practice of law hardly conformed to our criteria of a profession. For the Constitution of Indiana until 1932 provided that "every person of good moral character, being a voter, shall be entitled to practice law in all courts of justice" (Article 7, Sec. 21). My other grandfather was admitted to the bar in Kentucky, also without a college education, because the county court — the elected commissioners — merely examined candidates for the bar in a brief oral ceremony. Such procedure conformed to the populist prejudices against relying on any standards other than the will of the people as expressed through popular elections.

The same attitude had held back the development of professional standards in medicine, for it was considered undemocratic to enforce any standards. In Massachusetts the Federalists supported those who wanted to license only those medical doctors with a proper medical education, naturally enough at Harvard. But Dr. Waterhouse, who made some of the most notable contributions of the era to medical practice (especially with respect to vaccination for smallpox) fought that proposal on principle. In a powerful pamphlet he charged Harvard with being "one of the most nefarious and powerful engines directed by the detestable aristocracy and destroying the vital principles of Republicanism"[1] — that word then meant Jeffersonian democracy — and warned that its concerns for medical standards disguised its hypocritical desire for monopoly.

If the government service had trouble establishing professional standards for its members, it was different only as a matter of degree from the traditional professions. From the Jacksonian period on through the nineteenth century, the dogmas of direct democracy made it difficult to enforce any government regulation or to maintain standards in any public institution. It is significant, I think, that in the nineteenth century, as the nations of the Western world became more egalitarian in their politics by successive revolutions, they all except the United States became more centralized in their administrative institutions. America alone decentralized: the states and local governments undertook to elect by popular vote a great number of administrative officers, and the federal government by the spoils system equally destroyed any cohesion of policy or standards of quality among its executive agencies. Even more significant, the typical legislative body — including the Congress — broke itself down in specialized committees, with little regard for party doctrine but a great interest in party spoils, and concentrated its legislative attention not on policy issues, but on the detailed control of expenditures, of personnel actions, and of the organization structure by which patronage could be distributed.

It is hard to avoid the use of twentieth-century academic concepts and terminology which assume that from the beginning what we now call the spoils system was immoral in intent, as it came to be in effect. But at the outset it had its origins in something like a religious faith, derived from the early objections of New England Puritans—even while they still supported established Congregational churches—to anything like an episcopal or hierarchical establishment. The Puritans' commitment to an educated clergy was abandoned by the early nineteenth-century revivalistic churches that rescued the states west of the Appalachians from their frontier godlessness. It was the denominations that took literally the doctrine of the priesthood of all believers, and required no educational qualifications of their ministers, who converted most of those in the region that was to produce Jackson and Clay, Zachary Taylor and Abraham Lincoln. And it was the same doctrine transferred to the public service which affirmed that the performance of public duties was so simple a matter that it required no special qualifications and that rotation in office was the essential basis of democratic politics.

I must not suggest that the political patterns derived from the theology of the more evangelistic denominations were alone responsible for the democratic politics of nineteenth-century America. DeTocqueville came to the United States in the 1830s and gave the dissenting religious sects credit for America's dislike of political authority. But he went on to observe that the arrival of large numbers of Irish Catholics, in spite of their dedication to a quite different theory regarding ecclesiastical establishments, had only strengthened the general sentiments against hierarchical authority in politics; the Irish Catholics, he said, were "the most republican and the most democratic class of citizens which exists in the United States,"[2] because as a minority they knew that the rights of other minorities had to be respected in order to safeguard their own. I would add that on the basis of ancestral experience they were as suspicious as any Yankee Puritan of the English establishment and its political authority.

However idealistic the early conceptions of a pure democracy may have been, their effects in practical application were disastrous. To let the electorate select all minor officers did not make for greater popular control; it only made it possible for political machines to exercise irresponsible power through patronage. The system was morally wrong and ineffective, and its reform came about partly as a moral campaign, and partly by the pressure of scientific and technical and professional groups. These two approaches overlapped in time a great deal, but we may well describe them separately and in turn, because they had rather different effects on the professional status of government service.

THE MORAL APPROACH TO PROFESSIONALIZATION

First came the moral reform movement, which was supported by such organizations as the National Civil Service Reform League and derided by party regulars as the "snivel service" movement. It was hardly interested at all in the professional quality of the civil service but was primarily concerned with rescuing the electoral process from corruption by patronage. It therefore put most of its emphasis on rescuing from partisan spoils the greater number of jobs, which meant those at the lower levels—the less professional levels—of the hierarchy, and these reformers were willing to do so even by legalistic means that reduced the efficiency of the executive process. The key step was the Civil Service Act of 1883, which created the quasi-independent Civil Service Commission as a check on executive discretion as well as legislative patronage.

That act was ostensibly taken as an imitation of the British civil service reform, but with respect to its effect on the professionalization of the civil service it could hardly have been more different in its approach. The British reforms started with the top ranks and worked downward: the generalist administrators in the top ranks were the officer class. The system required that they be recruited at the age of leaving universities, on the basis of examinations related purely to their academic studies, and that the top jobs be reserved for them in order to encourage their development as a corporate establishment within the govenment. The American act wanted reform in a negative sense, to eliminate partisan patronage, but it was based on the same moralistic opposition to a professional approach that had been responsible for the spoils system. It required that every job be open to anyone from outside the service at any age, which made impossible any system of career development; and it required that tests for entry be based purely on the ability to perform the practical duties of the job in question, which discouraged any system of education either for the more general aspects of government service or for lifetime careers in it. Later the system of personnel classification had the same effect: it treated government service not as a coherent profession, but as a collection of miscellaneous jobs each of which could be filled by the test of the marketplace.

In one other way the general approach of the reform movement failed to encourage a sense of professional purpose within the government service. Its moralism was mainly negative; it identified morality, as New England Puritans had always been inclined to do, with a dislike for spending money. Later, as Yankees became richer in business, "economy and efficiency" became the slogan for governmental reform. This general approach became identified, in a more sophisticated form, with a doctrine that undertook to defend the professionalization of the career government service by setting limitations on its purposes, so as to reassure political leaders that their power would not be preempted. This was the doctrine of the distinction between policy and administration. In oversimplified terms, Woodrow Wilson, in his influential essay on "The Study of Administration" in 1887, was understood to argue that the field of policy decisions was to be reserved to the elected politician, while the job of carrying out those decisions efficiently was the sole duty of the career administrator. Actually, Wilson said nothing of the kind: he said instead that the first job of administration was to help decide what could properly and successfully be done, and the second was to do it efficiently. But a new generation of political scientists, led by Frank Goodnow of Columbia, made the distinction between policy and administration a fashionable one, and at Chicago some years later Leonard D. White, who wrote the first and most influential textbook on public administration, made it the basis of his approach toward professionalizing the government service.

White defended the distinction by the precedent of the British Civil Service. But here too I believe that Americans were misled by the British example. British administrators are elaborately deferential to political superiors, but they operate behind a veil of confidentiality that disguises their profound influence on policy. Indeed, as official statements by their professional society affirm, they are mainly interested in the formulation of policy, and hardly at all in management.

White's doctrine, however, was for a generation predominant in academic circles, and did much to influence the development of the early schools of public administration, which set the tone for the evolution of the profession of government service, especially in local government. The most influential part of this movement was the growth of the city manager profession. Woodrow Wilson had helped found the National Short Ballot

Association, which undertook to persuade local governments that they should elect not administrative officers, but only members of city councils or commissions. That movement, in later alliance with the National Municipal League, pushed the spread of the city manager form of government, which through the period between the two world wars did a great deal to build up the idea of government service as a respectable profession.

As it did so, it acquired or created two types of allies that are needed by any profession: schools for professional training, and societies of practitioners.

The professional schools were set up, usually on the initiative of professors of political science, who were challenged by the hope that the municipalities of their area might be rescued by this new profession from the dismal state that Lincoln Steffens had described in *The Shame of the Cities*. State universities like Texas and Michigan and Kansas, and private universities like Syracuse and Southern California, took the lead in this movement; and wherever their programs were effective the spread of the new form of municipal government was most conspicuous. Whether the university programs were the cause or the effect is hard to judge, but the result of the combination was to provide a new sense of professional self-respect within the municipalities, and a new source of trained personnel.

Public officials, like other groups in American society, had always had associations for their recreation and mutual comfort, but most had been the occasion for nothing more serious than annual sprees, sometimes at public expense. The city managers, with academic help, started something different. Professor John Stutz at the University of Kansas helped create in 1922 the permanent secretariat of what became the International City Managers Association. A few years later it moved its headquarters to the neighborhood of the University of Chicago, and with the help of small grants from the Spelman Fund of New York (an offshoot of Rockefeller philanthropy) a group of other associations of public officials were induced to move there into a common headquarters building. The national organizations of governors, mayors, finance officers, personnel officers, and others in the fields of planning, housing, taxation, and welfare, were brought together and encouraged to add a dimension of substantial professional research and publication to their programs.

These associations, it should be noted, included those fields that were most clearly engaged in what I have been calling general administration — the fields in which the practitioners were most directly involved in relation to general political issues, and under conditions of political accountability, cutting across specific functional fields or programs. (The distinction was not a rigorous one: governors and mayors were certainly not professionals by any definition, and housing and welfare officers were not complete generalists.) But the group did not include powerful groups of government officers in the more traditional professions that were restricted to specific programs: public health officers, or highway engineers, or those in the various scientific fields related to agriculture.

The associations were entirely independent of each other and controlled by their membership, but the most effective leaders in bringing them together were Charles E. Merriam, the political scientist who had founded the Social Science Research Council and was an influential advisor to the Rockefeller philanthropies, and Louis Brownlow, a former city manager who was to become President Roosevelt's pricipal adviser on issues of government organization and management. Between them, they had a clear concept of the purposes and limitations of professionalism in the government service. They were, somewhat grudgingly, allies of the government reform groups—of the National Municipal League and even of the various taxpayers' associations—but they were convinced that a more positive professional approach, led by public officials themselves, was even more necessary to improve the government service.

Such a positive approach, however, could not be extended to include our third criterion of a profession—the right of self-government. This came up in connection with the issues of the procedure by which various occupational groups try to convert themselves into something more like professions: the procedure of accreditation. As we have noted earlier, the development of the traditional professions met with considerable resistance in America from populist prejudices. In England, the medical and legal professions were conceded the right to govern themselves and to control the process of admission to their ranks. Generally in the United States, this was considered improper: it is the state that at least in legal form licenses doctors and lawyers to practice. Actually, of course, the professional groups themselves acquire substantial control over the procedures and the conduct of the examinations, or administer various means of accreditation that influence entry into the guild.

From the beginning, however, the city managers were clear that they could not control entry into their profession: its fundamental theory held that they were to be appointed by the elected city councils and serve at their pleasure. While they put a great deal of effort into defining the educational and other qualifications that they thought should be considered by appointing authorities, they held back from trying to exclude any duly appointed city managers for lack of prescribed qualifications. The kind of accreditation that has been found useful in many specialized fields of government service, including not only the older traditional professions but various fields of education and social work, was renounced on principle. And this precedent was followed by some of the city managers' sister societies, which operated in equally close relationship with political authority.

The desire for a professional society for all generalists in government service, cutting across all functional fields and all levels of government, finally led in 1939 to the creation of the American Society for Public Administration, in which Brownlow, the Director of the Public Administration Clearing House in Chicago, took the lead by discreet offers of small grants from philanthropic funds. Leonard White became the editor of the society's journal, the *Public Administration Review*. The society started operating almost as a subsidiary of the American Political Science Association, but soon began to run its annual meetings at separate times and in separate places, to put greater emphasis on practitioners rather than professors in its membership, and later to spawn two sister organizations that helped provide a professional base for the generalist in government service. One was the National Association of Schools of Public Affairs and Administration, which became a forum for the discussion of professional education in the field (which was growing more and more independent of the political science discipline, and reaching into others that seemed relevant to governmental problems). The second was the National Academy of Public Administration, which undertook to become a society with membership restricted to those who had made some distinguished contribution to the profession and could help contribute to the process of advising governments at high levels on their broadest problems.

One important issue of principle continued to be unresolved, and to plague the movement toward professionalism. This was the issue whether career officers should consider that their professional duty was to be neutral on issues of policy, and to concentrate on the efficient and economical execution of policies determined by their political superiors. On this, Brownlow and White, for all their mutual respect and cordial cooperation, differed fundamentally. As a city manager, Brownlow had assumed that even though his political superiors had the final authority, supported by the right to fire him at a moment's notice, it was his job—always without taking any part in electoral politics—to help think up and to advocate desirable new programs that were in the public interest. That was the doctrine that he and his fellow members of the President's Committee on Administrative Management embodied in their report to FDR, however discreetly and with due emphasis on the subordination of career officers to political authority.

White, however, held to the doctrine of neutrality in matters of policy. As late as the second Hoover Commission, in 1955, he and his colleagues on the Commission's Personnel Task Force defended that principle in their report, which was otherwise by far the best product, and the most sympathetic to the professionalization of the government service, of any part of the output of either of the two Hoover Commissions.

So much for the contribution of the moral reform approach—in later years the efficiency and economy approach—to the government service as a profession. It was a substantial contribution: it produced a great many dedicated and competent public officials, through education in a number of professional schools and political science departments, who served with distinction in local and state governments, and who during the New Deal and the second world war provided a great many recruits to the federal service. But the fields in which they served tended to be in those "tools of management" that were general to government agencies but did not bear directly on the substantive content of their major policies or their fundamental purposes. They accordingly tended to wind up as budget or personnel officers, or staff members in organization and managerial procedures. In these lines of work they were invaluable, but on crucial policy issues they tended to take second place to lawyers or to scientific and professional specialists. Which brings us to the second approach to government reform, namely, the scientific approach.

THE SCIENTIFIC APPROACH TO PROFESSIONALIZATION

The Civil Service Act of 1883 was enacted at a time when private businesses were managed by their owners, who would have scorned the notion that such management was a profession that could be taught in universities. Members of Congress would have been equally scornful of the idea that the general administration of a department was different enough from politics that their deserving partisans could not qualify for appointment. As the president and the department heads tried slowly over the decades to extend the merit system, it was impossible while complying with the Civil Service Act to prescribe tests for appointment or promotion for general administrators.

On the other hand, everyone recognized that the marine hospitals needed medical doctors, the Corps of Engineers needed civilians who could build dams and bridges, the state experiment stations needed agronomists, and every agency needed lawyers—and these skills, in the language of the statute, were directly related to the duties to be performed and, moreover, required some advanced education. The result was that the federal agencies as they grew in size found that the employees they were incorporating into a merit system of appointment, and taking away from party patronage, were disproportionately in scientific and professional fields. The outcome is that today something like two-thirds of the upper grades of the federal civil service—those that constitute the recently created Senior Executive Service —have come up in rank after an education in some scientific or professional field and experience in some program to which they were appointed on such specialized criteria. The contrast with most other major democracies is a striking one. The top ranks of the British civil service, for example, in spite of some recent efforts to include more scientific talent, are still dominated by those with an education in the humanistic disciplines; and the scientists and professionals are in categories of less influence, with little or no direct access to those in political authority.

In the federal government—and to varying extents at other levels—the government service became more professional more rapidly and extensively by the work of those in the other professions, especially in law and in various scientific fields, than by those who were interested purely in general administration as the basis for professional development. The habit of legislative committees in America (quite unlike those in Britain and even Canada) to insist on discussing policy directly with civil servants added to the status of those whose credibility as government officers was enhanced by some special expertise. With respect to their influence on the major issues of the day, the budget or personnel officer trained in a school of public administration did not carry the weight of an engineer from MIT or Cal Tech, or an agronomist from Iowa State, or a forester from Yale, or a lawyer from Columbia or Harvard.

The difference came in part from the superior prestige in American society of the professions over government service in general, and in part from the fact that in most professions an officer of some stature had ample opportunities for employment outside the government, and hence could afford to throw his or her weight around on controversial issues more freely than could one whose only marketable skill was restricted to public employment.

But it also came from the fact that the scientific professions, and even more the legal profession, had never been taught as a matter of professional ethics that they should abstain from taking public stands on policy issues. Their purposes were good: why should they not explain them to the voters whose support was needed? A county agent or a superintendent of schools or a highway builder was respected by politicians for affirming the value of his or her program. Legislatures, and especially the Congress, did not feel threatened by debates over policy; they controlled the substance of government not by parliamentary debates on policy, but by manipulating in committees the details of appropriations, and personnel ceilings, and patterns of organization. The generalist administrators, trained in the older-type schools of public administration, were therefore at least as likely to get into political hot water, for all their renunciation of policy advocacy, as were the scientific professionals who undertook to defend their programs' purposes. One may well reflect that if the traditional British civil servant gets away with the pretense of being neutral on policy, it is only because members of the House of Commons are neutral (or ignorant) on issues of administration and organization.

The structure and procedures of the American government service, or, if you like, its professional ethic, thus reflected what had become the popular political philosophy—a Jeffersonian belief in the possibility of permanent progress, based on the cultivation of the sciences and their practical application. This attitude was strong enough in the 1930s, but became immeasurably stronger after the Second World War. In that war, a decisive influence on the outcome was provided by the mobilization of the sciences for the development both of weapons and of the techniques and tactics by which they were used: radar, guided missiles, and the atomic bomb, but also the calculation by operations research and systems analysis of the procedures and patterns of organization for the use of new weapons, and the consideration by medical and psychological study of the way in which the human organism could control or adjust itself to its new tools.

In all of this business there was no separation between policy and administration. The traditional military doctrine had been that the general officers—generalists—should lay out the strategic and tactical doctrine, and define the "requirements" for weapons development, which the specialists would then undertake to meet. But as a British scientist remarked, invention is the mother of necessity: if scientists create weapons that the military could not have imagined, they have a decisive impact on high strategy.

The result was a fundamental change in the relation of government to science. Government was persuaded to accept the responsibility for the financial support of science, including even the social sciences. More significant for the professional role of the government service, the role of staff work in the development of policy—especially the kind of staff work that made use of the new statistical and mathematical techniques of systems analysis and economics—came to be more appreciated by politicians as well as by administrators. The older approach had assumed that new policies were produced by intuition in the minds of political leaders, embodied in party platforms, and enacted in statutes. The newer and more realistic assumption was that policies grew incrementally out of specific decisions, and that both the specific decisions and the general plans required complex and continuing staff work, commanding the new skills of the analytic sciences, as a basis for the ultimate decisions by elected politicians.

There was some fanciful fear that these new developments would lead to the creation of a science-based bureaucracy that would impose a tight ideological control on policy and political choice. Could the objective study by scientists of political issues lead to clear, unbiased answers that would constrain free political choice? In view of the Marxist effort to develop the sciences into a political ideology, the fear might not have seemed utterly fanciful. But it was not realistic in the United States. This was of course partly for fundamental philosophical reasons: an exact science must be too abstract to deal with the complex substance of a policy issue; while Marxist ideology may be in dictatorial control in some countries, it is not through the work of real scientists. But in the United States the major reason was institutional, and related to the way in which we think about the profession of government service.

The great invention of the Office of Scientific Research and Development during the Second World War was in the institutional system by which it worked. The OSRD controlled the allocation of funds, but the work was done through contracts with private institutions. This pattern was then imitated after the war by all the major new programs, from atomic energy and space exploration to Medicare, transportation, and urban renewal. As a result, something less than a tenth of all federal expenditures are now directly administered by federal civil servants. In the programs I just mentioned, the work of government is done by Union Carbide and Boeing, by Prudential Life and Amtrak and so on. Are their officers a part of the profession of government service?

The new system has been run with very little direct party patronage—at least in individual appointments—and in that way may be taken to justify the scientific approach to professional reform of the government service. Moreover, it has vastly increased the provision of scientific resources to the identification of policy issues, and the calculation of the best ways to deal with them, and thus it has begun to strengthen the weak research base of professional education in this field. In universities, the older schools of public administration, most of which were dedicated to the ethos of efficiency and economy, and to neutrality on policy issues, are rapidly taking up the teaching of systems analysis, applied economics, and other tools for the solution of public problems. They have joined with some of the newer schools to found new professional societies (notably the Association for the Public Policy and Management), emphasizing the study of policy analysis, and have developed new professional journals for the dissemination of their professional approach.

In these developments, the universities were generally not out ahead of governmental practice. The earlier seedbeds of the new professional approach were the research and analysis corporations, private institutions some of which were started by federal funds, such as the Rand Corporation and the Urban Institute. As their influence over policy became apparent, they were imitated by privately supported institutions that sought policy influence for one political end or another. So we have the paradox that the scientific approach to policy has led not to a unified doctrine, but to competition among dozens of institutions and associations, from Ralph Nader's Center for Responsive Law to the American Enterprise Institute for Public Policy Research, and from the Institute for Contemporary Studies founded by Caspar Weinberger and Ed Meese to the swarm of associations of scientists seeking to suppress nuclear weapons. The variety of competing scientific approaches to policy is almost as great as that of competing churches and religious sects in American society.

The competition in the use of the sciences (including the social sciences) for the development of policy extends within the government itself. The executive office of the president includes economic advisers, scientific advisers, and various specialist staffs. Congress now has a Budget Office to check on the president's economics, and an Office of Technology Assessment to check on the president's scientists, to say nothing of its use of the General Accounting Office that checks on everything. Altogether, Congress now operates on a billion dollar budget and has a staff of about 30,000 personnel. In addition it makes statutory arrangements with outside agencies for scientific advice: in the past decade it has employed the National Academy of Sciences to conduct more than thirty major studies on important policy issues, as independent checks on the executive. And the availability of funds for other policy studies, by contract with executive agencies, has vastly multiplied the number of consulting firms—more than a thousand were counted a few years ago in the field of ecology and the environment.

The scientific approach to the reform of the government service was more realistic than the earlier moral reform approach in its realization that the duty of the profession was to help in the formulation and development of policy as well as in carrying it out efficiently. This is what we might call the vertical dimension of professional responsibility: the ethical obligation of the professional in relation to political superiors. There is also a horizontal dimension of responsibility, and on this dimension too the scientific approach was superior. That is the dimension of the relation of an officer in one function or department to those in others. The moral or efficiency approach assumed that the key principle of government organization was the removal of overlapping and duplication among departments as the way of saving money. But modern science and technology scrambled the substance of government programs irretrievably: the protection of the environment from acid rain was in conflict with the expansion of industrial production, and the subsidy of highway construction destroyed the patterns of housing and race relations in our central cities—to say nothing of the conflict between our alliances for military security and our affirmation of civil rights throughout the world.

On the horizontal dimension of responsibility—the need to develop a coherent government-wide policy, reconciling the purposes of the competing departments—the scientific approach has been far more effective than the moral approach to professional responsibility in identifying the issues and measuring their comparative costs or risks against their benefits. It is by no means clear that it has been more successful in producing a system of genuine professional responsibility, or in achieving coherence and consistency in our public policy. It typically approaches a problem by treating it as an individual case and calculating its costs and its benefits. But theoretical calculations of the right answer may be less than half the battle, especially when several dozen competing calculators, working for different clients on different assumptions, are producing the figures on the bottom line. Rather more effective might be the development of a professional staff cutting across the competing departments, with some incentive to develop a common loyalty to a government-wide policy, and with a commitment to agree on assumptions before undertaking the systematic analysis.

In our present political situation, this may be a hopeless dream, although the enactment in 1978 of the Civil Service Reform Act, creating the new Senior Executive Service, was an effort in that direction. If it is to be made to work, we shall probably have to back up, so to speak, and try to put a new foundation under the splendid intellectual superstructure of the systems analysts and their scientific approach to public policy. That foundation needs to be what the old schools of public administration were trying, occasionally with some success, to help create: a pattern of government organization that would look beyond the efficient solution of individual problem cases, and make possible a comprehensive system of responsibility and a long-term career system for the general administrators. Professional responsibility—in both dimensions—depends not only on their intellectual competence in scientific analysis, but on their loyalty and motivation. Loyalty and motivation are hard to develop in our present riotous competition among the varieties of professionals who live on government money, but with little sense of obligation to a general public interest, and little appreciation of the need for an organizational pattern that clarifies the lines of authority and encourages the free flow of relevant information across the boundaries of specialized bureaus.

The scientific approach to the profession of government, by its encouragement of the system of "federalism by contract," has helped to confuse the source of the political pressure to spend government money. The "tax eaters" are no longer mainly the civil servants; the contracting out of government programs has produced powerful lobbies in private institutions for appropriations for the programs that they administer—which was of course one of the motives for creating the contracting system. As David Stockman remarked, "There is no such thing as a fiscal conservative when it comes to his district or his subcommittee";[3] and the contractors work in almost every congressional district.

The old efficiency approach of public administration assumed a clear distinction between the public and private realms, and thus gave general administrators an incentive for expanding the federal budget. The new system developed by the scientific approach has mixed the public and private realms together. It is indeed the duty of the professional generalist in government to help the elected politicians carry out their policies. For a political leader bent on saving money, it will be difficult to appreciate that the savings to be effected by efficient management are trivial, and the big savings must come in cutting out functions that compete with each other and cancel each other out. This calls for a higher government service that is professional in the sense of dedication to a lifetime career, immune to the temptation to look for the next job in corporations that are being subsidized or regulated, and still scientific in the ability to detect and analyze the ways in which programs interact with each other and in the long run produce unintended and undesirable secondary effects.

A recent director of the Office of Personnel Management has reproved the members of the career service for being tempted into the realms of policy as well as efficient administration. This, he argued, was against the principle stated so clearly by Max Weber: "The honor of the civil servant . . . is to execute conscientiously the order of the superior authorities."[4] One may sympathize with Mr. Devine's dislike for the tendency of romantic bureaucrats to push their own program regardless of political discipline, and still believe that the political problems of America today are not the same as those of Prussian bureaucrats in 1918. There is no question that civil servants must obey an order, nor (in my opinion) that they should stay out of electoral politics. But that does not mean staying out of policy. A concern for good administration requires a concern for the content of policies. Indeed, political authority needs the support of a career system of professional generalists if it is to enforce its policies and protect a system of true constitutional responsibility. Toward that end, we evidently in America still have a lot to learn.

NOTES

1. Joseph F. Kett, *American Medical Profession: The Role of Institutions, 1780–1860* (New Haven, Conn., 1968), p. 76.
2. Alexis de Tocqueville, *Democracy in America*, pt. 1, chap. 17.
3. *New York Times*, 9 September 1981, p. A28.
4. *Public Administration Times*, vol. 4, no. 9, 1 May 1981, p. 4.

GOVERNMENT SERVICE:
SUGGESTIONS FOR FURTHER READING

Aronson, Sidney H. *Status and Kinship in the Higher Civil Service*. Cambridge, Mass., 1964.
Better Government Personnel. Report of the Commission of Inquiry on Public Service Personnel. New York, 1935.

Dale, H.E. *The Higher Civil Service of Great Britain*. Oxford, 1941.

Fulton Committee of Inquiry into the Service, 1966–68, *Report of the Committee*, CMND 3638, June 1968, Her Majesty's Stationery Office.

Kellner, Peter, and Lord Crowther-Hunt. *The Civil Servants, An Inquiry into Britain's Ruling Class*. London, 1980.

Krislov, Samuel. *Representative Bureaucracy*. Englewood Cliffs, N.J., 1974.

Lynn, Laurence E., Jr. *Managing the Public's Business: The Job of the Government Executive*. New York, 1981.

Macmahon, Arthur W., and Millett, John D. *Federal Administrators*. New York, 1939.

Mosher, Frederick C. *Democracy and the Public Service*. New York, 1968.

Mosher, Frederick C., ed. *American Public Administration: Past, Present, Future*. University, Ala., 1975.

Reeves, Floyd W., and David, Paul T. *Personnel Administration in the Federal Service*. Washington, D.C., 1937.

Sayre, Wallace S., ed. *The Federal Government Service*. 2nd ed. American Assembly (Sixth). Englewood Cliffs, N.J., 1965.

Stahl, O. Glenn. *Public Personnel Administration*. 7th ed. New York, 1976.

Stanley, David T. *The Higher Civil Service*. Washington, D.C., 1964.

Task Force Report on Personnel and Civil Service. Commission on Organization of the Executive Branch of the Government. Washington, D.C., 1955.

Van Riper, Paul P. *History of the United States Civil Service*. Westport, Conn., 1958.

White, Leonard D. *The Republican Era: 1869–1901, A Study in Administrative History*. New York, 1958.

10. PSYCHOLOGY AND COUNSELING: CONVERGENCE INTO A PROFESSION

John C. Burnham

In the Dear Abby or Ann Landers columns of contemporary newspapers, problems appear frequently that are too difficult for Abby and Ann to solve in two column inches or less. In these cases the afflicted correspondent receives advice according to a standard formula: someone needs counseling. Usually exactly who is to do the counseling—physician, psychologist, minister, or personnel of schools or social agencies—is left up to the consumer of the services. But it does not matter, for in our times the term *psychologist* or *counselor*, meaning a person who furnishes psychological counseling or treatment, can, at least in the lay mind, apply to any of the lot. Nor are laypersons misled, for the psychologist or counselor in fact presents a new professional role, which Henry, Sims, and Spray have referred to as "the fifth profession."[1]

My assignment is to describe briefly how this new professional identity evolved. In order to do that, I shall trace four different streams—psychiatry/neurology, pastoral counseling, social work, and psychology—in order to show how all but the medical element coalesced into one generalized professional identity shortly after the middle of the twentieth century.

PSYCHIATRISTS AND NEUROLOGISTS

From the middle of the nineteenth century on, two specialty groups in medicine, psychiatrists and neurologists, worked with the mentally ill and other patients whose symptoms originated in the nervous system. Psychiatrists at first cared for large numbers of the mentally ill in huge, castlelike asylums located in the isolated, rural settings. Neurologists existed only in large urban centers, and their practice included office or home treatment of the "nervous," or what later would be called outpatient practice. The "nervous" were neurotic patients, too ill to function fully in life but not so ill as to be hospitalized. Both neurologists and psychiatrists served the important social function of alienist—a person who testified in court whether or not one was alienated from oneself, that is, was legally incompetent.

The distinctive aspect of the psychiatrists and neurologists in our narrative is that they were physicians. Fortunately, Professor Numbers has already discussed in this volume implications of membership in the medical profession, even as it existed in the nineteenth century. I need only to point out one special aspect of the M.D.'s in that period. An important segment of medical leaders embodied the cutting edge of the movement to secularize society: they represented, in their own eyes, science, and as such they wanted to advise everyone how to live according to the findings of science. In the case of physicians dealing with nervous and mental diseases, the urge to direct their fellow humans in the correct way to live was especially strong. In order to do so, they sensed that they had to replace the usual dispensers of advice and guidance, the clergy. As D. A. Gorton, one of these early mental hygienists of the medical profession, stated explicitly in 1873, "The custom of centuries has wrongfully confided exclusively to the profession of theology" the giving of advice on how to behave.[2] It was, as will become apparent soon, this social function that the later psychologist/counselor sought to inherit.

The role of physicians as secular priests was not entirely of their own making. The public came to expect it. In nineteenth-century American novels, for example, the physician typically appeared not so much as a technician as a friend and counselor, even when in the book representing "science." And this counseling role was doubly distilled for the wise man who could be a so-called alienist.

In the twentieth century two important developments greatly expanded the role of physician as counselor. The first was the coming of psychotherapy, which arrived in the United States suddenly, about 1905. Building upon the hypnotism that had been used in the 1890s, psychotherapy involved procedures such as persuasion, suggestion, and psychoanalysis. These new treatment modalities were a boon to that class of deeply troubled patients, the "nervous," who often came to be known in the Victorian age as "nervous invalids." Psychotherapy was also a boon to their physicians. The success of the new procedures showed that one person—the physician—could deeply influence the course of the life of another human being—the patient. After ages of medical impotence in the face of most nervous and mental diseases, physicians found psychotherapy an exciting innovation.

The second change in the twentieth century was the development of the outpatient specialists. The neurologists were already, of course, carrying office practices. But the psychiatrists, who started out with severely ill patients, also began treating less severely disturbed outpatients. At first various hospitals (especially in urban areas) opened outpatient clinics for ambulatory patients, and then psychiatrists established their own private practices. By 1930 half of the members of the American Psychiatric Association were in outpatient practice. They, along with the neurologists who had not gone into neurosurgery, constituted the model for the familiar cartoon figure, the psychiatrist, often identified by his technical equipment, not the stethoscope but the couch. To a large extent he or she provided the social model for the psychologist and counselor.

At this point our narrative leaves the physicians except for one dramatic event. During World War II physicians and service personnel in general discovered that psychiatrists and especially psychoanalysts provided both the rationale and the therapy that actually worked in myriads of cases of baffling disorders then called battle fatigue. This discovery on the part of both M.D.'s and other uniformed personnel gave a sudden impetus to a demand for outpatient psychiatric and counseling services, a demand that is still flourishing in American society.

Two observations are in order before the physicians leave our concerns. First, it did not take long after 1905 for others to figure out that people who were not M.D.'s could perform psychotherapy, and, indeed, even before World War I, one enterprising psychoanalyst in New York was training lay assistants to extend the benefits of the new method. In fact much of our narrative now will grow out of this insight that psychotherapy, if carried out with correct technique, or sometimes just plain enthusiasm, is effective whether or not the therapist holds a medical degree. The second observation is that the role of the psychiatrist in American society became distinctive: instead of being called upon to cure illnesses, he or she came to function as a person who could solve problems, usually personal problems but sometimes social problems. It is perhaps needless to add that a solver of problems need not be an M.D., either.

PASTORAL COUNSELORS

Theology, one of the original professions, gave rise to one of the streams that converged into the fifth profession. Christianity had a long tradition of healing and even specifically a tradition of the cure of souls, souls that represented the essence, unity, and responsibility of the person but which were not at peace with God, nature, and themselves. During the nineteenth century, many pious workers, under the influence of the new criticism, came to associate Christian healing with a literal belief in miracles, and as time went on this type of belief increasingly became unpopular among educated classes. But with psychotherapy, in the twentieth century, many of the clergy saw a way to continue the healing tradition and at the same time to be eminently "scientific" in the secular sense (as opposed to the then very important "Christian Science" sense).

The first major application came in the Emmanuel movement, named for the church in Boston where it originated in 1906, just as psychotherapy was stirring physicians. Elwood Worcester, the church rector, had started work with a group of tubercular patients and soon saw that in the tradition of Jesus he and his colleagues could bring a healing ministry to those who were unhappy and in need because of nervous and psychological problems.

Worcester and the other Emmanuel workers, it should be noted, were inspired by modernism in religion. They believed that Christians should work to bring the Kingdom of God into human society, and they tended to be optimistic about their fellow humans, to believe that souls could be healed. "The Emmanuel Movement," wrote a Brooklyn adherent, "knows nothing about and cares less for either original sin, or any other such theoretical redemption." (The therapeutic value of prayer he did not consider "theoretical.")[3] The Emmanuel movement died out within two decades but touched directly all of the alter leaders of pastoral psychology.

Modern pastoral counseling had origins not only in healing but in dissatisfaction with the ineffectiveness of the ordinary clergy. In the 1920s, seminary instructors, inspired by the popular psychology fad of the day, turned to psychotherapy as a model for ministers. The specific cases of counseling used as examples helped show students exactly what spiritual shepherds could do for parishioners. They were not so much curing or guiding, like the old evangelicals and preachers, however, as sustaining people who were damaged or broken by life. Such was the way that a number of crucial leaders, such as Seward Hiltner of Chicago, were conceptualizing their endeavors in the 1930s and 1940s. Only after World War II, however, did the movement become of major importance in the history of religion.

During the war, significant for religion as well as medicine, military chaplains found that they needed training such as clinicians had in order to cope with the personal and family problems the chaplains were called upon to deal with. As in medicine, this wartime experience transformed the field. Before the war, only one-tenth of the seminaries had qualified psychological faculty; by midcentury the proportion was three-quarters. Some of the pastoral counselors, as the new breed were labeled, became out-and-out Freudians; by the 1950s, however, Carl Rogers's client-centered therapy, for which technique was described clearly in the literature, dominated the field of pastoral counseling.

Shortly after World War II, then, pastoral counseling became recognized as a well-established subdiscipline, with two journals and substantial financing—financing that came particularly from sponsors who favored both modern psychology and the saving auspices of religion. There were also appropriate organizations, and beginning in 1944 professionals in the field held a series of national conferences that climaxed in 1967 in the formation of the Association for Clinical Pastoral Education.

Pastoral counseling flowered in America in spite of religious change. The new conservative theology that became fashionable in midcentury, neo-orthodoxy, involved a pessimistic view of humanity, but proponents found primitive drives and a saving ego, as taught in dynamic psychiatry, compatible with beliefs about the human potential of evil and at the same time useful in helping people seek beyond the self for a stabilizing faith. The sustaining—and hopefully reconciling—role of the clergy was no longer aimed at modernist social salvation but, in a conservative ethos, at the individual. Where pastoral psychology had once been almost exclusively a Protestant phenomenon, increasing numbers of Roman Catholics joined the ranks of Christian therapists.

By the late twentieth century pastoral counselors felt that they were reclaiming from secular psychologists and physicians the true function of the clergy: to remove neurotic barriers that kept people from accepting themselves and God alike. In the process they did do secular healing, and increasingly they tended to practice in clinics or elsewhere apart from the actual ministry of individual churches. They were, in short, becoming part of the fifth profession.

SOCIAL WORKERS

At the beginning of the twentieth century few people indeed would have expected that the settlement house workers and the "friendly visitors" to the poor, the ancestors, so to speak, of modern social workers, would have contributed to the fifth profession. Typically the early charity workers were volunteers concerned with uplifting people who were dependent, delinquent, and physically or mentally disabled. After the 1880s charity workers were defined by their association with the many charity organizations that sprang up in the great cities and gave a national identity to the work. The organizations also created a basis for the emergence of a social work profession by creating full-time, paid positions. Since the workers were in effect affiliated through the various charity groups, all that was needed for professional ordination was a set of special skills and institutions in which the skills were taught to new workers. In-service training began in the late nineteenth century in Boston. In 1898 the New York School of Philanthropy opened. Eventually schools of social work sprang up not only in connection with operating agencies but at colleges and universities (such as Smith College in 1918). The exact skills to be imparted were supplied by a series of gifted leaders who pointed out particularly that trained charity workers' classification of clients' needs was a prerequisite for effective philanthropic action. For decades, the struggle for public recognition as a profession was only partially successful. Social workers nevertheless tried to act in ways that professionals would.

Throughout the twentieth century social workers could direct their energies in three different directions: into social reform (particularly important in the Progressive and other reform eras), into administration of services, and into case work. The stream that led to counseling was the casework stream, and workers in it shared the belief of the reformers that without knowledge of cause no improvement was possible. Particularly in case work did social workers try to attain professional objectivity with which to apply their training to clients. Amos Warner, in the 1930 edition of his famous book *American Charities*, observed that "while the quiet, objective social worker of today may not be so spectacular as the enthusiastic reformer of a generation ago, there is good reason to believe that he is doing a much more effective job."[4]

The case worker from the beginning had to deal with the individual client. Dependency had long been ascribed to character, classified by a worker in 1907 as "(1) inefficiency, (2) improvidence, (3) immorality, (4) stupidity,

(5) intemperance, (6) shiftlessness, (7) ignorance."[5] But with the publication of Mary Richmond's *Social Diagnosis* in 1917, a new approach to the individual case crystallized: the client had social problems, and the goal of the social worker was to help the client adjust or adapt to his or her personal social environment; the focus was now emphatically on individuals or, at most, on families, and especially within a social environment.

In part the casework emphasis grew out of two types of social work new in the twentieth century, medical social work and psychiatric social work, and one not so new, school social work. Medical and psychiatric social work started formally about 1906 and derived from physicians' convictions that patients could be treated only within a social context; it did no good for a physician to advise a workman barely supporting six children that he needed a three-month cruise in order to recover from his illness. Psychiatric social work developed particularly from the work of William Healy and others with delinquent children, work in which each case appeared to be unique in the combination of factors that caused social maladjustment. School social workers were influenced by similar conditions and ideas to concentrate on the individual child in an individual social setting. In all three instances the social workers retained their identities and did not view themselves, for example, as nurses or teachers.

Under the influence of colleagues who practiced with M.D.'s, social workers saw the advantage of high professional status and used the physicians as professional models. Ida Cannon, a pioneer of medical social work, declared in 1917 that she wanted social workers "to share with the skilled men of the medical profession the great responsibility that social medicine is now placing upon us all."[6]

As the decades passed, psychiatry more and more influenced medicine with the idea that all physicians should be solvers of problems and should cure laziness and misbehavior with prescriptions or treatments; in so far as this tendency characterized medicine, physicians were indeed appropriate professional models for social case workers. Moreover, other events and circumstances affected social work. During World War I Red Cross workers assigned to service personnel made a favorable impression with their family social work. Then later the generally rising levels of affluence in the United States stimulated social workers' interest in social maladjustments other than economic poverty, particularly those in the areas of health and education, areas in which by midcentury the best-trained social workers were concentrated (as opposed to those in welfare agencies). There were still "system changers" as well as "people helpers" among social workers, but the latter, now with professional identification as social workers, had become an important segment in the counseling personnel of American society.[7] They continued to operate within the general field of social work, which began to take on its present contours in 1955 when a number of social work organizations representing special functions and ad hoc services to the profession merged into the National Association of Social Workers.

In the modern configuration, the exact arena within which social work counseling took place varied. Within a few years of the founding of NASW, the organization recognized private practice as a legitimate field, established standards for it, and finally, in 1967, issued a *Private Practice Handbook*. At the same time the national group continued to maintain that social work counseling should occur primarily within "socially sponsored organization structures."[8] Throughout the 1960s and 1970s the number of social workers doing counseling in private practice as well as in institutional settings increased greatly. When demand for psychotherapists greatly outstripped supply, social workers filled the role in both independent and institutional settings. By the mid-1970s as many as ten thousand social workers were doing counseling either part-time or full-time in private practice, and they were successfully collecting payment from health insurance agencies—one of the most important badges of professional status.

CLINICAL PSYCHOLOGISTS

The group around which the various streams of counseling converged was the clinical psychologists. Unlike members of any other practicing profession, clinical psychologists had their origins in an academic discipline, experimental psychology. Having started with one kind of professional status, that of academic, they subsequently developed another.

The evolution from discipline to profession, as Donald Napoli points out, followed the appearance of applied psychology, which was very much, as the psychologists at first intended, like the application of any science. In the last decades of the nineteenth century experimental psychology had developed as a new academic discipline, distinct from philosophy and physiology. The discipline flourished in American universities, where by the 1900s psychology tended to take on national emphasis, namely, the study of human development and adaptation to the environment; and Americans therefore contributed especially to the fields of child development and individual differences. Many pioneer American psychologists were very ambitious for psychology, and they believed—at first only rather vaguely—that their science could be helpful in a variety of areas of life: education, organizational management, and manipulation of masses of people. Early in the new century the psychotherapy movement helped confirm the belief of psychologists, too, in the potential of using psychological forces to predict and control human behavior. In 1923 pioneer clinical psychologist Shepard I. Franz wrote that "the rapidly growing appreciation of the value of psychological facts and principles in directing individuals who are poorly adjusted to their environments has opened up many lines of psychological research and practice."[9]

At first the applied psychologists of all kinds concentrated on individual differences. The mental tests (of which the IQ test is the best known example) came to constitute applied psychologist's most widely used and effective tool. The first significant sign of a new professionalism, then, was the claim of some psychologists that they and only they were qualified to administer the so-called mental tests.

Meantime the term *clinical psychology* had been introduced effectively by Lightner Witmer, who founded a psychological clinic, as he called it, at the University of Pennsylvania in 1896. He addressed particularly problems of school children, checking their perceptual and cognitive processes and recommending for each individual such correctives as eyeglasses or special educational procedures. Simultaneously other psychologists urged that the newly formed American Psychological Association, an academic group, standardize tests that were then available so that psychologists could better assess just what mental and perceptual abilities and disabilities a person had. Already by that time (1895) they could identify tests for two dozen separate areas such as memory, color vision, perception of time, will power, and rapidity of movement. Then a decade later the graded intelligence test came in, and within another few years the IQ was established as part of the general American vocabulary.

Applied psychology, then, in the early twentieth century consisted primarily of aiding educators and business executives and sometimes physicians in assessing any particular person to decide the best way to educate or treat or use the person; only occasionally did the person himself/herself seek out the services of a psychologist. During World War I the extensive use of psychologists in the armed services gave a dramatic impetus to the use of mental tests, again particularly in both education and industry. Success was so considerable that in the 1920s a substantial number of quack psychologists appeared against whom trained psychologists tried to protect the public, but with little success, since psychologists had no official and legal social recognition enforced by sanctions.

Meantime a new dimension appeared with the full development of the so-called personality test, with which the psychologists attempted, with growing sophistication, to chart the life patterns of each individual. Under the influence, often, of psychoanalytic psychology, psychologists even devised tests to elicit life patterns that were hidden from the person himself or herself, and practitioners therefore sometimes took on an uncanny aura. It was against this background that events of World War II in effect created an important new profession, for beginning in 1941 the armed services, far more than in World War I, utilized psychological knowledge and personnel to the extent that both numbers and status of psychologists were greatly enhanced.

There was one background factor of crucial importance. In the 1920s and 1930s many psychologists had seen the implications of the development of psychotherapy, especially psychoanalysis, and in fact a few psychologists had already undertaken to learn and practice psychotherapy exclusively. After all, the founder of a dominant variety of psychotherapy, Sigmund Freud, himself encouraged the training of nonmedical "lay analysts" in Europe (although the M.D. was generally still necessary for recognition as a psychoanalyst in the United States). But the practice of psychotherapy by psychologists was not of great moment until wartime needs pressed many into practice. Mostly, before then, clinical psychology meant testing and diagnosis, and direct competition between psychiatrists and psychologist therapists was so irrelevant to clinical psychologists that only in the hard times of the Great Depression of the 1930s did the clinicians begin to organize effectively. At that time and for some years it appeared that clinical psychologists—those doing testing (chiefly in the schools), diagnostic work, and sometimes psychotherapy—would break away from the academic psychologists and form a separate professional organization that would include all applied and not just clinical psychologists. But during and after World War II the American Psychological Association reabsorbed the clinicians and the others, and the academics successfully kept the clinical training programs within psychology departments in the universities.

The World War II experience that created so much demand for psychotherapy had two major effects on psychology. First, as I have suggested, psychologists willy-nilly won the right to perform psychotherapy in the armed forces, and this shifted the emphasis in clinical psychology from diagnosis to therapy. As early as 1945 a survey showed that clinical psychologists were spending an average of 25 percent of their time doing psychotherapy. And as psychotherapy rose into national prominence in that period, psychologists such as Carl Rogers at the University of Chicago and Albert Ellis in private practice in New York contributed major types of psychotherapy, utilized widely by many types of therapists—M.D. and Ph.D. alike, as well as the pastoral counselors I have already mentioned.

The second major wartime development was in organization. As the conflict ended, an alert group of academic psychologists saw their opportunity and seized it by teaming up Veterans Administration and other training grants with the university clinical psychology graduate programs. Where once the Ph.D. in psychology consigned the holder to institutional and, frequently, teaching employment, now it often led to private or hospital practice. In the years following, other kinds of applied psychologists and academic psychologists diminished proportionately to only a fraction of those in clinical pursuits, thus completely reversing the earlier relationship between the two groups. The American Psychological Association, as many traditionalists lamented, became more and more a profesional rather than a scientific organization.

At many points the M.D.'s, especially the psychiatrists, objected that clinical psychologists were practicing medicine without a license and at least ought to give therapy only under the supervision of a licensed physician. The psychologists, who of course were particularly well trained in psychological diagnostic testing, replied that their knowledge and skills were in many ways better than those of M.D.'s, which was true, for even psychiatrists were generally not as expert as psychologists in interpreting Rorschach tests, for example, or distinguishing cognitive functions. The physicians continued to fight tenaciously against recognition of psychologist therapists, but the doctors' cause appeared hopeless, if for no other reason than that studies over several decades confirmed that even very well educated people could not or would not distinguish between the M.D. psychiatrist and the non-M.D. psychologist. When both performed skilled psychotherapy, what, indeed, was the point of a distinction? For the psychologist, of course, what was most important was that not only government agencies but third-party payers in health insurance recognized the psychologists' professional status. The ultimate in professional recognition for psychologists, however, came in 1972 when American television confirmed the role of the psychologist psychotherapist in a popular series, "The Bob Newhart Show."

Meantime, again shortly after World War II, another group, the counseling psychologists, had split off from the clinical psychologists. The clinicians came more and more to be identified with diagnosing and treating the abnormal; beginning particularly in the early 1950s counseling psychologists distinguished their area of practice as normal people, clients who needed psychological measurement, vocational guidance, and advice about normal development and adjustment. Counseling psychologists utilized insights and techniques from psychotherapy as well as more traditional psychological tests and techniques, but they were not primarily concerned with mental illnesses. An early official statement (1956) described the subspecialty goals in general terms as:

(a) the development of an individual's inner life through concern with his motivations and emotions,

(b) the individual's achievement of harmony with his environment through helping him to develop the resources that he must bring to this task (e.g., by assisting him to make effective use of appropriate community resources), and,

(c) the influencing of society to recognize individual differences and to encourage the fullest development of all persons within it.[10]

Although there were special training, certification, and other professional identifications for counseling psychologists, again the general public did not make distinctions between one kind of psychologist and another.

CONFLUENCE AND TRANSFORMATION

By the time Bob Newhart was conjured up to answer the referrals from Abby and Ann Landers, the various streams of nonmedical counselors and psychologists were in confluence (and I have not mentioned yet another stream, psychiatric nurses in private practice). The actual functioning of the various streams was not distinguishable from the functioning of many M.D.'s, although physicians practiced under very different social and professional auspices. Because the nonmedical practitioners shared with each other professional goals and provided services that appeared to outsiders to be identical, the generic psychologists and counselors tended to converge; and, as I shall suggest, their confluence was validated by the appearance of a new kind of training program and a new graduate degree, the doctorate of psychology. Only in institutional settings, where, for example, social workers and psychologists worked side by side under physicians, did the relationship to the M.D. dominate so as to underline the separateness of the paramedical personnel. In private practice such bureaucratic considerations became irrelevant.

The origins of the new relationship go back to the team concept originated by a physician, William Healy, whom I have already mentioned. Healy in 1909 set out to discover why children in juvenile courts in Chicago had gone astray. He studied physical causes and had the help of a psychologist for mental diagnosis. He also sometimes utilized case workers from social agencies with which the child had been involved. By the early 1920s his psychiatric case conference was becoming standard practice in institutions everywhere in the United States. The psychologists, the social worker, the nurse, various medical specialists, and anyone else who had studied the case sat around a table and on an equal and professional basis discussed the patient's case and as a team recommended treatment strategies. In 1935 a parody on "Men of Harlech" showed the new relationship. After solos by the Social Worker, Pediatrician, Psychologist, Recreation Worker, and Psychiatrist, all joined in this harmonious chorus:

> Thus we pool each contribution,
> Synthesize a true solution,
> Engineer a revolution
> Of Personality.[11]

This model was absorbed into the whole mental hygiene movement into which both medical and nonmedical professionals were drawn. The M.D.'s often protested over the years that they were supposed to be in charge and/or do the therapy, but in the end, as I have suggested, the claims of the "lay" professionals persisted.

Conflict showed up most clearly in the area of licensure. For decades after World War II psychologists attempted with varying degrees of success to obtain official and final professional recognition, namely, licensing by the state, with exclusive rights to practice within the area of competence. M.D.'s consistently opposed licensure for psychologists as an infringement of the medical monopoly. And the conflict extended even to certification, as physician groups at times opposed state-sponsored certification as a step toward licensure. Within medicine itself, to this day specialists are merely certified by specialty boards and on that basis recognized by government agencies and third-party payers, but those specialists are not licensed as such—the only license held is the general one of an M.D. Like the medical specialists, psychologists and counselors sought certification of one kind or another from the 1920s on so as to bolster their claims to competence and just compensation. One of the major significances of the professional organizations of social workers, pastoral counselors, and psychologists alike, therefore, was the implicit certification that membership conferred. Or professional organizations could set up independent certifying machinery, as the American Psychological Association in 1946 set up the American Board of Examiners in Professional Psychology, in close imitation of the medical specialty boards. The other important type of certification has always been training, and establishing proper educational programs was long a concern among psychologists, clergy, and social workers.

But the truth was that the public paid little attention to the kind of diploma or certificate that hung on the wall of the counselor or therapist. With the post–World War II explosion in demand for their services, precise training or background in the long run was largely irrelevant, even, in the late 1960s and 1970s, going to the point that some people with very little training at all claimed the right to offer counseling and psychotherapy. At that point sociologists such as Harold Wilensky could talk about "the professionalization of everyone," suggesting more precisely that bureaucratic and client control of a therapeutic situation subverted traditional professional functioning in which the client purchased the very freedom of the professional to use his or her skills.[12]

It was the logic of the convergence of the psychological professions in their actual practice, plus the need for maintaining professional standards, that led people to talk of a new training program and a new degree to recognize the fifth profession. As early as 1954 the famous psychoanalyst, Lawrence S. Kubie, proposed establishing a new doctorate of medical psychology that combined psychology and medicine but left out much somatic medicine and academic experimental psychology. Nothing came of such suggestions, however, until 1968–70. In those years the University of Illinois began a Psy.D. program, and the independent California School of Psychology was founded to award the doctorate in professional psychology. The California School was the most significant, for it was independent, and soon there were East Coast and other imitators. By the 1980s officials of the California School estimated that they were furnishing one-fifth of the new psychological practitioners produced nationally each year for what appeared to be an insatiable demand of Americans for guidance, therapy, and sustaining. Graduates of CSPP in fact functioned in social agencies, in schools, under religious sponsorship, in hospitals, and in private practice. Such new degree programs were of course successful only because others had already set up machinery for the recognition of professional status in various areas.

THE SOCIAL FUNCTION OF THE PSYCHOLOGIST/COUNSELOR

Let me conclude by briefly discussing two of the social forces that pushed the generic "psychologist" to an almost omniprofessional eminence after the mid-twentieth century.

The first was the rise of the so-called bureaucratic or organizational society, in which industrial age Americans in all of their social roles more and more became part of bureaucratic organizations in industry, charity, and other parts of the private sector and private life as well as government. I am referring of course to the familiar cog-in-the-machine phenomenon. The implicit strategy of managers in bureaucracies was to keep the system functioning by dealing with each person on a case-by-case basis so that his or her personal problems would not disrupt the functioning of the system. Thus institutions tended to respond to needs or wants, not on the basis of general social change, but rather on the basis of how each person could be cured, satisfied, or adapted to the system. Very early in the twentieth century psychotherapy began to provide a model whereby a professional could deal with individual "maladjusted" people in the direction of helping them "adjust." The development of a casework emphasis in social work was a dramatic application of this model, and in a slightly more subtle form pastoral counseling was not far behind.

Beginning especially in the 1920s, and culminating in the 1970s, this general cultural emphasis on the individual evolved into an extreme emphasis on the self, in what Christopher Lasch later referred to as "the culture of narcissism."[13] One of the aspects of narcissism was concern about "the real me" and the relationship of this self to immediate surroundings—at the expense of concern with institutions and values. Much of the popularity of psychology and counseling derived from this intense American concern with the maladjusted self, alienation, and personal feelings—for all of which the appropriate professional to deal with problems on a one-to-one basis, or as leader of a group of mutually helpful selves, was the generic psychologist. This popular concern with self also showed up in the holistic health movement in which physical functioning per se was often considered strictly secondary to a subjectively happy, integrated self. In fact, a significant segment of the professional psychologists of the 1970s and after explicitly connected themselves to the holistic health movement.

A very large proportion of psychologists and counselors had always considered themselves humane and liberal and were actually highly ethical, conscientious, and socially concerned. They were therefore bewildered and hurt when in the late 1960s radicals began denigrating them and their work as tools of the establishment and the system, typical band-aid cover-up for the failures of society. While psychotherapy and counseling that were centered on the self in a bureaucratic system could serve conservative purposes, other valid perspectives existed. Most of the members of the fifth profession instead viewed their function in the progressive tradition in which an initially paternalistic figure helped a person develop independence and self-respect regardless of environmental impingements. They—and many other Americans—hoped that society was affluent enough that everyone with problems could have professional help (the profession not stipulated) with significant cumulative effects. In 1971 a set of textbook authors confidently summarized by declaring flatly, "Professional workers are problem solvers."[14]

Psychologists and counselors could in fact draw on their antecedents and see their functioning as one that partook of the traditional minister, social worker, and healer as well as applied scientist. In times of fragmentation and crisis they seemed to be able to resolve and combine science and humanism for many people. Psychologists and counselors could themselves provide models of ego strength and love that everyone agreed made a better society. The continued growth of numbers of members of the fifth profession and their usefulness suggested that most Americans of the 1980s, like Dear Abby and Ann Landers, tended to consider psychologists a necessary and decent element in a world full of crumbling institutions and evaporating values.

NOTES

1. William E. Henry, John H. Sims, and S. Lee Spray, *The Fifth Profession: Becoming a Psychotherapist* (San Francisco, 1971). These authors viewed the new profession as a fifth in addition to psychiatry, psychoanalysis, social work, and psychology; it will soon become clear that I use the idea but in a broader context of professions.

2. D. A. Gorton, quoted in Barbara Sicherman, "The Paradox of Prudence: Mental Health in the Gilded Age," *Journal of American History* 42 (1976): 891.

3. Robert MacDonald, quoted in Raymond J. Cunningham, "The Emmanuel Movement: A Variety of American Religious Experience," *American Quarterly* 14 (1962): 60.

4. Amos Warner, quoted in James Leiby, *A History of Social Welfare and Social Work in the United States* (New York, 1978), p. 182.

5. This summary of W. H. McClain's material is taken from Virginia P. Robinson, *A Changing Psychology in Social Case Work* (Chapel Hill, N.C., 1930), p. 12.

6. Ida Cannon, quoted in Roy Lubove, *The Professional Altruist: The Emergence of Social Work as a Career, 1880–1930* (Cambridge, Mass., 1965), p. 33.

7. Katherine A. Kendall, "Signals from an Illustrious Past," *Social Casework* 68 (1977): 328–36.

8. Paul Kurzman, "Private Practice as a Social Work Function," *Social Work* 21 (1976): 366.

9. Shepard I. Franz, "Clinical Psychology," *Science* 57 (1923): 430.

10. "Counseling Psychology as a Specialty," *American Psychologists* 11 (1956): 183.

11. R. L. Jenkins, quoted in John C. Burnham, "The Struggle Between Physicians and Paramedical Personnel in American Psychiatry, 1917–41," *Journal of the History of Medicine* 29 (1974): 98.

12. Harold L. Wilensky, "The Professionalization of Everyone?" *American Journal of Sociology* 70 (1964): 137–58.

13. Christopher Lasch, *The Culture of Narcissism: American Life in an Age of Diminishing Expectations* (New York, 1979).

14. Arthur W. Combs, Donald L. Avila, and William W. Purkey, *Helping Relationships: Basic Concepts for the Helping Professions* (Boston, 1972), p. 3.

PSYCHOLOGY: SUGGESTIONS FOR FURTHER READING

Aubrey, Roger F. "Historical Development of Guidance and Counseling and Implications for the Future." *Personnel and Guidance Journal* 55 (1977): 288–95.

Burham, John C. "The New Psychology: From Narcissism to Social Control." In *Change and Continuity in Twentieth-Century America: The 1920s*, ed. John Braeman, Robert H. Bremner, and David Brody, pp. 351–98. Columbus, Ohio, 1968.

Goode, William J. "Encroachment, Charlatanism, and the Emerging Profession: Psychology, Sociology, and Medicine." *American Sociological Review* 25 (1960): 902–14.

Henry, William E., Sims, John H., and Spray, S. Lee. *The Fifth Profession: Becoming a Psychotherapist*. San Francisco, 1971.

Holifield, E. Brooks. *A History of Pastoral Care in America: From Salvation to Self-Realization*. Nashville, Tenn., 1983.

Kemp, Charles F. *Physicians of the Soul: A History of Pastoral Counseling*. New York, 1947.

Lasch, Christopher. *The Culture of Narcissism: American Life in an Age of Diminishing Expectations*. New York, 1979.

Leiby, James. *A History of Social Welfare and Social Work in the United States*. New York, 1978.

Levenstein, Sidney. *Private Practice in Social Casework: A Profession's Changing Pattern*. New York, 1964.

Levine, Murray, and Levine, Adeline. *A Social History of Helping Services: Clinic, Court, School, and Community*. New York, 1970.

Lubove, Roy. *The Professional Altruist: The Emergence of Social Work as a Career*. Cambridge, Mass., 1965.

Napoli, Donald S. *Architects of Adjustment: The History of the Psychological Profession in the United States*. Port Washington, N.Y., 1981.

Reisman, John M. *A History of Clinical Psychology*. 2nd ed. New York, 1976.

Thorton, Edward E. *Professional Education for the Ministry: A History of Clinical Pastoral Education*. Nashville, 1970.

11. THE PROFESSION OF MANAGE- MENT IN THE UNITED STATES

Harold C. Livesay

Twenty years ago, in a burst of nationalistic naiveté, I might have called this paper "Management, the *American* Profession." Twenty years ago American business straddled the capitalist world, basking in the glow of global envy. Its magic—"professional management"—unraveled the mysteries of running a profitable business, transmuting them to a set of equations, some more complex than others, a few as yet unsolved. It seemed only a matter of time, however, until the profession and its pundits conjured up case studies and computer programs, creating an "off-the-shelf" (they created jargon too, of course) sorcery for the corner grocery or the global enterprise.

No problem stymied this American science. No challenge could long resist its overwhelming logic and flow of ideas, machines, and wealth it generated. Poverty, hunger, cold, underdevelopment, the "Communist menace," dread disease, the quality of life, "blue-collar blues," "rape of the environment," population explosion? Just management problems, all of these, and if the answer had not yet appeared, just wait, and watch the pages of the *Harvard Business Review*. From Ford, IBM, Xerox, and Boeing the missionaries carried the gospel hither and yon, and how the heathen did marvel. Flocks of pilgrims sought this miracle at its source, and twenty years ago half of the Harvard Business School students were respectful Japanese, manicured Germans, and—miracle of miracles—an occasional grudging admirer from England or France. Foreign journalists warned of "the American challenge"[1] that might reduce the world's enterprises to a set of American subsidiaries. Under the onslaught of English, the language of American managers (and they would learn no other), French relinquished its traditional place as the international *lingua franca* and receded toward parochial oblivion, like Albanian or Portuguese.

The flood tide of American management's success swept its historians from their perch of objectivity. The histories they wrote, and to a remarkable extent still write, reflect the outlook of the profession they chronicle: doing business in America and then in the world presented a series of challenges and American management solved them, developing itself into a profession along the way. Myriad case studies and biographies of business leaders fused into "institutional history" that documented the emergence of the institutions—big business, big government, big labor—that housed American professional management and sent it forth to civilize the world. Although the great architects (white males, every last one of them) who created these massive structures—the Andrew Carnegies, the Henry Fords, the Pierre Duponts, the Alfred Sloans—captured historians' imaginations now and then, with the passage of time the history of management focused increasingly on the history of institutions and their behavior, most particularly on the bureaucracies they embodied. Thus historians reinforced the illusion that such institutions exist within but apart from the society that surrounds them, influencing the people but uninfluenced by them, exerting control but too powerful to be controlled, a view that paradoxically surfaces in American management's most admiring apologists as well as its most caustic critics. For all one can tell from their histories, the General Motors system could have developed as well in Dakar as in Detroit and the IBM mindset could have flourished as well on the banks of the River Lena in Siberia as it did on the shores of the Susquehanna in Endicott, New York.[2]

In such an intellectual climate, the history of management became a subset of the history of institutional behavior patterns. The managers themselves, stripped of individuality by the omnipotence of the agencies they serve, emerge as human blanks, once identified by their grey flannel uniforms, now marked by styled hair, health club memberships, and obligatory ownership of a blow dryer. Here, too, friends and foes coalesce, for the same qualities that typify the ideal manager to some characterize the robotized capitalist to others.

Rank nonsense, much of this. Those of us who propounded it have gotten a rude comeuppance in the last twenty years.[3] The Japanese have performed the function once discharged by the slave who rose on the Roman conqueror's chariot, tempering the euphoria of the triumph by whispering in his master's ear, "All glory is fleeting." Slave, where were you when we needed you? Why did you let us write all those success stories? One by one the citadels of American professional management have crumbled, and some have fallen. The Pennsylvania Railroad, once admired as the most perfectly managed enterprise on earth, was bred to its lifelong rival, the New York Central, producing a monstrosity that survived only as a ward of the taxpayer. U.S. Steel, built on the foundation of Andrew Carnegie's hyper-efficient empire, cannot compete in its own backyard with producers located ten thousand miles away. The automobile industry, long an unassailable bastion of American managers' skills, slides on down the razor blade of corporate life. Indeed, survival of the American automobile industry seems to depend on learning to build American cars that blend European body design with Japanese engine technology. American managers still swarm abroad, but they have as much to learn as to teach. The management systems now most admired and emulated developed, not in Cambridge, or Detroit, or Palo Alto, but in exotic places such as Zama, Yokohama, and Nagoya. American academics, as enterprising a group of entrepreneurs as any we have left, have developed a whole industry that translates Japanese methods into forms compatible with the American milieu.[4]

The point of all this is not to write an obituary for the American economy, nor to denounce American professional management, but to argue that much of the history of the management profession needs rewriting, and perhaps to excuse in advance the inadequate discussion that follows here. Stripped of the oversimplification that success seemed to allow, the development of American management reveals a history as complex as that of any other social phenomenon. Indeed, the first lesson of failure may be one that every historian should have known all along: the profession of management is a social (or cultural, if you prefer) phenomenon, not an economic one.[5] The paths to understanding its development lead outside the neat, well-defined perimeter of business, government, and labor institutions into the broader reaches of history that grapple with the development of the American character. It is not enough to understand the role of cost accounting in tuning production to the fluctuations of the market. We have to understand as many aspects as we can of the society that produced the individuals who used these methods. This involves such issues as the American obsession with individuality and the struggle to preserve it in the face of ever-increasing need for group cooperation and the emergence of larger institutions. We need to understand the American definition of social mobility, and comprehend what defined *status* and how it took over the role played by *class* in Europe. We must grapple with the history of American education and the values inculcated; we must consider traditional American biases: racism, sexism, veneration of youth, and repugnance for age. These are only a few examples, and beyond these daunting but relatively well-charted regions lies a trackless wilderness that may have played even more important parts. Who, for example, could spend five minutes in any American institution and not sense the overwhelming behavior force exerted by American concepts of sexuality, male and female?

American society generally has confounded explanation or manipulation by simplistic theory, and the history of professional management in America, as a subset of the history of the larger society, proves no exception. Indeed, professional managers now and in the past reflect the gorgeous and befuddling complexity that is and was America. The validity of that proposition soon emerges when one confronts the first task involved in an essay like this one—identifying the set of people to be discussed. Tackling this chore soon reveals management as the quintessentially American profession, for no encompassing generalization specifies much about the population it identifies. Managers, it seems, are those who hold managerial positions; that is, they supervise others. Beyond that, definition leads to a string of heavily qualified statements: most managers now work for others, but many are self-employed; most are male, but the number of exceptions grows daily; most are white, but fewer all the time; many are Anglo-Saxon Protestant, but most are not; many went to college, but unless one excludes foremen, the overwhelming majority did not; some who went to college studied management, but most did not; a few belong to the American Management Association, but far more belong to the American Automobile Association; some read professional journals, but most do not; a majority work for private enterprise, but a growing minority do not.

All of these people, presuming they get paid for what they do, think of themselves as professional managers. The term *profession of management*, however, implies something quite different from an abstracted summary of the tasks hired managers perform. Management as a profession emerged only in the twentieth century after some business schools and some managers concluded that management was an art that existed independently of specific business situations. Masters of this skill could transfer their talents as readily from one firm to another as pianists could move from one piano to the next. The present-day profession of management consists of those employees who occupy bureaucratic supervisory positions requiring training in no specific discipline other than the discipline of management itself. This population includes increasing numbers of people formally trained in management, holding bachelor's, master's, or doctoral degrees, as well as executives trained in applied fields, who absorbed the principles of professional management while on the job. In theory this definition includes some civil servants and a few trade union officials. In practice, however, the guild consists almost entirely of business executives who regard the others as camp followers or poor relations at best.[6]

Management thus differs from most other professions, which consist of people trained specifically and exclusively in medicine, law, dentistry, or engineering. Its sloppy definition (and I can do no better) excludes, in addition to government and trade union officials, most proprietors and partners, as well as most executives of small and medium-sized businesses (and thus most of the managers in the most dynamic sector of the economy). It does encompass, however, more than the army of business-school-trained grey flannel suit stereotypes who swarm through the halls of corporate America, for it includes thousands of managers who do not have WASP pedigrees, did not go to Ivy League Schools, and hold degrees not in management, but in engineering, physics, law, computer science, or chemistry, as well the increasing cadre of managers rising from the shop floor as American business learns its Japanese lessons. The Jewish lawyer who heads Dupont, the salesman son of Italian immigrants brought in to resuscitate Chrysler, and the up-from-the-blue-collar-ranks president of Delta Airlines exemplify such exceptions.

Heterogeneity, in fact, characterized American management long before it anointed itself as a profession. At times certain types of people and methods dominated, but by the time their supremacy became self-evident, their heyday had passed; their guiding principles, developed to solve problems in the past, had become blueprints for imminent failure; and the future could most accurately have been discerned among the mavericks, the misfits, and the dissenting minority.

The present seems no different. In energy, for example, big business and its professional management have given us Three Mile Island, while using its profits, not to search for better energy sources, but to buy Montgomery Ward. For imagination, initiative, and a hint of the future one has to look to innovators like Dan Ben-Shmuel, an Irish immigrant blacksmith turned metal sculptor turned inventor, who developed a gadget that recovers heat and pollutants from power house smokestacks, or to Michael Zinn, product of a vocational high school, whose hostility to nuclear energy led him to perfect a plastic solar collector that unrolls like a garden hose and can be installed by any reasonably handy person around the house.

Ben-Shmuel, Zinn, and hundreds like them keep small and mid-sized firms the most dynamic sector of the American economy in terms of technological innovation and job formation. Between 1953 and 1973, for example, more than half of all major innovations came from firms smaller than one thousand employees. These firms also made a far more effective use of research and development dollars than their giant counterparts—by a factor of four to one compared to firms with one thousand to ten thousand employees, and by an astonishing twenty-four to one over firms with more than ten thousand employees. Between 1969 and 1976, firms with fewer than twenty employees created 69 percent of all net new jobs; companies with fewer than five hundred employees contributed 87 percent. Recent investigations suggest that these figures have risen, not fallen, since the 1970s. Such firms, however, generally disdain professional managers.[7]

Ben-Shmuel, Zinn, and their colleagues, moreover, turn out, on close inspection, to belong to the category of *entrepreneurs*, in the sense that Joseph Schumpeter defined it; that is, they are innovators who find new products or new ways to manufacture or merchandise existing products. These innovators, Schumpeter argued, supplied the dynamic force that drove capitalism forward. Ironically, as we might see it, or dialectically, as Schumpeter argued, these entrepreneurs' very success inevitably sounded the death knell of capitalism, for it led to the creation of bureaucratic management structures that ultimately extinguished innovation, leading to capitalism's senility and, eventually, to its transmogrification into some species of socialism.[8]

Until the late 1960s or early 1970s, one could argue that American businesses had proven Schumpeter wrong by achieving what he thought impossible, the bureaucratization of entrepreneurial energy. The predicament in which we now find ourselves, however, suggests that he may have been right after all, and that our national success proved our undoing. It is in the light of this current concern that I wish here to explore briefly the history of management in the United States, concluding with some speculation on the lessons we may learn from the Japanese and on what reply, if any, might be made to the Schumpeterian pessimism. Although no history falls neatly into periods, the history of management passed through four discernible stages of development, emerging as a distinct profession only in the last. The first of these, from the foundings of American business—essentially coterminous with the founding of American society—until about 1850, embodied an extension of the business structure dominant in the Western world from the Renaissance on. Families owned businesses; family members managed them, drew replacements from family ranks, and trained their junior colleagues on the job. These methods proved practical enough through the early stages of industrialization in the United States because of the simple structure of even large businesses such as the New England textile mills, the low technological content of most manufacturing processes, and the relatively restricted market in which most firms operated. Aside from owner-managers, the number remained small. Alfred D. Chandler, Jr., the most eminent historian of American business, has argued that through the 1840s every hired manager in the United States—ships' officers, plantation overseers, and factory foremen, the bulk of them—could have been housed in the Dupont Company's present-day office building in Wilmington, Delaware.

The second period, 1850–1900, saw the proliferation of salaried managers in American firms, usually in coexistence with members of the owning family. The institution that necessitated change and pioneered the development of the bureaucratic management was the railroads. Spread over a large geographic area, raising millions of dollars to build a technologically complex operation requiring hundreds, then thousands, of employees (many of them highly skilled) to operate, collecting its revenues literally in a river of nickels and dimes and dollars that had to be carefully accounted for, the railroads needed financiers, accountants, technicians, lawyers, civil and mechanical engineers, an enormous stock of persons and skills far beyond the capacity of any family to supply. From the outset, railroads had to find ways to run the trains without running them into one another, and then had to find people to administer the system. American railroads, and the Pennsylvania Railroad in particular, developed the bureaucratic structure of management that, in one form or another, has guided America's big businesses ever since.

Four principal factors necessitated a bureaucratic structure of management and specialists to operate it. These factors were: the increasing size of business firms; growing technical complexity; the growth of the American market in population, purchasing power, and area; and, most important though perhaps least obvious, costs—the needs to learn them and the increasing necessity to reduce them. Indeed, I believe that the individuals most responsible for the development of American management structures and the management profession—the two cannot realistically be seen in isolation from one another—adopted new strategies and created new structures primarily under the compulsion to reduce the costs to maintain or increase profits, and not to solve problems of bigness, technology, mass production, or distribution. In fact, outside of areas such as steel and petroleum refining where technology inherently demanded it, mass production appealed to entrepreneurs and managers primarily because it offered enormous cost reductions.

As the pioneering big business firms, railroads hired the specialists they needed: civil engineers to survey the right of way, lay track, and build bridges; mechanical engineers to design equipment and supervise its maintenance; accountants, first to keep track of the income and outflow, later to track down costs in increasing detail; lawyers to do the things that lawyers do in the always litigious American environment. From the ranks of these specialists, trained in their specialty before joining the railroad, emerged many of those who became managers, supervising not only their own departments, but assuming general change of other departments as well. Others, who joined the firm with no training, often as errand runners or laborers, rose through the ranks in true Horatio Alger style to fill the managerial complement.

After the Civil War, bureaucratic management and the specialists who operated it spread from the railroads to American industry, first to steel and then into any enterprise too complex to be staffed by family members alone. The evangelist who carried the gospel from the railroads to manufacturing was Andrew Carnegie. Tom Scott, superintendent of the Pennsylvania Railroad's Pittsburgh Division, hired Carnegie as his personal telegrapher. Scott, a protégé of J. Edgar Thompson, a civil engineer and the Pennsylvania's president, taught Carnegie the cost-based management methods perfected on the Pennsylvania. Carnegie, who rose in turn to superintendent of the Pittsburgh Division, carried those techniques into the steel industry when he opened his first mill in 1873 and hired W. P. Shinn, an experienced railroad executive, as works superintendent.

Carnegie Steel's success — by 1900 it produced more annually than the entire steel industry of Great Britain — made cost-based management a standard procedure in American business. The firm's ownership-management structure typified that of many large American firms of the time in that it contained a mixture of family members, trained experts, and people who came up through the ranks. Carnegie himself remained controlling owner, set policy, kept a narrow eye on the weekly cost sheets, and served as super salesman. His brother Tom and cousin Dodd Lauder held high executive positions. Carnegie employed Alexander Holley, foremost Bessemer expert in the world, to build his mill. Chemists and accountants became managers, joined in the executive offices by men such as Captain Bill Jones, who learned steel making as a formal apprentice, William Borntrager, a German immigrant who rose from laborer to partner, and Charles Schwab, who began by holding Carnegie's horse and ultimately became president of U.S. Steel.[9]

A similar mixture of family and nonfamily members ran most of the country's largest firms in the late nineteenth century, including such giants as the McCormick Farm Machinery Company. In fact, only the railroads, among America's large transportation and manufacturing industries, presented an exception to the pattern. Virtually all American managers of the period, however, had one important experience in common: whether they owed their success to family position, professional training, apprenticeship, or a climb from the bottom, they learned the business from the shop floor up, acquiring through practical experience a knowledge, not only of the firm's products, but also of the workers who made them.

By the end of the nineteenth century, the situation prevalent in 1850 had reversed. Family members had become the exception, not the rule, in the executive offices of American businesses. Managerial authority rested firmly in the hands of outsiders who worked for salaries and had little or no ownership stake in the firm.

A variety of factors diminished the family as a source of managerial talent. In addition to the sheer size of firms which necessitated bringing in outsiders, the proliferation of ownership among thousands of stockholders through growth or mergers often eliminated individual families as controlling owners and with it their ability to dictate the choice of family members as executives. Some companies, like the McCormick Company, passed through all these stages successively, expanding the numbers of nonfamily managers at each step, finally disappearing into J. P. Morgan's creation, International Harvester, the last step eliminating the family from management altogether.

Other firms, while retaining family ownership, found the continuance of family management a luxury it could no longer afford in an increasingly competitive environment. For example, when Pierre Dupont and two of his cousins took control of the family firm in 1902, they eliminated the long-standing policy of automatically hiring and promoting relatives into positions of responsibility. Thereafter, kinfolk had to stand the same scrutiny as outsiders. Soon only a handful of the family's hundreds of members could be found among the ranks of the company's managers, although they retained firm control of the ownership.[10]

In a surprising number of cases, the controlling family simply failed to produce its own successors. Unlike the prolific Duponts and McCormicks, for example, Carnegie had no male heirs and had little choice but to sell out on retirement. In other firms, the founder's descendants proved inept or uninterested, prompting the late nineteenth-century American proverb, "From shirtsleeves to shirtsleeves in the three generations." Together these factors diminished the role of owner-managers in American businesses employing more workers than a handful of managers could supervise.

Within the ranks of the hired managers themselves, changes took place that continued into the third period of development of American management, which began around the turn of the twentieth century and lasted until shortly after World War II. In this period, owner-managers disappeared almost entirely in large American corporations. In addition, formally trained professionals—first engineers, then accountants and marketing specialists—pushed blue-collar aspirants off the ladder of success. For the first time, a college degree became a key to the executive suite. Turning to people with formal training, business reflected the trend toward professionalization that emerged in the larger American society toward the end of the nineteenth century. Doctors, lawyers, engineers, and scientists (among others) organized themselves in professional societies, promulgated codes of ethical behavior, standardized nomenclatures and specifications, established formal criteria for certification, abandoned the apprenticeship method of training recruits in favor of supporting the proliferating professional schools, particularly those affiliated with a college or university. By the time the complexities of the twentieth-century economy forced big business to promote specialists in a proliferating range of disciplines, American universities stood ready to supply them.

In the 1850s, '60s, and '70s, management tended to be production oriented. Whether formally trained as engineers or not, men who battered down the obstacles to large-scale production generally predominated and often rose to the top ranks. After 1873, increasing competition put a premium on the skills of cost analysis, efficiency through engineering, and marketing. Successful management increasingly demanded, not simply an ability to turn out products in large volume, but rather the knack of producing at minimal cost and peddling the results in the expanding mass market. The pre–Civil War generation of entrepreneur managers—typified, perhaps, by the Yankee mechanic locomotive builder Matthias Baldwin—gave way after the war to the cost-obsessed generation of Andrew Carnegie, which in its turn yielded supremacy to formally trained engineers on the order of Pierre Dupont. Following them came the master organizer, the true founding father of American managerial capitalism, Alfred P. Sloan of General Motors, an MIT-trained engineer who believed that survival depended on an organization which harnessed managers' talents while eliminating their personalities as influences on the firm's behavior.

In a sense, the profession of management, as I have defined it here, began with Sloan. Before considering his impact, however, I want to sketch the circumstances that demanded a leader of his temperament and abilities. By 1873, American business had assembled the prerequisites for mass production, including financial and transportation infrastructures. Thereafter, the problem that vexed management, whether family or hired, was the market. Unlike production levels, money, labor, or technology, the market defied rational control. Like the tides, demand rose and fell to a rhythm of its own, susceptible to no one's will; unlike the tides, however, demand had an unpredictable beat. Managers' attempts to combat the menace of falling markets by controlling production through pools or cartels failed by and large, while generating public hostility that triggered legislative attempts at regulation, such as the Sherman Anti-Trust Act of 1890.

Carnegie and others like him responded to the market with a different strategy that enabled them to prosper despite the vicissitudes of the late nineteenth century, which included the two major depressions of 1873 and 1893.

Carnegie thought the market almost infinitely elastic; that is, he believed that regardless of prevailing economic conditions, at some price one could sell all the goods or services one could produce. When demand fell, it simply signalled that the prevailing price was too high. The proper response was to slash prices until they "found" the market again. Dropping prices without simultaneously plunging the firm into bankruptcy required cutting costs; cutting costs required knowing what they were and how to reduce them; this in turn required sophisticated accounting techniques and the constant installation of more efficient technology. Following this creed, mercilessly forcing his managers into line, Carnegie made his firm the most efficient steel producer on earth and himself the richest man in the world.

Henry Ford's Model T and assembly line pushed this nineteenth-century doctrine to the limit, cutting the price of the flivver and finding, in fact, an ever larger market until 1921. Ford went the Carnegie view one better. He saw no need to wait for demand to fall before reducing prices. If the market lay waiting, thought Ford, why delay? Cut costs and prices, right now. The success of Ford, Carnegie, and others who espoused this view of the market masked for decades the fact that it embodied a basic fallacy. The market, of course, was never as elastic as they thought. A combination of the huge cost reductions that technology yielded with the swift expansion of the American market, fueled by rising prosperity and an expanding population, postponed the day of reckoning, the day when even the most efficient manufacturers learned that markets were finite, that even at rock-bottom prices they could become so saturated that customers would fail to appear.

For the automobile industry the awakening came in the early 1920s. Both Ford and General Motors discovered that sales volumes fell below a level that would cover the costs of production. Ford postponed disaster first by shutting down his plant for a year in 1921, then by his creative genius that produced two new cars, the Model A in 1928 and the V-8 in 1932. Events of the 1920s, however, exposed the shortcomings of the nineteenth-century view of the market and the inadequacy of even its most efficient proponents to cope with twentieth-century realities.

The managerial philosophy that replaced the anachronism emerged from the systematic, engineering mind of Pierre Dupont and the staff of professionals he assembled at Dupont after taking over the company in 1902. Ironically, Pierre led American management into the future by devising a strategy to preserve a structure rapidly becoming, in 1902, a relic of the past—family ownership. Raised in the Dupont enclave on the Brandywine in Wilmington, Delaware, Pierre saw the company as his heritage. He meant to keep it in the family, even if that meant banishing family members from its management. Recognizing that if he were to avoid going to the capital markets, he would have to confine the company's investments in new technology, new products, or research and development within the limits imposed by the family's resources and the firm's profits, Pierre insisted on the development of a managerial art hitherto thought impossible—market fore-casting. No proposal, no matter how promising, gained approval unless accompanied by estimates of potential sales and the costs, prices, and profits that would accompany them. With limited capital resources, the company could fund only those projects that promised high rates of return.

Driven by the boss's determination, the Dupont staffs of accountants, chemists, and engineers had raised this new art from educated guesswork to a promising if not unerring accuracy by the time the First World War erupted in Europe. As a manufacturer of gunpowder, the Dupont Company amassed enormous profits during the war, some of which it used to diversify into the manufacture of plastics, paints, industrial chemicals, and dyes, making its choices and managing its operations on the blend of cost accounting, market forecasting, and rate of return estimates it had perfected. Seeing in the automobile industry an enormous market for paints and plastics and having, after all, plenty of money to go around, Dupont poured millions of dollars into General Motors between 1918 and 1922. When the crisis of 1920–21 threatened GM with bankruptcy, Pierre Dupont assumed the presidency and appointed Alfred P. Sloan to restore order and profitability.

Dupont and Sloan were kindred spirits. Both MIT-trained, systematic, unassuming, preferring the background to the limelight, they presented a stark contrast to the flamboyant, self-trained characters like Carnegie and Ford who preceded them. Sloan embraced the Dupont management creed absolutely and installed it swiftly at General Motors, aided by an army of Dupont accountants headed by Donaldson Brown. The precise nature of the structure he developed to articulate his management philosophy mercifully need not trouble us here, but the philosophy itself proved momentous, for it led to the supremacy in big business of the modern professional manager.

Sloan stated his philosophy in simple terms: "The primary object of the corporation was to make money, not just make motor cars," a striking reversal of Henry Ford's observation that if one employed "a great army of men at high wages" to make a good car "that a lot of people can buy . . . at a cheap price . . . the money will fall into your hands; you can't get out of it." In fact, Sloan had seen in his own career—building Hyatt Roller Bearing from a tiny job shop to a huge supplier of mass-produced components, merging it into GM, and watching the corporate high jinks of his flamboyant predecessor in the GM presidency, Billy Durant—that money could pour out of careless hands even faster than it fell into them. Sloan had no use for flair, "hunches," "genius," people who made decisions based "on some intuitive flash of brilliance," or flashy characters who "could create but . . . could not administer." He wanted managers like himself, who had "an engineering care for the facts."

Sloan's management methods required subordinating all decisions to the principle of maximum return on minimum investment, achieved by yoking engineering efficiency to market forecasting. In the complex modern economy this required an administrative structure not subject to the vagaries of the human personality. "It is imperative for the health of the organization that it always tends to rise above subjectivity," he declared. After installing—or so he thought—such a structure at GM, he observed: "One of the . . . great strengths is that it was designed to be an objective organization not the type that gets lost in . . . personalities."[11]

The "objective organization," however, must strip out the effect of personalities without leeching out individual initiative in the process. The danger of such a loss Sloan saw as clearly as his contemporary Schumpeter. "General Motors," he declared, "was built on initiative." In Sloan's mind, the corporate structure could preserve individual initiative (and thus nourish entrepreneurial energies within the bureaucracy) in two ways. First, the corporation's resources multiplied the possibilities of individual achievement. Backed by GM, Charlie Kettering rose from a Dayton, Ohio, tinkerer to the presiding genius of automotive technology; Alfred Mellor's "idea" surrounded by "a lot of junk" (as Billy Durant described it) grew into the first commercially successful mechanical refrigerator and ultimately the Frigidaire Division; the Winton Engine Company became GM's Electro-Motive Division, the world's largest manufacturer of diesel locomotives.

Sloan's second way to preserve individual initiative involved "placing high salaries and bonuses based on company performance." Together these two ploys encouraged executives "to relate their own individual efforts to the welfare of the whole corporation."

Reflecting on his career after his retirement in 1946, Sloan understandably judged his system a success. GM didn't just survive the Great Depression; it made a profit and paid a dividend in every year of it. American business generally endorsed Sloan's ideas by copying them in one form or another. The precise structures that firms adapted varied widely from highly centralized to widely decentralized authority, from functionally to geographically departmentalized, with myriad hybrids in between. The axiom that cost control, market forecasting, and rate of return could be embedded in an administrative structure that operated independently of administrators' personalities without the loss of individual initiative took hold across the broad spectrum of American business. The three decades of prosperity that followed the Second World War seemed proof positive that American business had elevated management to a science—or an art, as some called it—in its own right, with principles that could be taught as abstractions with general validity.

This concept had enormous impact on the career paths of prospective managers. If management in fact was a discipline unto itself, not related to any specific manufacturing process, accounting method, scientific training, or marketing wisdom, and if its principles could be enumerated and taught, then managers could be trained without reference to specific, practical business situations. Managers themselves could forego the period of practical, shop-floor experience that had customarily initiated their careers throughout American history until after the Second World War.

Since the 1920s Harvard Business School and its imitators had advanced precisely this proposition and had developed curricula to articulate it. Wallace Donham (Harvard Business School's dean in the 1920s) and his successors concentrated on training students to make the kind of decisions that upper-level managers made, a skill Donham thought more an art than a science, dependent more on general and theoretical knowledge than upon specific or practical experience. Professional managers no longer solved practical problems; they devised organizations and hired specialists to solve them; their art was knowing what structure and which experts to use. When American business at last embraced this doctrine after World War II, the business schools of America stood ready and eager to supply this new breed of cat, the professional manager, the man or woman trained not in some specific skills, but in the art of general control of business policy. In addition, the lean depression years, followed by the wartime hiatus, meant that American business confronted a dearth of trained managers after the war. With the rest of the industrial world flattened, the global market lay open to American business. The resultant demand for executives, the swarms of veterans anxious to make up for lost time, and the GI Bill that financed their educations coalesced to nurture the first generation of pure professional managers and thus ushered in the final period, the era dominated by the profession of management.

Together Sloan's theories, their practical realization at General Motors, the educational philosophies developed by sequestered pedagogues, and the postwar economic climate swiftly reshaped the executive cadres. Certainly some people continued to emerge from specialized departments into the upper echelons of management. Here and there a talented individual still made it from the factory locker room to the executive dining room, but the numbers of such people diminished steadily in the first thirty years after World War II, with results that now raise questions which would have been dismissed as absurd twenty, or even ten, years ago. In the era of the professional manager, American industry has dropped from its global pinnacle into a spiral yet to be arrested.

Not all American firms have stagnated, of course. But the basic industries on which the country's industrial prosperity rests have drifted into imminent peril, while most of the energizing thrust in the economy now comes from those small and medium-sized firms where the professional manager remains a rarity and old-style entrepreneurs still abound.

Something clearly went haywire somewhere. In a mere twenty years the combination of Sloan's organizational principles with the most aristocratic of business pedagogues, bolstered by the most sophisticated research and information technology on earth, which seemed powerful enough in 1962 to take over the entire European economy, no longer competes effectively in a galaxy of industries in their home markets. Such a collapse presents an enigma, particularly, it seems, to those who presided over it; however, a combination of historical perspective and an analysis of the simultaneous and astonishing Japanese success unravels much of the mystery.

In the first place, after the 1920s American business was never quite as good as it thought it was. Insulated from foreign competition by high tariffs and the limited capacity of producers overseas, American firms had only to be efficient enough to profit at the high price levels afforded by the prosperity that prevailed with brief exceptions from 1900 to 1929. Even in those halcyon days a good many failed, and the number of competitors in such basic industries as automobiles, tires, steel, and petroleum dwindled steadily. In the 1920s, the question "How did General Motors do so well?" implies the reality that most companies in fact did badly, and many, of course, disappeared altogether. During the Second World War losing money became a near impossibility. Afterwards, the prostration of friends and foes alike added much of the world market to the domain of American industry, which probably reached the height of its prosperity about 1965. Thereafter, through a process too complex to elaborate here, the American market increasingly became part of the world market. For the first time, American business faced stiff competition for customers at home as well as abroad. With such an enormous advantage in terms of wealth and technology, and with professional management firmly in place, American business should have held its own and then some. Instead, it faded away.

Business itself likes to place most of the blame on a combination of expensive, intractable labor at home in contrast with cheap, docile workers abroad, and American governments hostile to business in contrast with foreign governments that aided and comforted their home producers. In fact, American management itself deserves most of the blame, for it abandoned profit maximization for risk minimization, long-term competitiveness for short-term profits, and the speed of individual initiative for the sluggishness of committee responsibility. Though these debilitating processes have deep historical roots, they blossomed as a result of shortcomings in Sloan's logic, shortcomings built into his organizational structures and transplanted with those structures into much of American big business.

Ironically enough, Sloan, who prided himself on having created an organization immune to the influence of personality, didn't see that the thing functioned optimally only when his own forceful personality headed it. When he left, the firm ran on its own momentum for many years; but his determination to force the best ideas out of his subordinates' minds into the firm's operations succeeded so well that his successors shifted, perhaps without knowing it, to a policy designed, not to maintain constant improvement, but rather to keep things as they were. In addition, smugness about the ability of American management methods to solve quickly any problems that might arise led to a focus on short-term earnings, the profits that kept stockholders tranquil and on which this year's executive bonuses depended.[12]

Hired managers, moreover, were workers just as much as the folks on the assembly line, and behaved accordingly. Far from convincing the blue collars to embrace management's long view, Sloan's successors themselves abandoned farsightedness in favor of labor's traditional obsession with "More, more, more. Now." This development Sloan did not foresee. He himself owned a massive share in the company and cared nothing for the limelight. ("All I had in the world was in General Motors," he once remarked.) His successors, on the contrary, holding minuscule shares and anxious to sport the baubles of status, soon looked on the annual bonus not as a reward for extraordinary effort, but as part of their normal salaries, a routine payment for routine services. Thus policies designed to encourage daring and initiative in fact stifled them into conformity and caution. Rather than relating their "individual efforts to the welfare of the whole corporation," many executives saw the profession of management as a way to use the corporation to their own benefit.

The opportunity to avoid dirty work in the shop by getting on the "fast-track" shortcut to the top appealed to the American mentality, traditionally obsessed with quick fixes and instant gratification. The absence of a European class structure, moreover, while it fired ambitions and facilitated social mobility, led Americans to an obsession with rising status. Deprived by corporate capitalism of the prestige of ownership, executives yearned for gewgaws to impress the neighbors and corner offices on the upper floors to awe their peers. In addition, the professionalization of management subdivided executives' duties as surely as the assembly line broke down workers' tasks. Thus deprived of fulfillment on the job, the bosses, like their underlings, had to look for satisfaction in the form of opulent offices, high salaries, conspicuous consumption.

The final shortcoming of professional management I want to address concerns the state of labor relations. We have in the United States the ridiculous situation of having the most educated, innovative, and imaginative labor force in the world and making almost no creative use of it. American industry, on the whole, has created an adversarial system of dealing with its workers, suppressing their talents and strangling their creativity, thus minimizing the enormous contribution workers could make to the vitality of American industry.

It was not always so. Even a cursory tour of American business history before the mid-1870s shows workers and bosses cooperating to an extent that astounded European visitors. Industrialization changed the picture—not, as some have argued, because big firms drove wages to subsistence levels or below, or because skilled workers were "deskilled" and turned into mindless machine tenders. In fact, wages rose, slowly but steadily, and American workers improved their physical standard of living generation by generation. Moreover, industrialization, while decreasing the percentage of skilled jobs among all jobs, increased significantly the absolute number of jobs for skilled artisans.

What *did* happen, we now know, was that in order to install cost-saving technology and mass production methods, management took from workers a time-honored prerogative, the right to control the workplace. Before industrialization, workers themselves largely determined the organization and pace of production and decided who got hired and how they were trained. During industrialization, these things became matters of managerial prerogative. The struggle that accompanied the transition didn't center on money; it didn't take management long to learn that rock-bottom wages cost more than they saved. The actual conflict revolved around power. It exacerbated as owner-managers gave way to professionals. Owners always had the psychological assurance of their ownership. Nothing workers could do, short of bankrupting the firm or burning down the works, could deprive owners of their status.

For professional managers, however, their self-respect depended upon authority and the ability to exercise it. Jealous of their fragile superiority, they reacted hostilely to any workers' attempts to encroach on managerial privilege. Consequently, even after the struggle to reorganize business along modern industrial lines had been won, the adversarial relationship continued. Worker suggestions were rarely solicited and even more rarely welcomed, an attitude that preluded a symbiotic relationship between workers and management that might have benefited both. Sloan, for example, could see the need to stimulate managerial initiative, but workers, he thought, should satisfy themselves with steady employment, good wages, and increased leisure time, leaving the running of the company to their betters. That labor relationships remained adversarial throughout the twentieth century could scarcely be denied by anyone who spent fifteen minutes on an American factory floor or read Harvey Swados's *On the Line*.[13] The fact that increasing numbers of managers rose to positions of great authority without having spent time getting their hands dirty out where the work got done meant that management got more and more out of touch with reality.

Happily, events of recent years have forced on American business an awareness of this hostility and its costs. Many companies have recently taken steps to involve workers in decision making and to tap the reservoir of experience and imagination dammed up in the people who actually do the jobs. Whether American industry can reverse its decline depends critically on the success of such worker involvement programs as the Ford Motor Company's "Quality Circles." Should they succeed, it will mark yet another lesson painfully learned from the current epitome of industrial efficiency, the Japanese.

The ironic thing about the Japanese miracle is that there turns out to be so little about it that is exclusively Japanese. For some time we comforted ourselves with wild notions about the docility of Japanese labor, wailing "Hail to Honda" or some such while bobbing up and down to company calisthenics fueled by a handful of fish heads and rice, somehow converted through an Oriental gastric miracle into boundless energy. In fact, Japanese labor peace dates from the mid–1950s when Japanese industry accepted the principle of lifetime employment. Watching Japanese workers and managers doing exercises *does* disconcert the Western visitor at first, but scarcely creates a more repressive atmosphere than the pseudocollegiate exhortations that ring through the halls of IBM.

Japanese success in fact stems from two factors: low costs and high quality, both achieved through methods that used to be common in American business. I can cite only a few examples here. The first is the Japanese focus on automation and the most efficient sequencing of operations, skills pioneered by Americans since Eli Whitney. Frederick Taylor would feel right at home in a Japanese factory. A second example is Toyota's so-called *kanban* ("just in time") system that minimizes inventory by stocking just enough material at the plant to keep the assembly line going. This permits an inventory cost about a quarter as large as any American plant of similar capacity. Japanese genius? Hardly. Recently, after an hour and a half of answering questions from a group of Western academics, Eiji Toyota, the company chairman, said, "Now I have question for you. Who invented 'kan-ban' system?" "Your grandfather?" guessed one of the visitors. Smiling seraphically, Mr. Toyota replied, "No. Henry Ford. River Rouge, about 1915."

These two examples of Japanese use of methods made in the United States could be extended almost indefinitely. One thing, however, that the

Japanese have not imported is the professional manager. Japanese executives begin their careers on the shop floor and spend eight to ten years there. They then rise vertically through single departments to the upper echelon, where they pool their expertise with colleagues who have come up similarly in other departments. This melding of talents is facilitated by the fact that the Japanese don't believe in executive offices and put the bosses together in large rooms, rather than walling them off from their responsibilities.

I believe that as we learn more about the Japanese, we will realize that American industry needs, not some new magic, but a return to some old principles. In the process, much of what has come to characterize the "professional manager" will have to go on the scrap heap. We cannot expect a nation of self-styled individualists to adopt the organic conception of society innate to Japanese, but we can reinstall in the workplace that respect for the dignity of the individual that we have long trumpeted as one of our abiding virtues. Managers have to learn that they don't need to exalt their own positions by denigrating the workers. One way to achieve this is to get managers into the plants before they disappear into the executive suite.

We must return to a longer view of what constitutes profitability and couple that to renewed attention to costs. If workers can be persuaded to identify their welfare with that of the company, something that profit-sharing plans would accelerate, then they can facilitate the improvements in cost and quality required to remain competitive in the world market, of which the United States has become a permanent part.

Meanwhile, we can count ourselves fortunate that we still have a significant sector in which professional management has never taken hold. The owner-entrepreneurs supply most of the drive that keeps the economy going. If we learn well the lessons they offer and the lessons inherent in the Japanese success, we can perhaps yet confound Schumpeter, discredit the notion that no nation can recover once it stumbles into industrial decline, and create a better society in the bargain. These lessons should not be beyond our capacities to absorb; they are, after all, largely the lessons of our own past.

NOTES

1. Jean-Jacques Servan-Schreiver, *The American Challenge* (New York, 1968).
2. I can think of no major exceptions in the literature of the history of American management. The very best of the lot is Alfred D. Chandler, Jr., *The*

Visible Hand (Cambridge, Mass., 1977), an encyclopedic work with notes that list most of the literature of management history.

3. See, for example, my own book *American Made* (Boston, 1979).

4. These books seem to multiply without end. For two of the better known examples, see William Ouchi, *Theory Z: How American Business Can Meet the Japanese Challenge* (New York, 1981), and Richard T. Pascale and Anthony G. Athos, *The Art of Japanese Management* (New York, 1981).

5. As Thomas C. Cochran, a pioneer business historian and one of the best, has been arguing for forty years, most recently in *Frontiers of Change* (New York, 1981).

6. Chandler's work, for example, restricts itself to this group, and it goes without saying that the literature of management scholars restricts itself similarly to the group of people that they themselves train.

7. These statistics or some variation of them have appeared frequently in popular literature in recent years. I drew these from "Small Business' Big Clout," *Dun's Review,* March 1980.

8. Joseph Schumpeter, *Capitalism, Socialism, and Democracy* (New York, 1957).

9. The most comprehensive Carnegie biography is Joseph Wall, *Andrew Carnegie* (New York, 1970). In my own *Andrew Carnegie and the Rise of Big Business* (Boston, 1975), I emphasize Carnegie's place specifically in the development of American management.

10. Chandler elaborates the Dupont story in *Pierre S. du Pont and the Making of the Modern Corporation* (New York, 1971), and in *Strategy and Structure* (Garden City, N.Y., 1966).

11. These arguments about the development of management can be followed briefly in Livesay, *American Made,* or in detail in Chandler, *Visible Hand.* Sloan speaks for himself in two autobiographical works: *Adventures of a White Collar Man* (New York, 1941) and *My Years with General Motors* (Garden City, N.Y., 1964).

12. Pat Wright (with John Z. DeLorean), *On a Clear Day You Can See General Motors* (Detroit, 1980). The reader has to strip off a layer of DeLorean's wounded vanity from this work, but underneath lies a perceptive analysis of the GM system's shortcomings after Sloan.

13. Harvey Swados, *On the Line* (New York, 1978).

MANAGEMENT: SUGGESTIONS FOR FURTHER READING

Abegglen, James. *The Japanese Factory.* Rutland, Vt., 1986.
Cochran, Thomas C. *Business in American Life: A History.* New York, 1974.
Cornuelle, Richard. *De-Managing America.* East Hanover, N.J., 1976.
Halberstam, David. *The Reckoning.* New York, 1986.

Livesay, Harold C. *American Made*. Boston, 1979.
Montgomery, David. *Workers' Control in America*. New York, 1979.
Porter, Glenn. *The Rise of Big Business*. Arlington Heights, Ill., 1973.
Servan-Schreiber, J.J. *The American Challenge*. New York, 1968.
Sloan, Alfred P. *My Years with General Motors*. Garden City, N.Y., 1964.
Swados, Harvey. *On the Line*. New York, 1978.
Townsend, Robert. *Up the Organization*. New York, 1978.